Jin – Kindness, caring, benevolence*

---

* *The kanji Jin is composed, on the left, of the character for "human" and, on the right, of two horizontal strokes that represent the number two. The whole symbol evokes the benevolence that unites human beings to one another.*

Christian Vanhenten

In search of Martial Kindness

Principles of
Aiki*do* Com*munication*

Translated into American English by
Theodore Kendris, Ph.D.

Editions de la Bienveillance

Original book

Ne cessez pas d'être gentils, soyez forts
Les Principes de l'AïkiCom
Une approche de bienveillance martiale
ISBN : 978-2-9601476-0-5
Editions de la Bienveillance, 2012

Editions de la Bienveillance, 2016
(c) 2016 by Christian Vanhenten

All rights reserved. No part of this book may be reproduced in any form or by any means, electronic or mechanical, including photocopying, recording, or by any information storage and retrieval system, without permission in writing from the publisher.

ISBN : 978-2-9601476-2-9

Table of content

Table of content 5
Acknowledgements 10
Translator's Note 10
About this book 12
About AikiCom and Aiki-coaching 12
Introduction 13
    Cautions 15
        Caution #1 15
        Caution #2 15
        Caution #3 16
        Caution #4 16
        Caution #5 16
Chapter 1 The Birth of *AikiCom* 17
    My First Steps in Aikido 17
    NLP and Méta-PNL 19
    Hypnosis and Aikido 20
    NLP and Méta-PNL Workshops 21
    Modeling Aikido 22
    Testing the Concept 24
    From Aikido to *AikiCom* 24
    The Child Resembles Its Parents 25
    My Life Changed 25
Chapter 2 AikiCom 27
    Definition 27
    Why AikiCom 30
    Aiki, Philosophy of *Being* in Action 34
        The Martial Kindness of *Aiki* 36
        The Reversal of the Body-Mind Relationship 37

- Connecting Oneself with the World.. 41
- Ethics According to Edgar Morin.. 42
- The Martial Dimension of the Kind Warrior..................................... 44
- The *Aiki* Attitude 46
- The Premises of the *Aiki* Attitude... 48
  - Premise 1 (P1): Being in the Flow... 48
  - Premise 2 (P2): Awareness of My Condition as a Learning Being 50
  - Premise 3 (P3): Awareness of Being a Connected Individual... 52
  - Premise 4 (P4): Awareness That the other Person Is Also a Being 53
  - Premise 5 (P5): The Connection Nurtures Life 55
  - Violation of These Premises 56
    - Violation of Premise 1 "Being in the Flow" 56
    - Violation of Premise 2 "Awareness of My Condition As a Learning Being"... 56
    - Violation of Premise 3 "Awareness of Being a Connected Individual"... 56
    - Violation of Premise 4 "Awareness That the Other Person Is Also a Being".. 56
    - Violation of Premise 5 "Connection Nourishes Life"................ 57
- The Qualities of the *Aiki* Attitude 57
  - Flexibility 57
  - Respect.. 58
  - Kindness 60
  - Martial-ness 60

Chapter 3 Coming back to myself... 63
- Centering 64
  - The Three Centers.. 64
    - The Cognitive Center... 65
    - The Emotional Center.. 65
    - The Somatic Center... 66
      - The Enteric Brain... 67
      - Center of Gravity.. 68
      - The Symbolism of the Hara 69
    - The Three Centers and the Temporal Dimension 73
      - The Cognitive Center and Time... 75
      - The Emotional Center and Time 75

- The Hara and Time ... 76
  - The Three Centers and the Triune Brain ... 77
  - Centering Oneself Is a Process ... 80
  - Centering Yourself with the Three Centers ... 82
  - I Am Multifaceted ... 84
    - A Lively Discussion ... 86
    - Centering Oneself as a Multifaceted Being ... 87
- Verticality ... 92
  - The Sky ... 94
  - The Cognitive Center ... 95
  - The Emotional Center ... 95
  - The Somatic Center ... 96
  - The Earth ... 97
  - Vertical Axis, Axis of Energy ... 98
- Coming into the World ... 102
- The Axis of Action ... 104
  - Orienting the Axis of Action ... 105
- The Relationship Axis ... 106
- The Aikisphere ... 107
  - Being in the Moment and Outside of Time ... 110

Chapter 4 Taking Action ... 115

- The Geometry of Conflict ... 116
  - Non-meeting, Parallel Paths ... 117
  - Frontal Opposition ... 117
  - The Standard Conflict ... 118
  - Facts and Emotions ... 119
  - We Are More Sensitive to Differences than to Similarities ... 122
- Perceiving ... 123
  - When Should We React? ... 124
  - How Should We React? ... 126
  - To Whom Do We React? The Enemy Within ... 129
  - React to What? ... 134
- Getting off the Line of Danger ... 136
  - Getting Out of Trench Warfare ... 139
  - Rendering the Attack Useless ... 139
  - The Need for Impact ... 140
  - Not Withdrawing, Going Toward the Attacker ... 140
  - Starting the Wheel of Transformation ... 140

- Summary 141
- Connecting Yourself, Linking Yourself 141
  - Establishing Contact 141
  - The Link Maintains Security 142
  - Connection Before Action 143
  - The Right Tension, the Right Perception 144
  - Deciding and Acting with the *Aikisphere* 147
- Dialogue in the Present Moment 153
  - Shoshin: Beginner's Mind 154
- Necessary Vulnerability 155
- The Aiki Fundamental Options of Action 157
  - The Triangle 159
    - Embodying the Triangle 159
    - The Triangle in Daily Life 160
  - The Circle 165
    - Embodying the Circle 165
    - The Circle in Daily Life 166
  - The Square 168
    - Embodying the Square 170
  - Decoding and Choice Grid 173
  - The Three Shapes Are Present Within Us 173
- *AikiCom:* Testing through Conflict 174
  - Randori 174
  - Physical Aggression 178
  - The Verbal Attack 179
  - Internal Conflict 187
  - Struggling against Events 189

Chapter 5 The *Aiki* Attitude 191
- Martin Buber's Reciprocity 192
- The Quadrants of Kindness 197
- Rapoport and Axelrod 199
- The Conditions of Pragmatic Kindness 201
  - Clarity 201
  - Reciprocity 201
  - Lasting Relationship 204
- *Ai* and *Ki*—Love and Power 205
- The Stages of Dialogue 208
- Living in the Flow 212

Conclusion 219
Illustrations... 223
Terminology.. 224
Bibliography 226

Acknowledgements

The first person I would like to thank is my father, for the brilliant idea that he had to one day tow me along in his wake on the way to aikido and for the love of learning that he passed along to me. I would also like to thank the aikido masters who have crossed my path and influenced my practice, as well as the students at my dojo, Kimochi de Namur, who have been first-rate partners and teachers.

This work would not have seen the light of day without the encouragement of my spouse Blanca throughout the long adventure of writing a book. Together, and with the participation—more unconscious than intentional—of our children, we experienced *AikiCom* in our daily life and saw that it allowed us to make it through the vicissitudes of life with kindness and created a quality of life that I would never have thought possible before.

Finally, I would like to thank Ted Kendris, the translator of this book. We worked together for several months with a wonderful rapport. Ted's interest in AikiCom was surely an asset that helped us arrive at a faithful translation, in addition to making the process more inspiring. I would also like to thank Maria Vilar Badia and Jack Richford for their valuable comments on the first draft of this translation.

Translator's Note

I am very grateful to Christian Vanhenten for the opportunity to translate his fascinating work. It was a wonderful experience for me, not only on a professional level but on a personal one. The *AikiCom* approach, which I had the good fortune to experience firsthand at a seminar in Belgium, has already had a positive influence on my interactions with others. The vast amount of research carried out by Vanhenten Sensei bears witness to his passion for *AikiCom* and the application of martial kindness. I encourage you to explore the footnotes and bibliography as you study this book and use the suggested readings as a starting point on your own path.

Ted Kendris

About this book

This book was written to offer you an overview of *AikiCom* and how the approach was born at the crossroads of Aikido and various communication approaches. The physical dimension of *AikiCom* cannot, of course, be rendered by a written text. This book will therefore lack a significant part of what *AikiCom* can offer. It is only through physical practice during *AikiCom* workshops and regular courses that you can fully appreciate the Aiki attitude presented in these pages.

About AikiCom and Aiki-coaching

AikiCom is protected by international law covering intellectual property in order to prevent the dilution of its principles and patterns [paradigms?] and to ensure the quality of its teaching. Nevertheless, *AikiCom* is intended to be an approach that is open to any contributions that respect its spirit and philosophy. Future development will include the contributions of other developers in the same way that open source software is developed.

Similarly, the term *Aiki-coaching* is also protected and is reserved for therapists and coaches who have been trained in *Aiki-coaching*.

To make this book more readable, we decided not to add the symbol © after the terms *AikiCom* and *Aiki-coaching*.

If you are interested in *AikiCom* and want additional information, we invite you to visit our website http://www.aikicom.org. An *AikiCom* Facebook page is also available, along with a Twitter account (@laikicom and #aikicom). You can also subscribe to our newsletter to stay informed about the development in *AikiCom* and receive the schedule of workshops and activities.

Introduction

Originally, the aim of this book was to introduce a special way of handling conflict based on the principles of aikido. Nowadays, interpersonal conflicts are more verbal than physical, but they still retain all the characteristics of the struggle that our ancestors had to face against savage beasts or against enemies who were determined to kill or enslave them. We all react in our own unique way when faced with conflict or with the frustration of not seeing our wishes met.

Conflict is inevitable as soon as someone blocks the path that leads to carrying out our plans. Generally, there is conflict as soon as two different intents meet: mine and *the* other's.

In this book, we'll call the *other* (in italics) anyone or anything that is not me as long as I give him (or it) a certain level of autonomy and willpower. It is essentially a person but it can also be a group of persons, an organization, or a thing that I am personifying (and thus I perceive as acting as a person with his or her own willpower). It can be Society or the State when I see it as an abstract person. At work, it can be a department or the staff. The *other* is also within me. It can be an illness I am struggling against or a part of myself that wants to do or stop doing something. It can also be the self-judging part of me that is criticizing me. I notice these parts of myself each time I am in a dilemma, facing a choice, or when I hear that little voice inside my head that judges me or lectures me.

AikiCom is about handling the inevitable conflict that arises each time I meet the *other*.

Aikido is not only a martial art, but a tremendous metaphor for life. It allows us to discover how to handle conflicts in a constructive and creative way. Instead of thinking of the *other* as an adversary, the aikidoka approaches him[1] as a partner. The *other* gives us a chance to learn, to grow.

Starting with bodily experience – by practicing movements that are based on aikido – we can go beyond intellectual experience that is not very effective in bringing lasting change to our daily lives. The concepts of centering, of rooting oneself to the ground, and of verticality are the preludes to meeting the *other* without fearing that he will unbalance us. We can then explore how to transform unavoidable conflictual energy, and do so in synergy with self-respect and respect for others.

If handling conflict was at the start of AikiCom development, over the course of my research, this theme very quickly grew broader to touch on what is at the center of this book: the *Aiki* attitude.

One possible definition of "attitude" is "the arrangement of the parts of a body or figure" (*Merriam-Webster's Collegiate Dictionary, Eleventh Edition*, page 80). This is one's bearing, posture, or appearance. It is also a mood, a set of judgments and tendencies that push us to adopt a given behavior.

AikiCom defines the *Aiki* attitude and offers, by physical and mental exercises, to integrate it into our daily life, into our way of being.

We are communicating beings and it is through our way of interacting with others that we take our place in the world. Every experience is an experience of communication with our environment. This communication feeds on an exchange of information. However, our potential well-being depends above all on the energies involved. We are reminded of this by the terms "Ai" and "Ki," which mean respectively *harmony* and *energy*.

---

[1] Translator's note: the masculine is generally used in this book in order to avoid complicated constructions in an attempt to be gender inclusive. This is an especially tricky topic since the French masculine plural can also include female individuals.

Cautions

Caution #1

This book is the result of more than forty years of aikido practice and more than twenty years of exploration of the human dynamic in its capacity to learn, to change, and to evolve. This book furthers the goal of gathering together some of the main concepts that are presented during *AikiCom* workshops. I am entirely aware of the fact that it deprives the reader of what makes up the very foundation of *AikiCom*: bodily practice. Practice must absolutely be supervised by an experienced trainer so that physical practice goes beyond the simple mechanical execution of a set of movements and brings about the integration of *AikiCom*'s concepts into one's body. This is just as true for participants who have no aikido experience as it is for aikidokas who have not been trained to give meaning to their aikido practice. Purely mechanical repetition of movements is a waste of time. Although I know that it is pointless to try to make the "perfect" movement (assuming it exists), I was able to see that sometimes it sufficed to make some micro-corrections in order to perceive that little something that can lead to many changes. It is the trainer's responsibility to notice and suggest those corrections.

Caution #2

With seven notes and twelve half tones, people can create symphonies, heartbreaking blues music, or simple little tunes. It's the same for human beings as it is for music. The infinite number of combinations of simple elements build the complexity and richness of our experience. Can we pretend to invent something new while exploring what makes us human? I don't think so. The most we can hope to offer is a new interpretation of the way we function. With *AikiCom*, I don't claim to bring anything more than a synthesis based on my own experience and learning. I'm foolish enough to believe that this synthesis is unique because it builds bridges between different approaches and because it took a long period of practice to "fine tune" the method—a long period in our modern world, where urgency and impatience encourage short and immediate learning.

Caution #3

I don't pretend to offer any sort of truth. When I discovered NLP (neurolinguistic programming), I was seduced by the intellectual audacity of its two co-creators, who did not hesitate to proclaim their lack of interest in any form of truth. The only thing that mattered for Bandler and Grinder was whether a model was useful or not. They thus preferred a useful lie to a so-called truth that does not help a person to change. *AikiCom* is the product of Méta-PNL², which focuses on modeling human skills in order to integrate them in our daily behavior. In this approach, I am trying to offer maps of the world that are more useful than true. The models and explanations that will be recommended to you throughout this book are an attempt to share a vision for a better life in a world that is not always easy.

Caution #4

AikiCom is learned through practice. The goal of this book is to present the spirit and the principles of the *AikiCom* approach. It is neither a method nor a set of exercises. Workbooks will be published at a later date to present a variety of exercises applied to real-life situations, as well as suggestions for exercises aimed at using *AikiCom* in daily life. You will also find illustrations, videos, further explanations, and various commentaries on the *AikiCom* web site at http://www.aikicom.eu

Caution #5

Certain passages in this book are fairly dense. This is especially true for the topics related to Ueshiba's philosophy and the philosophical reflections tied to Martin Buber's thoughts. They are the result of very complex material and I did my best to synthesize it all. These chapters underwent several rewritings and I hope that the version that I am passing along to you will help you see some basic principles that are essential in order to understand the spirit of aikido, despite our Western cultural baggage.

---

² See NLP and Méta-PNL, page 23.

Chapter 1

The Birth of *AikiCom*

My First Steps in Aikido

When I began practicing aikido, at the age of twelve, I wanted to learn to defend myself. At the time, my practice put a lot of emphasis on arm locks and twists. Aikido had to prove to me that it was an effective martial art. That suited me perfectly. One day, after lunch, a boy who was two years older than I—a significant difference at that age—wanted to challenge me and grabbed me by my shirt. We were in the entry of the hallway leading to the classrooms and behind him there was a wall of schoolbags stored in the space underneath the main staircase. The movement began with the extension of his hand. At the moment when I felt the material of my shirt twist in his fist, my right hand was already on his. A slight movement of my hip brought my left hand to the same level as his elbow, then the wrist lock known as *nikkyo* drew a surprised grimace out of him. A second later, Daniel (if he reads this book, he'll recognize himself) was lying on top of the schoolbags mumbling: "What did you do?" I calmly answered: "Don't ever do that again!" and left the hallway under the stunned gaze of the other boys. At the age of fifteen, this kind of experience leaves an enduring memory. I was far from being the strongest boy in school, but aikido allowed me to gain the respect of those who were looking to assert themselves through force. Since my first day on a *tatami*, my father had repeated to me only to use the techniques when necessary and only to defend myself. During practice, there was always an air of secrecy that I found pleasing. Beyond these feats of strength, the act of putting on a *keikogi* once or twice a week to learn aikido had given me self-confidence so that I never needed to be aggressive or seek to impose myself. I was sociable and friendly, and the other boys knew that I would not cave in to violent intimidation. Aside from some rare moments such as the one that I have just described, aikido offered me the privilege of being respected without having to fight.

What makes aikido original is this subtle association between the martial dimension and the philosophy of peace and harmony. At the age of twelve, it was very difficult for me to make the connection between this search for peace and actual self-defense practice. To be honest, I was more interested in physical practice and learning defensive techniques. After years of practice, the spirit of aikido slowly percolated through me. To twist an attacker's arm changed from being a solution to being an opportunity that I could either seize or ignore. I was discovering that aikido offered me the luxury of choosing to do harm or *not* to do harm. Then, gradually, it was my response to the attack that changed. The self-defense aspect faded, leading to a more subtle search to find a way to feel better in one's body, with oneself, and with others.

After more than forty years of aikido practice, I have integrated this martial art so deeply in my being that I can no longer say what, in my life, comes from this practice and what does not. I often say that I don't know what life would be without aikido. When I was living with my parents, aikido was an activity for the whole family, the most frequent topic of discussion. I could never thank my father enough for introducing me to aikido. Today, this journey seems to be a path, a

Do,[3] that allowed me to make it through the trials and tribulations of a childhood that was spent in a difficult family situation, even though it took me several decades to arrive at some form of inner peace.

NLP and Méta-PNL

Aside from aikido, I have accumulated over twenty-five years of knowledge and experience in the areas of well-being and communication. On this path, NLP played a great role in contributing to giving meaning to my life and to the events that I experienced.

When I discovered NLP in 1989, I saw it as a technique to communicate better with others and to understand better how we function. Five years and several dozen books later, I decided to get training as a practitioner and then as a master practitioner of NLP. This training curriculum shattered the limits of what I had believed to be possible. Of course, I was far from the promises of "unlimited power" proclaimed by Anthony Robbins in his book of the same title,[4] which for me was just another self-help book. NLP practitioner training opened me up to a sort of personal sensitivity. I was beginning to glimpse the possibility of looking within, of opening up this space that I had learned to protect so ferociously. I was beginning to believe that I could one day take off my heavy protective armor in order to be better able to feel life flowing through me.

While the applications of NLP contributed to changing my life, it is the modeling process that captivated me. Most of my research was focused on the beginnings of NLP[5], when its cocreators, Grinder and Bandler, became partners to model the practices of the remarkable therapists Fritz Perls, Virginia Satir, and Milton Erickson. The modeling of these exceptional communicators gave birth to the techniques and tools of NLP that forged its reputation. The more I sought to understand this period of the beginnings of NLP, the more I understood the evolution of NLP, which limited itself more and more

---

[3] *Do* = way in Japanese
[4] Unlimited Power: The New Science of Personal Achievement, New York: Free Press, 1986.
[5] I had a chance to collaborate with Monique Esser, author of several essays on NLP, who opened my eyes to the richness of the beginnings of NLP.

to conveying the models and techniques that had been developed by its major trainers and developers. The business of NLP training mainly provides ready-made solutions to a public that wanted quick answers. To highlight this drifting off course and put modeling back at the heart of the debate, I developed Méta-PNL[6] to stress the different levels of NLP from the simple application of techniques to the definition of the paradigms underlying the actual modeling process[7].

Hypnosis and Aikido

Even though NLP had opened a range of possibilities, I felt that I would need something more to set out on the path toward transformation. Ericksonian hypnosis seemed to offer this extra dimension to me. However, for this I needed to find a trainer, a practitioner in whom I could put my full confidence.

I remember signing up a bit by chance for a seminar given by Stephen Gilligan in Belgium in 1996. This three-day seminar had a major influence on the rest of my development, as much on my personal growth as on the steps that led me to create *AikiCom*.

My meeting with this exceptional trainer succeeded in breaking down the walls of control that I had erected for myself. Hypnosis struck me like a bolt from the blue, giving me permission to look at the protective shadow zones that I maintained within myself. I could finally look tenderly at the behaviors that I wanted to change, at these beliefs that were so strong that they seemed permanent. At the same time, I was discovering that it was possible for me to enter into deep communication with others, I who had always had the impression of only touching them superficially.

The subject of the seminar was the presentation of self-relations psychotherapy, which Stephen Gilligan had described in his book *The Courage to Love,* which had just been published. Stephen Gilligan was an aikidoka and he made numerous allusions to this martial art for which we both shared a passion. During a discussion with Stephen while we were taking a break—just like the images of the left and right

---

[6] Méta-PNL (Méta-pratique neurolinguistique/Neurolinguistic meta-practice) is a field of NLP that is devoted to the modeling process of NLP. (www.metapnl.com)

[7] On http://www.metapnl.com you will find a description of the logical levels of NLP which led to the birth of Méta-PNL.

eyes converging to form three-dimensional vision—my development in the world of communication, and in particular NLP, merged with aikido, the martial art that I had been practicing since the age of twelve. How come I hadn't gotten it sooner?

This realization was similar to our reaction to the following figure (Figure 1).

Figure 1 : Illusion

As long as you only see one of the two women, whether it's the young one or the old one, there is nothing worth mentioning. Then, after you make the effort to see the other woman, you wonder how you didn't see her in the first place.

This encounter with hypnosis and with Stephen Gilligan was to radically transform my vision of aikido. The following year I opened my own *dojo* in Namur, Belgium, determined to teach aikido while further blending its martial applications with communication.

NLP and Méta-PNL Workshops

At the same time that I was starting up the Kimochi *dojo*, where I was exploring the connections between communication and aikido, I started *l'Atelier PNL* (the NLP Workshop). My goal was to maintain and perhaps develop the expertise that I had acquired during my NLP practitioner and master practitioner training. Very quickly, the social impact of this group was to go beyond the simple desire to practice NLP techniques. This was a chance for extraordinary encounters with NLP practitioners from all of its schools. It was also an opportunity for debates and experimentation that must have been similar to the group spirit that drove Grinder and Bandler when they created what was eventually to become NLP. It was in the setting of these workshops that I met Monique Esser, who shared with me her knowledge of the history of NLP and of its paradigms. My discovery of the early days of NLP led me to become aware of the importance of modeling. This importance is even more crucial since modeling is only partially taught by current NLP schools, who prefer to teach more short-term techniques.

The *Atelier PNL* took place until the early 2000s. My interest in modeling pushed me to various research activities and led to the creation of Méta-PNL.

During this time, I continued teaching aikido while searching to apply it in my daily life. Naturally, I felt compelled to model my aikido practice, or at least the practice that I was teaching in my *dojo* in Namur.

Modeling Aikido

Modeling aikido was a great challenge because NLP does not offer any tool to decode a bodily practice such as aikido. NLP was conceived in the bosom of linguistics[8], and it was developed in the neurological realm[9]. It made only minor incursions into the physical domain[10]. The GDS muscular chain approach developed by Godelieve

---

[8] John Grinder was a linguist who applied Chomsky's transformational grammar to therapeutic practice (see the first book on NLP: *The Structure of Magic, Vol. 1, A Book About Language and Therapy*).
[9] By neurological, I mean the concern that Bandler and Grinder had to return to the level of the most elementary sensory operations: what I see, I hear, I say to myself, I feel. In NLP these sequences of operations are called "strategies" (see Robert Dilts et al., *The Study of the Structure of Subjective Experience*, Vol I, Meta Publications 1980).
[10] Physical mimicry is the stroke of genius that permitted the creation of NLP. Richard Bandler had the gift of being able to put himself in the shoes of the people he imitated and John Grinder could structure what Bandler reproduced. Calibration is one of the essential processes of NLP, allowing one to synchronize both verbally and nonverbally

Denys-Struyf played a decisive role in my work of decoding movement as well as the psychological repercussions of movement.

In *Méta-PNL*, the process of modeling a person's behavior of excellence requires the identification of the structure[11] of his experience and the separation of the aspects that are specific to him as an individual from the general aspects that are needed to allow everyone to reproduce the modeled behavior.

As for structure of experience, we can, right from the start, distinguish the external behavior—this is the visible part of the iceberg and in the case at hand, the physical practice of aikido—from the internal process, that is to say, the thoughts and the beliefs that are behind it.

Starting off with the modest goal of modeling conflict management and communication while respecting the principles of aikido, I gradually realized the depth of the martial art that had been created by Morihei Ueshiba. The founder of aikido was an individual of great spirituality. Many writings indicate that he always wanted to go beyond the scope of mere martial training. Ueshiba strove to achieve his vision of spreading peace and harmony through physical, martial training.

Modeling involves isolating the universal dimension of aikido from what was specific to its creator, Morihei Ueshiba, as much in its physical dimension as in the patterns of thought that give aikido its unique character. This eventually led to the approach that I call *AikiCom*, which, following the example of aikido, allows one to develop human qualities that make up what I call the *Aiki attitude*, an attitude of martial kindness that expresses, in my opinion, what the founder of aikido wanted to pass along to us[12].

---

with the person with whom one is speaking in a way that creates a favorable relational framework.
[11] I could have written "the identification of *a* structure" because the structure that is identified is a process of co-emergence: the observer influences what he/she observes.
[12] This interpretation was developed from countless works describing the philosophy of aikido, from the accounts of those who had a chance to find it and to learn aikido firsthand, but above all through the work carried out by Bruno Traversi's team, published in the works titled *Takemusu Aiki*.

Testing the Concept

Once the concept was in place I examined it tirelessly[13] in order to put it to the test. Wherever possible, I tried to apply it to my daily life. It was amazing that life seemed to provide an endless number of chances for me to test my way of managing conflicts.

This was my crossing of the desert, my "temptation of Mara," on a different scale, of course. I would return home in the evening exhausted from conscious efforts to manage conflict in a positive manner, that is, without seeking victory but rather seeking a common ground where each person involved could meet in mutual respect. This research was tiring, but I felt in harmony with myself and with my environment. As the "serenity prayer" advises, I accepted that which could not be changed and changed that which could be changed. Then, after several weeks, I experienced a great surprise. Suddenly, there was calm and the frequency of conflicts diminished drastically. The nature of my exchanges with my loved ones, my colleagues, my friends—and those who were less than friends—changed. One stage had been completed, one onion skin had been peeled away. I could delight in beginning to peel the next layer. After all, this exploration never ends. Quite the contrary, dare I say. And in a certain sense, this is a good thing. Every day, I delight in this feeling of making progress on my path, one step at a time. Sometimes radically new scenery reveals itself, like when you cross over the crest of a mountain and a valley that had been invisible until that moment reveals itself to you. This valley is vast, covered by a soft, light mist that doesn't block the sun. The landscape generates a physical sensation of my rib cage opening up, along with a call to move forward.

But not alone!

From Aikido to *AikiCom*

My *dojo* in Namur had already existed for ten years. Ten years of practice and teaching and exploration with, as a bonus, a growing enthusiasm among the *dojo's* students, who played a key role in my

---

[13] The test phase is essential in the process of modeling. It allows you to make sure that the model that is constructed is not only an acceptable intellectual creation, but also a model that allows you to reproduce the skill that is modeled while obtaining similar results, considering the context, of course.

approach. The more I progressed in my approach, the more I felt a sort of rupture. It was becoming more and more difficult to pursue what was turning into two objectives that were leading to two different paths. On the one hand, I was teaching aikido while respecting the standards and requirements of both the Belgian Federation and the world headquarters in Tokyo. On the other hand, my training was becoming more and more refined, centered on communication and self-awareness. The gestation period was reaching its term and had to give rise to a birth. The newborn baby was baptized "AikiCom." Simultaneously resembling and different from its two parents—aikido and communication—it longed to follow its own path. As Khalil Gibran wrote in *The Prophet,* "Your children are not your children. They are the sons and daughters of Life's longing for itself. [...] You are the bows from which your children as living arrows are sent forth."

The Child Resembles Its Parents

As is the case with all births, everyone tries to find family resemblances. Just as one will recognize that the child has its father's eyes, its grandmother's nose, its aunt's ears, everyone will recognize in *AikiCom* the concepts that one finds in different approaches, schools, methods, and even spiritual movements that I was brought up on. It's certainly what I desire the most. The more connections you make, the more *AikiCom* will be easy to apply to your daily life. It's the concept of cross-fertilization that was so dear to the anthropologist Gregory Bateson[14].

My Life Changed

Since developing *AikiCom*, my life has changed radically. I broke from a harmful relationship, I met my companion—who eventually became my spouse—and together we are building a life as a couple with respect for our differences and with a kindness that creates a space of peace and security that allows us to move through the world with a very stimulating inner strength. My two sons from my first marriage witnessed my sometimes chaotic progress and today I realize how much my role as a father was a chance for constant self-

---

[14] Gregory Bateson was an English anthropologist who contributed to what is nowadays called the Palo Alto School of brief therapy.

questioning. Today I take pleasure in seeing them transition to adult life. We continue to practice aikido together as I did with my father when I was a child. *AikiCom* has brought me this wave and I take pleasure in letting myself be carried away by the flow.

Chapter 2

AikiCom

Definition

*A**ikiCom* can be defined as an approach that invites us to discover and live the *Aiki* attitude. This attitude is characterized by a form of martial kindness. *AikiCom* is a personal development approach advocating the application, in our daily lives, of the principles of aikido to communication—with communication being understood in the broadest sense of the term. By this, I mean any form of exchange with others, with the environment, and with ourselves. We are communicating beings, the product of a long period of evolution that gave us awareness, the ability to conceptualize and to give meaning to our experience and to share it with others.

Thus, when I communicate with a person, I share my view of the world and I express what I want as an autonomous being, endowed with awareness and therefore able to express my free will. Without the awareness of being me, I cannot even imagine the meaning of "to want," "to feel like," or "to desire." My awareness lets me know the meaning of the word "I." This concept contributes to forming my identity, which distinguishes me from the rest of the world. It makes me unique throughout my life, even if I change physically, my feelings follow one another, and my thoughts evolve over time as a result of my experiences.

I also communicate with my environment. I am constantly subjected to an unceasing stream of stimuli that will confirm or disprove my internal representation of what I believe the world to be. This map of the world that I keep in my memory allows me to give meaning to my experiences and, depending on whether this meaning is agreeable to me or not, sensations will arise in me that create my emotions. If the stimuli call to my mind something dangerous, I will feel fear; if they make me think of unfair treatment or a frustrating situation, I will feel anger; if they make me aware that I have lost something, I will feel sadness, etc.

Finally, I communicate with myself when I am torn between different options and I'm having difficulty deciding what to do. We often live as though we were made up of several parts. There are frequently times when we want to change something in our life and come to the bitter realization that, in spite of our desire to change, we are continuing to behave as we did before. Everything plays out as though a part of ourselves wanted to change and another acted to maintain the status quo. Our mind is the product of the incredible ability of our brain to connect experiences with each other. We are thus able to think, but also to think that we think and even to think that we think about the fact that we think. This is what mathematicians call recursiveness, which can be defined as the ability to apply a function to itself.

All these forms of communication connect us with others, with the world, and with ourselves.

We are aware and unique beings. The part of ourselves that we call the *ego* tends to intensify this feeling of being unique, of being endowed with willpower that we bring to the world in order to control our experience. However, very early in our childhood, we become aware that we do not master everything. We do not even master what takes place within us.

It is at this moment that the *Aiki* attitude comes into play in our relationship with the world, as an individual, in our interactions with our environment, and with ourselves. We can rebel and struggle against everything that thwarts our wishes or look for the path that blends energies and allows us to go with the flow of life.

As you will have guessed, *AikiCom* unwaveringly chooses the second option, to "go with the flow." It's not about letting things happen, or enduring, or being passive, but rather doing the right thing. It is about not forcing the course of things, but to make us be a part of life's flow, aware of the fact that we are not as separate from the rest of the world as our ego believes.

If it were limited to these slightly "New Age" philosophical considerations, AikiCom would be nothing more than a pleasant way of filling late-evening conversations. The issue for us is to live our daily life according to aiki principles. Our relationship with the world can either drain our energy and exhaust us or give us the impression that we are surfing on a wave that is carrying us along. *AikiCom* helps us to move away from the first option so that we can live in the second one.

Let's look at a few examples.

> Andre wants to control everything and everyone. At work he has difficulty delegating responsibility and spends his time controlling his subordinates. In the evening, he checks his children's homework and then shuts himself in his office to carry out the household administrative duties that he wouldn't even dream of leaving to his spouse. His life is full of constant tension that he won't call into question until his first warning signs of heart disease.

> Nathalie feels like the victim of an infinite series of blows that life has dealt her. She fights, but then she fails and starts again with a new experience that leads to the same result.

Jim is living with Julie, but he feels bad when he sees Julie living her life fully as an independent woman.

Eric has just been fired. He is crushed and keeps repeating: "This can't be true; this can't be true." Rejecting reality, he continues to struggle to deny the obvious instead of focusing his energy to recover and look for a new job.

Steve is torn. After spending fifteen years in administration, where he worked in an especially boring occupation as an accountant, he dreams of quitting his job and taking up painting and selling his artwork. He has always painted and, after exhibiting in several galleries, some experts took notice of his work and bought several of his paintings. His job does not give him the time to paint, but it assures him financial security that he is afraid to let go of by embarking on a career as a full-time artist.

These examples show the energy that we can expend while remaining in situations that do not suit us, but in which our ego pushes us to keep ourselves instead of listening, of perceiving, when the world invites us to let go so that we can move forward.

Why AikiCom

It all starts with aikido, which gives us a philosophy of life through bodily practice. This martial art teaches us how to restore harmony within ourselves and with others. Aikido offers a subtle combination of meaning and movement; it is practiced throughout the world and everyone who practices it finds what he is looking for. The vast majority of aikido practitioners seek above all to learn a technical discipline, a perfection of movement that combines elegance and martial effectiveness. For them, the spirit of aikido is connected to its practice only by a few slogans that they read here and there in books or fliers handed out to advertise dojos. Other aikidokas seek a path of harmony of the body and mind, following in the footsteps of the Founder.

Teaching aikido in a primarily technical way resonates particularly with our Western sports mentality. The spirituality of aikido has been put on the back burner and pushed away from the *tatamis*, no doubt because it confused the technically-minded practitioners in their teaching and in a way it harmed the reputation of aikido as a sport, albeit a sport that is practiced without an emphasis on competition. The problem is that in separating the spirit of aikido from its practice, we take away the substance from the martial art. Why practice for so many years? To keep in good physical condition?[15] To achieve a hypothetical perfection of movement? Physical performance is not eternal. Our body ages. Small injuries add up and progressively limit our freedom of movement. I believe that there is a fundamental misunderstanding in the comprehension of what Morihei Ueshiba, the founder of aikido, meant when he urged us to practice continuously. Training for the sake of training is not an end in itself. To do something just for the sake of doing it only passes the time. Ueshiba urged us to practice in order to realize what he called the finality of aikido: reversal. According to him, practice was supposed to bring a radical shift, the reversal of the primacy of the *body of flesh*[16] that is engraved in material reality—in space and in time and therefore subject to the laws of causality—with the primacy of the *spiritual body* that unfolds outside of time and does not need to *do* in order to *be*. In general, materialistic concerns take up our time and do not satisfy us. It is by working on ourselves with both mind and body that we can realize our full potential.

Aiki practice leads us, through the body in movement, to experience this development, and in this way to transform how we see and experience things. The reversal happens when we become aware of being in the world in a new way—connected to the world and to others—and of being able to contribute to more harmony within ourselves and around ourselves. In Buddhism, this reversal is called "awakening" and it calls to mind the experience of becoming aware of the illusion in which our ego plunges us, which makes us believe that

---

[15] Aikido is an excellent physical practice because it respects our body, it is complete on a muscular level, and it is balanced in its intensity, which can be adapted to our physical condition and our age. It can nevertheless cause injuries, especially to joints, when it is practiced in an athletic manner instead of a harmonious way.

[16] This expression was used by Morihei Ueshiba in his works.

we are distinct from others and from the world. In becoming aware of this illusion, we realize that we are living beings interconnected with others, with life, and with the world. This is how fighting becomes useless, Ueshiba tells us. If I am One with the Universe, to attack me is to attack the Universe. Obviously, there is no hope of victory. And if fighting is useless, let's move on to something else!

The physical practice of aikido is futile if it does not lead to something else. But to what? Do we need to immerse ourselves inexorably in Eastern culture and spirituality to attempt to understand the thoughts of the founder of aikido, although even the Japanese who followed his teachings had trouble grasping the deep meaning?

Personally, I do not think so. The fact that aikido is practiced throughout the world certainly proves to us that you do not need to be born on the Japanese Islands to feel what aikido can provide. The meaning of a physical practice such as aikido takes on its full magnitude if it leads to a way of being, an attitude toward life that puts into practice the principles that led Morihei Ueshiba to create aikido. This attitude stresses the reality of being connected to other people and to our universe. We are in permanent interaction. One cannot not communicate.[17] This leads us to the heart of the creation of *AikiCom*: **the physical and mental exploration of a mode of communication with oneself and with others, while applying the principles of aikido.** Our goal is to define the outline of what I call the *Aiki* attitude, which consists of centering ourselves to develop more harmony without losing the martial dimension because the world in which we live is far from being ideal; but it is the only one that we have and we can contribute to making it better. Martial kindness is clearly the main issue. That is to say, it is a struggle that mobilizes our energy to aim for more harmony, a commitment to action in order to instill kindness in our relationship with other people and with the world.

Regular practice of aikido promotes the integration of its principles through movement and offers extraordinary physical anchoring to

---

[17] This quote by Paul Watzlawick and Don Jackson in *The Pragmatics of Human Communication* (1967) became one of the presuppositions of Neurolinguistic Programming (NLP).

experience them in daily life[18]. But even if aikido is undoubtedly less demanding than other martial arts in terms of flexibility or force, it remains a practice that calls for good physical conditioning[19]. As an aikido instructor, I have had many opportunities to see men and women give up practicing aikido because their bodies no longer allowed it[20]. I have also shared the grief of people who, having discovered aikido late in life, had to give up learning the spirit of aikido because of failing health. One of the objectives of *AikiCom* is to allow those who cannot afford to commit to regular aikido practice, to physically experience the application of *Aiki* principles.

AikiCom was born at the crossroads of two paths that were not meant to meet, that of forty years of aikido practice, including twenty spent teaching it, and that of NLP[21]—the goal of which is the modeling of human skills.

The modeling of the physical practice of aikido allowed me to identify, isolate, and formalize sequences of movement that are drawn from aikido techniques which illustrate the principles of kind communication.

By creating *AikiCom* as an approach that is tied to—but distinct from—the martial art created by Morihei Ueshiba, a tremendous field of experimentation was opened in the area of communication and life skills. *AikiCom* allows the mixing of physical and language exercises, work with weapons and role playing, an area of cross-fertilization whose limits I have not yet finished exploring.

---

[18] Provided that the teaching gives meaning to the movement that is taught and that the techniques are executed only as opportunities to experience the fundamental principles of aikido.

[19] And this is true even though aikido can be practiced at the pace that suits us the best. It is not rare to find aikido practitioners who are over 70 years old on the *tatamis*.

[20] A checkup at a doctor's office is a prerequisite for practicing aikido.

[21] NLP as it is currently taught has become a study of tools and techniques for change rather than the learning of modeling. For more information on this topic, I refer the reader to the Méta-PNL site www.metapnl.com. I coined the term Méta-PNL in the year 2000 to return modeling to the heart of NLP.

Aiki, Philosophy of *Being* in Action

There is a controversy in the world of aikido concerning the heritage of Morihei Ueshiba. Some tell us that he had a deeply religious and spiritual vision that was entirely unique and Japanese. This vision, as such, couldn't pretend to become universal. The Japanese themselves admit that they had difficulty grasping the Founder's way of thinking[22]. If Kishomaru Ueshiba, his son, had not formalized aikido by structuring the practice—separating, along the way, everything related to this line of thought—it is likely that aikido would not have experienced the development that it is seeing today. Ueshiba's heirs, those students who had the privilege of following his teaching, carried on his memory, or at least what they grasped and made an impression on them. While practicing, each of them was seeking answers to personal questions, so it is normal that they all found different answers. When observing as a whole the schools or styles of aikido that followed in the footsteps of the Founder's direct students[23] we find the elements of the philosophy that Morihei Ueshiba wanted to pass on because the spirit of aikido is inseparable from its practice. Chase it out the door and it comes back in through the window.

Those who focus mainly on the technical practice of aikido are often ill at ease when facing the challenge of joining the spirit to the movement. They prefer to argue that there is no aikido without the perfect mastery of movement and that it is itself an endless path. Just because the path of technical progress is long does not mean that it has no end. We are limited by our physical ability, which evolves following a bell curve: we progress in technical mastery and physical condition until a peak, around the age of thirty or forty, then our abilities naturally decrease over the years. We can adapt our aikido practice to our physical condition and thus be able to practice for a long time. Although we can be delighted about this, we cannot hope

---

[22] Aside from two or three older students who are no longer with us, the direct students of Ueshiba were young Japanese, around twenty years old, who had difficulty understanding his speech and focused on the practice of techniques (according to the eyewitness account of Seishiro Endo, current technical director of the Tokyo Aikikai, during seminars that he has led in Belgium.)

[23] Traditionally, a master's students (*deshi*) who lived in his house (*uchi*) were known as uchi-deshi.

to reach our golden years without experiencing its effects. The myth of eternal youth still has a bright future ahead of it, especially when it is perpetuated by the advocates of our consumer society. One can consequently wonder if this sort of aikidoka isn't on a quest for some Holy Grail of perfect movement and nothing else. Most will stop along the way because of weariness or after the accumulation of small injuries and sprains or the consequences of thousands of falls they have taken during their long career on the mats.

It is surprising that we can talk so much about the virtues of peace, harmony, and nonviolence in aikido. However, these qualities appear very little in our behavior. Obviously, the very act of practicing does not inevitably bring the virtues of peace and harmony that everyone sees in aikido. As a result, there is a strong temptation to take refuge in a form of practice that has lost its martial qualities and retains only the spirit. There again the result will not materialize. By cutting off aikido from its physical dimension, you take away what makes it special, that is, the embodiment of a philosophy. The answer is to be found in the joining of the two aspects that make up the essence of aikido: movement and meaning, body and mind. I often illustrate this with the metaphor of two-part adhesive that is used, for example, to repair kayaks. These glues are made of two tubes containing products which, taken separately, cannot glue anything at all. However, once they are combined and applied together they have exceptional adhesive characteristics. It is the same for aikido: movement without meaning is simply gymnastics, meaning without movement is just useless talk .

While the physical dimension has been the subject of a precise formalization and worldwide consensus[24], we must wonder about the meaning of aikido practice. What do we mean when we talk about the meaning of aikido?

The primacy of physical practice has often reduced the spirit of aikido to a few slogans that are repeated in *dojo* advertisements. To avoid clichés and fancy words, it is necessary to look at the message that Morihei Ueshiba wanted to give to us and to separate what belongs

---

[24] The quarrels between schools come more from questions of style and variations than from disagreements on the fundamentals.

to the esoteric Buddhism that moved Ueshiba, from the universal aspects that could touch every human being.

The Martial Kindness of *Aiki*

"In my opinion, it [aikido] can be said to be the true martial art. The reason for this is that it is a martial art based on universal truth. This Universe is composed of many different parts, and yet the Universe as a whole is united as a family and symbolizes the ultimate state of peace. Holding such a view of the Universe, aikido cannot be anything but a martial art of love. It cannot be a martial art of violence.[25]"

> *Aiki is the power of harmony,*
> *Of all beings, all things working together.*
> *Relentlessly train yourself—Followers of the Way.*
> Morihei Ueshiba[26]

What distinguishes aikido from all the other martial arts is its philosophy, which aims at restoring harmony in combat situations. In concrete terms, the aikidoka will lead the attacker, the *uke*, in a circular movement that will neutralize the attack and thus render it pointless. The goal is therefore not to destroy or injure the attacker, but to lead him toward a new situation. Born from the synthesis of combat martial arts whose goal was to be able to vanquish adversaries who were physically stronger, aikido developed by applying the principle inherited from jiu-jitsu according to which the soft person controls the stiff and the flexible person conquers the rigid. The aikidoka is in the center of the movement, this immobile space that connects him to the universe and allows him to develop the harmony of the body and spirit in accord with "the truth of the universe[27]." Aikido practice is more than the search for mere personal balance. To take on its full magnitude, it ought to be part of a more universal balance.

---

[25] Excerpt from an interview with Morihei Ueshiba and his son Kisshomaru by two anonymous journalists, and published in Japanese under the title "Aikido" by Kisshomaru Ueshiba, Tokyo Kowado 1957. Japanese translation by Stanley Pranin for the periodical *Aiki News* No. 18, August 1976.
[26] Kisshomaru Ueshiba quoting Morihei Ueshiba in *The Spirit of Aikido*, page 31.
[27] *Ibid.*, page 36.

> *"Nen[28] is never concerned with winning or losing, and it grows by becoming properly connected to the ki of the universe."*[29]

Aikido as it was conceived of by Morihei Ueshiba truly proposes a martial ethic: the aikidoka trains for combat but from a perspective of kindness. That is to say, he is always aware that victory is attained through peace and harmony.

The true challenge of the aikidoka is therefore not technical mastery with the intent of assuring him supremacy in combat, but the mastery of himself, of his emotions, and of his desire to resort to violence as a response to his opponent's attack.

> *"The state of mind of the Aikidoka must be peaceful and totally nonviolent. That is to say, that special state of mind which brings violence into a state of harmony. And this I think is the true spirit of Japanese martial arts. We have been given this earth to transform into a heaven on earth. Warlike activity is totally out of place."*[30]

The Reversal of the Body-Mind Relationship

The fact that aikido has always refused to go along with a sports and competition mindset has allowed it to preserve its very spirit even if it is difficult to make the connection between effective physical training in aikido dojos and aikido's underlying philosophy. It remains difficult to go beyond this duality between body and spirit—here, I mean the duality between physical practice and the philosophy or spirituality of aikido.

Morihei Ueshiba was not only an expert in martial arts. His practice was an integral part of a spiritual search. His teaching did not separate

---

[28] *Nen* is a Japanese term that is difficult to translate. According to Kisshomaru Ueshiba, it evokes the concentration of the spirit in the search for a certain form of unity of order in the universe. It is, for this reason, the heart of aikido practice. It is the principle of true practice. Without nen, practice cannot hope to go beyond the simple stage of technical prowess and could even lead to tragic consequences that can lead to destruction.

[29] *Ibid.*, pp. 36-37.

[30] *The Spirit of Aikido* by Kisshomaru Ueshiba, Tokyo, Kowado, 1957, pages 198-219.

the physical dimension (*keiko* or training) from the spiritual dimension. In the first volume of *Carnets de Takemusu Aiki*[31], Bruno Traversi gives us an interesting interpretation of the thoughts of the Founder of aikido in order to understand the connection between physical practice and the spiritual dimension of aikido.

For Ueshiba, aikido was above all a physical art but Traversi warns us: "...for Ueshiba, the body does not present itself as a fixed reality but as a reality that is open to changes, and even to transmutation.[32]" To avoid being too wordy, I will sum up what I gathered from Traversi's analysis while inviting you nevertheless to read his analysis in its entirety.

For Ueshiba, the body is both an obstacle and a medium to allow the soul to attain its fulfillment. Ueshiba mentions two psychic entities to be aware of when talking about the human being: the *physical soul* and the *spiritual soul*. The *physical soul,* also called the body of flesh, is sensitive. It is connected to the world in which it is immersed. It makes distinctions between things and it separates them. Very often, it acts in reaction to events and it is subject to the laws of cause and effect. This *physical soul* is, according to Ueshiba, created by the center, but it is directed toward the outside. The *spiritual soul* is intimately connected to the center. It is connected to the unique, to the universal, and it is located in the timeless. According to Ueshiba, progress on the *Aiki* path must lead us to what he calls inner reversal or internal revolution by inverting the dominance of the *physical soul* over the *spiritual soul*. This reversal leads to a transformation of our way of *acting*. The *physical soul* acts in the temporal, by an action-reaction process; the *spiritual soul* acts spontaneously, in synchronicity. This is what Ueshiba calls "marvelous action

---

[31] A team of professors and graduate students under the direction of Bruno Traversi carried out a systematic exploration of Ueshiba's explanations. Their work was published under the titles *TakeMusu Aiki*, Éditions du cénacle, 2006, 2008, and *Les carnets de Takemusu Aiki, Carnet d'étude fondamentale sur la pensée de Morihei Ueshiba, Volume 1, Le Corps et le Sabre, Éditions du cénacle, 2010.* The original writings, some of which were translated into a Western language for the first time, were accompanied by commentaries and explanations.
[32] Translated from *Les carnets de Takemusu Aiki, Carnet d'étude fondamentale sur la pensée de Morihei Ueshiba, Volume 1, Le Corps et le Sabre, Éditions du cénacle, 2010*, page *19*.

[*myōyō*],³³" the coincidental juxtaposition of things and events. The simultaneously universal and unique nature of the center allows us to go beyond the Japanese concept of *Mâ*, which can be described as space-time. When we watch films showing Ueshiba practicing, we intuitively grasp this notion of simultaneity, this moment where the attack and the defense are no longer part of a causal sequence, but seem to happen at the same time. In this particular dimension of practice, the attack no longer has a *raison d'être* and neither does the fight. The universe regains its coherence and harmony is reestablished.

The challenge of practice is to bring about this reversal, giving the *spiritual soul* its dominance over the *body of flesh*. Discipline and training perform this switch: instead of the aikido practitioner executing the movement, a state is reached where the movement springs up spontaneously. This can only happen when the practitioner maintains his center, in contact with everything that surrounds him.

It is clear that this practice described by the founder of aikido is a highly spiritual view that can seem very distant from today's practice. However, many aikidokas who have reached a certain level have already had this sort of experience during *randoris* or moments of intense practice. During these moments that are often very brief and even furtive, time seems to no longer exist or it gives the impression that everything is happening in slow motion; movements seem to emerge without having been decided consciously and they meet uke's action in a perfectly synchronized way. These extraordinary moments have been studied by Mihaly Csikszentmihalyi and are called "flow experiences."

Csikszentmihalyi studied flow experiences (or optimal experiences) for over twenty years throughout the world, in various areas, and with people who were both exceptional (mountain climbers, musicians, great sportsmen) and ordinary (surgeons, teachers, retired people, workers, etc.).³⁴ The result of these observations reveals that one of the characteristics of these experiences results from a state of

---

33 In French "agissement merveilleux", *Ibid.*, page 30.
34 Mihaly Csikszentmihalyi, *Vivre, la Psychologie du bonheur*, Éditions Robert Laffont, Paris, 2004. Jean-François Vézina, *Les Hasards nécessaires,* Les Éditions de l'Homme, Montréal, Québec, 2001.

concentration that transforms the perception of time and creates the feeling of spontaneous action.

The new paradigm of quantum physics also confirms temporal switching through the notion of emergence that underlies two levels of reality: that which is apparent, evident, and visible, and that which is not but could become so. David Bohm formalized these two realities by defining the notions of explicate and implicate order. Implicate order contains the seeds of what can spring up in our reality. This emergence will not take place except under certain favorable conditions:

> *"The logic of the emergent process is an attempt (a temporary one) to translate the movement of life. To take up one of Francisco Varela's expressions, it has to do with a 'logic of viability.' Could this viability correspond to a sort of organic intelligence by which the Universe and the human being, in particular, were shaped? Ephemeral events and configurations are the visible vestiges of this and their linking together is a confirmation."* [35]

The internationalization of aikido necessitated setting aside Ueshiba's thinking, which was judged to be too obscure and without a doubt was mistakenly considered not to be universal enough. By doing this, the baby was probably thrown out with the bath water a little too quickly. While it is clear that it is idealistic and useless to try to grasp all of Ueshiba's thought, given that our Western reference points (in terms of language, nationality, culture, generation, and spirituality) are so different, it is still interesting to take a look at the message that he left us. Otherwise, all we would have left would be to content ourselves with repeating overly simplified messages of peace, universal harmony, and love along with a physical aikido practice that has become more and more disconnected from its philosophical messages.

Now, at the beginning of the third millennium, we must admit that the philosophy that inspired aikido is the subject of renewed interest.

---

[35] Translation of a passage from: Bernadette Lamboy, *Devenir qui je suis, une autre Approche de la Personne*, 2003, Desclée de Brouwer, page 87.

The twentieth century saw Mankind commit unspeakable atrocities and develop weapons that are capable of destroying all of humanity several times over, before throwing itself into a capitalist, financial, and consumerist tailspin that is exhausting the planet and threatens to throw it irreversibly out of balance. In this crazy and foolish race, we have seen men and women stand up against inevitability and restore respectability to the notion of combat. People like Gandhi, Martin Luther King, and Nelson Mandela paved the way for a struggle that espouses nonviolence, in a form of combat where force is of another nature. It is not about responding to violence with violence, but rather about using strategies that will transform violence into an unacceptable behavior and prevent it from producing its anticipated effects.

On an individual scale, we notice the evolution towards a senseless individualism. The rejection of any form of authority or imposed truth led to a loss of reference points, a loss of meaning. Life seems to have been reduced to the slogan "work more to consume more." The cult of essentially materialistic individual success destroyed numerous forms of solidarity. This trend has revealed its limits and many voices have risen up to change this race that is leading us straight into a wall. The end of the 1960s made us want to believe in the slogan "peace and love" but this cry was crushed by the steamroller of mass consumption.

The Occupy Wall Street movement[36] is a significant modern example of the expression of a desire for widespread change and a wish to obtain it without resorting to violence, a revolution without a bloodbath. After powerlessness there seems to come a desire to act, to become a player again, to carry on a fight, but without violence. A mobilization centered on kindness, a kindness born from the vague feeling that our species is threatened, that our children will inherit a world where it will be difficult, even impossible, for them to live if nothing changes.

Connecting Oneself with the World

Ueshiba's thought is an extraordinarily modern response to today's challenges. Starting with a return to oneself through centering, his

---

[36] This movement was an offshoot of *el movimiento de los indignados,* which sprang up in Spain in 2011.

vision relies on the awareness of our individuality to connect ourselves to the universe that surrounds us. The process implies a softening of the boundaries of our ego that supports the feeling of being distinct, isolated, separated. We reconnect ourselves, or rather regain awareness of being connected to others and to the world. Martial combat becomes the place for a metamorphosis where conflict turns into a meeting. The meeting of energies does not lead to defeat; it becomes a place for transmutation, so that life may nourish life.

In my vision of aikido, combat creates the framework that permits the development of our humanity through the indispensable encounter with another person—in his difference—and through confidence in the transformational potential that is born from this meeting. The important thing is to accept the inherent risk of being alive. We mobilize our vital energy to struggle against entropy, the disorder whose inescapable nature was revealed by the second law of thermodynamics. This contribution of energy creates the order that emerges from chaos. This is the combat of life, where we find the *ki* of *Aiki*.

This is clearly a mechanism that is quasi-biological in nature.

Ethics According to Edgar Morin

While aikido is essentially a humanistic, humane, martial approach, we realize that it embraces an ethical standard in the sense described by Edgar Morin. In the last volume of *La Méthode*, the French sociologist and philosopher explains how the Big Bang, the event that gave birth to the Universe that we know, caused incredible forces of dispersion. Matter organized itself into atoms, stars, and planets, including the Earth. In this extraordinarily exceptional environment, what Morin describes as the unexpected victory of the forces of connectedness in their pathetic struggle against dispersal[37] has permitted the birth of macromolecules and then created conditions that were favorable for life. The first single-cell organisms became diversified to create flora and then fauna, forming what we call the biosphere. Astonishingly, the weak binding forces—source of life—continued to develop by resisting the incessant forces of separation. The diversity of species, and then demographic growth, gathered

---

[37] Edgar Morin, *La méthode volume 6, Éthique*, Éditions du Seuil, 2004, page 28.

individuals into packs, troops, communities, villages, and families, thus creating new forces of separation. In order to continue, life integrated death by assuring the survival of the species through reproduction and death, as well as through the food chain, which turned certain species into predators and others into prey. Through the course of evolution, rivalries were passed on within communities. Survival was only assured at the price of an improbable balance between competition, rivalry and a feeling of belonging. We retain within ourselves a vague feeling of being connected to others through a common ancestor. Deep down within us, there echoes a vague impression that our own survival depends on the survival of others. And despite this, we remain tempted by an instinct of rivalry, a desire to distinguish ourselves, to be different, to show our freedom to be an independent being. It is the unique individual who is distinct, and wants to be free, but whose survival depends on that of his species. This is the eternal struggle between solidarity and the devil[38]. Edgar Morin defines ethics as being, " the expression among independent and responsible individuals of the imperative of connectedness ".[39] The more the individual becomes conscious of being distinct from others, the more he feels isolated, worried, and uncertain, and the more intense will be his feeling of interconnectedness. As a conscious being, he feels lost in the immense universe and has a cruel need to feel connected to his brothers and sisters. The feeling of belonging, of family, of paradise, and of general harmony are thus only the manifestation of a vital necessity. By giving birth to beings that were more and more complex, life created the most elaborate form of interdependence. It is known as solidarity, friendship, and love. The history of the Universe, which has never ceased to expand since the Big Bang, is only a frantic search for an invisible form of interconnectedness, for the memory of its constituent particles of having been connected, infinitely near, beyond time and space.

---

[38] In French, the word *diable* is based on the Greek *diabolos*, which means "he who separates."
[39] *Ibid.*, page 114.

The Martial Dimension of the Kind Warrior

From the great cosmic mirror
Without beginning and without end,
Human society became manifest.
At that time liberation and confusion arose.
When fear and doubt occurred
Towards the confidence which is primordially free,
Countless multitudes of cowards arose.
When the confidence which is primordially free
Was followed and delighted in,
Countless multitudes of warriors arose.[40]

Warriorship here does not refer to making war on others. Aggression is the source of our problems, not the solution. Here the word "warrior" is taken from the Tibetan "pawo," which literally means "one who is brave." Warriorship in this context is the tradition of human bravery, or the tradition of fearlessness.[41]

"Granted that you may, in fact, experience the mind of a warrior on occasion; resolute, flexible, clear, and free of doubt. You can develop the body of a warrior, lithe, supple, sensitive, and filled with energy. In rare moments, you may even feel the heart of a warrior, loving everything and everyone who appears before you. But these qualities are fragmented in you. You lack integration. My task is to put you back together again, Humpty."[42]

The term *warrior* will not fail to make some of you shudder, as it continues to do for me as I write these lines. Nevertheless, the term deserves some attention. Several authors who are far from warmongers have gone so far as to write books about the subject: Chögyam Trungpa, author of *Shambhala, The Sacred Path of the Warrior;* Paulo Coelho, with his *Le Manuel du Guerrier de la Lumière;* Carlos

---

[40] Chögyam Trungpa, *The Sacred Path of the Warrior*, page 9.
[41] *Ibid.*, page 12.
[42] Dan Millman, *The Way of the Peaceful Warrior*, page 16.

Castaneda in his introductory books about Don Juan, the Yaqui sorcerer; Fabrice Midal, author of *La voie du Chevalier;* and Dan Millman with his book *The Peaceful Warrior,* which was made into a Hollywood movie.

The warrior is an archetype that symbolizes valor, courage, and commitment. There emanates from him an energy that he embodies through action in the service of a cause. The warrior knows that he will not shirk a responsibility and it is by this path that he hopes for victory. Carlos Castaneda maintains that, " The basic difference between an ordinary man and a warrior is that a warrior takes everything as a challenge, while an ordinary man takes everything either as a blessing or as a curse. "[43]

Whatever happens to him, he takes charge of it. If the word "warrior" evokes war, it is in order to understand the capacity of combat to reestablish peace, justice, and harmony. The warrior is not a frustrated and insensitive being; he lives out the experience of the tender heart. This sensitivity is the root of the bravery that permits him to open himself up to the world without resistance and to face it[44].

We find the warrior archetype in all civilizations: among Native Americans, but also in South America, in Europe (with the image of King Arthur, who exemplifies the knightly ideal), in the *Bible* (with King David), and even in Japan among the *samurai*.

The image of the warrior is used more and more as a model of commitment, of desire, and of courage whether in business or, especially, in the world of sports. The warrior's training is both physical and psycho-spiritual. The martial arts are the archetypal image of it. In Japan, the martial arts are rooted in the combat arts that taught people how to survive and be victorious on the field of battle (*Bushido*). With the Meiji era[45], Japan came out of its isolation and opened itself up to the world. The warrior arts then evolved to become a way, a path to personal and spiritual fulfillment (*Budo*).

---

[43] Carlos Castaneda, *Tales of Power,* page 61.
[44] Chögyam Trungpa in *The Sacred Path of the Warrior.*
[45] The Meiji era lasted from 1868 until 1912 (Wikipedia, Meiji period; consulted August 3, 2015).

Training in the martial arts is training in victory over oneself even more than over another person. The warrior is not spared by fear; it is by overcoming fear that he shows his courage.

Fabrice Midal's knight[46] is a man who is driven by hope and courage. He tries to make his action meaningful for himself, but also for others. According to Midal, the knightly ideal is now more necessary than ever. It is accessible to everyone in order to wage a new form of war: the economic war. Society confines its individuals to a grey uniformity, a forced egalitarianism from which it seems the only way out is through competition. However, Midal asserts that this competition aims less at bettering ourselves than pitting us against each other. The peace in which we live is managed like we manage our budget, our emotions, our stress. Even politics seems resigned to managing the State. Midal calls on knightly heroism to come out of this accounting perspective that makes our modern life so dull. For the knight, the choice is not between action and contemplation. Thought and action are inseparable. He thus escapes from the trap of feverish action, of escaping into doing. The knight is not a restless activist. He is ready for what arises and he acts when he feels that it is right to act. He has a sense of duty, refuses to yield, and devotes himself to ambitious goals while remaining worthy in all circumstances. It is Nietzsche who gives the best description of his dragon:

> *"Apathetic habit, all that is base and petty, filling every corner of the earth and billowing up around all that is great like a heavy breath of the earth, casts itself across the path that greatness has to tread on its way to immortality and retards, deceives, suffocates and stifles it.*[47]*"*

The *Aiki* Attitude

The conscious (that is, aware) practice of aikido leads to noticeable changes in our way of being, a consequence of the repeated practice of gestures and movements[48]. An *aiki* manner of behaving, of

---

[46] Fabrice Midal, *L'esprit de la chevalerie*, Paris, Presses de la Renaissance, 2005.
[47] Friedrich Nietzsche, *Untimely Meditations*, edited by Daniel Breazeale, page 68.
[48] This form of learning is illustrated in the movie *The Karate Kid* (1984), when we see the instructor train young Daniel Larusso by giving him tasks of cleaning or painting in order to teach him how to fight.

observing and feeling the attack when it comes, the indispensable relaxation that allows an optimal management of muscle tone, the perception of the other person and the *aiki* way of blending with the other person's energy in order to transform it are qualities that can only be learned through repetition. If we add to this the mental dimension that conditions the intent at the heart of the movement and the will to not turn to violence, we construct, from the *body in movement*, a philosophy of *being in action*. The embodiment of this philosophy of *being* makes up what I call the *Aiki* attitude. This attitude includes the physical dimension and transcends it[49] to encompass an ethics of life, and in a more general way, a manner of understanding the world and our experience. *AikiCom* goes beyond the physical learning of aikido and ties it to our mental experience in order to apply its principles. A radical change follows from it in our manner of seeing the world and giving meaning to our experiences. Simultaneously more present and in harmony with ourselves, we can control our action without expending our energy struggling to exhaustion against the elements, but in perceiving the subtle variations of our environment that allow us to act with a minimum of effort in order to reach our objective. Water that meets a rock goes around it to return to the sea, without clashing or giving up. In the same state of mind, we slip into the flow of life while breathing our kind influence into it. A feeling of ease and well-being, difficult to put into words, flows from it. We have the feeling of doing the right thing and doing it at the right moment. It is not surprising that our life is punctuated by synchronicities[50], events that occur, not by a causal connection, but rather by a connection of meaning. It is as though chance took it upon itself to make a new order emerge in nature, in a creative way.

To define an attitude is not easy. I have chosen to present it to you in the form of five premises and four qualities.

---

[49] On this subject, one can talk about the *holon*, a term invented by Arthur Koestler, which defines an entity that is both a part of something and, in and of itself, a totality. *AikiCom* is an approach in its own right and includes the practice of aikido itself.
[50] It was Carl Gustav Jung who defined synchronicity as being a phenomenon that is produced when an external, objective event coincides with a specific psychic state. For example, you are thinking about a person when suddenly the phone rings. You answer and it is that very person who is calling you.

The Premises of the *Aiki* Attitude

> *Premise: From Medieval Latin premissa ("set before") [premissa propositio ("the proposition set before")], feminine past participle of Latin praemittere ("to send or put before"), from prae- ("before") + mittere ("to send").*
>
> *A proposition antecedently supposed or proved; something previously stated or assumed as the basis of further argument; a condition; a supposition.*[51]

Premise 1 (P1): Being in the Flow

> *"My God, grant me the courage to change*
> *the things I can change,*
> *The serenity to accept the things I cannot change,*
> *and the wisdom to know the difference."*[52]

Feeling that things are "flowing" naturally, that they are moving with ease is a great pleasure in life. On the other hand, if an event or a project seems to run into countless obstacles, if the energy to carry it out is particularly intense, even excessive, perhaps it would be better to reconsider it, postpone it, or even cancel it. As with any form of popular or ancestral wisdom, there's many a slip 'twixt cup and lip. The practice of *Aiki* movements makes us experience this premise through our bodies. When my partner grabs me by my shoulders, I can resist and try to push him back. If I am stronger than he is, I will succeed. On the contrary, he might push harder and make me lose ground. In the flow approach, when I feel a push I don't try to resist or confront—which would have the effect of strengthening the push. Instead, in the same way as water that moves around a rock, I explore movement that will use this energy and transform it without ever trying to oppose it. Regular practice of the movements of aikido etches this principle in our neurological system and in our muscles, which makes it easier to use in other life events, and not only physical ones.

---

[51] Wiktionary, premise, consulted on June 4, 2015.
[52] The author of this stoic quote, which is sometimes called the "serenity prayer" has not been confirmed.

Most of the difficulties that we experience find their roots in a lack of fluidity. We hold onto thoughts, beliefs, and situations that immobilize us even though they do not suit us. We very often do not even notice these inflexibilities because they have become so habitual for us. And when we become aware of them, the fear of letting them go can prevent us from moving forward and finding new options. We are then like the creatures who populate the bottom of the river in the following story:

> Migar belonged to a very special tribe. This tribe lived at the bottom of a pretty mountain stream that tumbled joyously down to the river and then the sea. The members of the tribe had learned to resist the flow of the water by hanging onto small branches that grew at the bottom of the stream. This had become second nature and Migar really didn't think about it anymore. But from time to time it so happened that some people, because of fatigue, let go of the branches that kept them with the tribe and found themselves carried far away, in the flow of the stream. The others said that dreadful misfortunes, incredible pain and torment befell those people and that one had to remain solidly attached to avoid meeting the same fate. Migar respected this rule that had been handed down by the elders, but he did not feel happy in this situation. One day, he decided to let go of the branch and go through the experience himself. When he relaxed his hand, it was with an inexpressible fear and the clear feeling that he would never see his loved ones again. However, this fear changed very quickly. When the flow carried him away, he had a feeling of great lightness, of relief. His mind was full of uncertainty and he recalled the dreadful stories told by the Elders, who had never let go of their own branches. As he flowed along, he was astonished to discover wondrous scenery. He found new peoples, fish, frogs, and loads of new things. He found all the food that he desired while floating with the current. One day he discovered a welcoming bank where the current had calmed and where he could live without having to hang on as he had in the past. There, he met other beings, some of whom had, before him, let go of their branches. He lived happily, but not without thinking regretfully about his companions upstream who, by hanging on to

the plants of the stream had deprived themselves of seeing all these new worlds[53].

Premise 2 (P2): Awareness of My Condition as a Learning Being

Warriorship is a continual journey. To be a warrior is to learn to be genuine in every moment of your life. (Chögyam Trungpa, Shambhala, The Sacred Path of the Warrior, page 31)

Living beings can only survive by learning. Humberto Maturana and Francesco Varela, in their effort to define living systems, defined the concept of *autopoiesis*. *Autopoiesis* is the characteristic of living systems that must unceasingly react to disruptions of their environment by compensating for them or by replacing some of their components to assure the stability of their own organized structure.

A living system that does not learn is doomed to die.

> *"In a living thing, all organizing activity is cognition, as much in its internal development as in its interactions with the environment. One can therefore say that the mind is more a process than a thing. But what is cognition? Maturana and Varela developed the Santiago theory, which defines cognition. This theory considerably broadens the process of cognition and even that of the mind. According to the authors, the brain is not necessary for there to be cognition. A bacterium is endowed with a mind even though it has no brain. The process of cognition is seen in a very broad sense. It includes perception, emotion, and action, in addition to the thought process. For the human being, cognition also includes language, conceptual thought, and all the other attributes of human awareness. The entire living thing is involved in this process of cognition. It is no longer limited to the brain alone, nor to the nervous system. Recent studies have shown that the nervous system, the immune system, and the endocrine system, which are traditionally seen*

---

[53] This is my adaptation of a story that is often told in hypnosis sessions to help a client learn to "let go."

> as three separate systems, make up, in reality, a unique cognitive network."[54]

This concept of a learning system was applied by Peter Senge[55] to the business world. Learning organizations make their members' learning easier and enduring in order to favor a sort of continuous improvement. The quality of *being* a learner guarantees our integration in an environment that is essentially changing.

The premise of the *Aiki* attitude emphasizes the indispensable curiosity that makes it up. Rather than projecting all my presuppositions onto the other person, I develop what the Japanese call *shoshin*, or the beginner's mind. I approach the other with an open mind.

Nan-in, a Japanese master of the Meiji era (1868-1912), one day received a university professor who had come to learn about Zen. Nan-in served him tea. He poured a full cup for his visitor and then continued to pour. The professor watched the tea overflow until he could no longer restrain himself.

"It's full. No more will go in!"

"Like this cup," Nan-in said, "you are full of your own opinions and speculations. How could I show you Zen unless you have first emptied your cup?"

Buddhists tell us over and over that all is impermanence. Heraclitus said the same thing when he wrote, "No man ever steps in the same river twice.[56]" When I live through a new experience, when something disturbs an order that seemed to be unchanging, I can see this change as a threat and turn to reptilian survival reflexes. If, on the other hand, I have the awareness of being in the flow, I do not struggle against what comes my way; I accept it and I am delighted by what that can teach me, even if the experience is difficult, indeed even if it is painful. Premises P1 and P2 plunge me into a fluid life dynamic, in a constant search for the best way to fit into my environment.

---

[54] Christian Vanhenten in *Au-delà de la Magie, la Méta-PNL*, Ed. La Bienveillance, 2001.
[55] Peter Senge, *The Fifth Discipline,* Currency Doubleday, 1990.
[56] Wikipedia, Heraclitus, consulted June 29, 2015.

Premise 3 (P3): Awareness of Being a Connected Individual

The ego is the representation that we have of ourselves[57]. It is the crystallization of our identity, that which makes us unique and different from the rest of the world. This representation is the fruit of the awareness that we have of ourselves, this view we have of ourselves that gives us the feeling of existing as a being. Its anthem is Guy Béart's song "Parlez-moi de moi."

Talk to me about me,
That's all that interests me
Talk to me about me
That's all that excites me
About my loves, my moods, my affections
About my changes of heart, my fits of rage, my weaknesses
Talk to me about me
Sometimes roughly
But talk to me, talk to me about me[58].

The ego is characterized by an urgent need to exist and to assure its survival. Everything that contributes to connecting me to other people, to these beings who are different from me, constitutes a threat to my ego. The ego is also very resistant to change. It is the defender of what is identical, that is, of what does not change.

I experience being me when I can say, "I" or "me." This experience of being oneself is twofold in nature. It is both authentic (who am I really?) and illusory. The ego is this illusory part.

In numerous spiritual approaches, the ego is seen as a false, or at least limited, representation of ourselves. It can be compared to a veil, a screen that masks our authentic self, emerging from the depths of our nature. It deprives us of the freedom to evolve toward who we really

---

[57] The *ego* is often translated in literature as the "self." I do not intend to go into any scientific explanations which would weigh down the discussion and would not be of any help in understanding what I would like to communicate. I will therefore use the term *ego* to talk about the concept of the part of me whose goal is to create and maintain my awareness of being me as a distinct and unique individual in the universe. The *ego* only exists as the effect of a certain phenomenon among human beings: the awareness of self; the self can be defined as the subject of the process that is called cognition, a fundamental process that defines living systems.
[58] "Parlez-moi de moi" (Loose translation; lyrics and music by Guy Béart, 1980)

are by keeping us in conditions of difficulty and suffering. Freeing ourselves from the domination of the ego can thus be seen as the act of lifting the veil to reveal our authentic self.

The ego is a part of the duality that creates our feeling of being separate, to the same extent as the authentic self is non-dual and connects us. Love, compassion, and true presence are just as much expressions of our true self. Our true self is sometimes called the "non-self" or the "non-ego."

The ego is quite logically at the root of our egoistic (selfish) attitudes by isolating us from others. The "self" takes up all the room and makes us inaccessible to others; it isolates us.

Numerous scientific studies arrive at the same conclusion as do Buddhists: the ego is an illusion. Awareness of self is a virtuality.

> *"The existential concern that animates our entire discussion in this book results from the tangible demonstration within cognitive science that the self or cognizing subject is fundamentally fragmented, divided, or non-unified"*[59]

In this age of virtual reality and of films with special effects that have become undetectable, it is not surprising that an illusion may seem more real than reality. It is the same for the ego, which assures our feeling of being a person. The main thing is to not let ourselves be pushed to the limit of the ego's reasoning, all the while keeping our awareness of being individuals who are endowed with our own will and of living this incredible phenomenological experience that permits me to say "I."

Premise 4 (P4): Awareness That the other Person Is Also a Being

While it is relatively easy to admit that I am a person and that I am endowed with a view of things and of my own will, and while in return for a certain amount of effort I can contemplate being connected with the universe that surrounds me, it is sometimes difficult for me to recognize, to admit, and above all to accept that the other person may be a person like me—above all when I am in conflict with him or her.

---

[59] Francisco Varela, Evan Thompson, Eleanor Rosch in *The Embodied Mind*, Introduction, page xvii.

In conflict, I tend to want to master my environment and put it at the service of the satisfaction of my needs, of my desires. The other person is then no more than a troublemaker. I do not understand that he may not see things as I do and that he may not be going along with my wishes. It is far easier for me to accept that an *object* can resist my desire than to see a *person* oppose it deliberately.

> Etchemin was impatient to find his lover. Just one more hour of paddling his canoe and he would hold her in his arms. The usually peaceful river seemed to be angry. The rain pattered on the waves and Etchemin had to row energetically to offset the effects of the current. Suddenly, Etchemin saw another canoe approaching in the distance and heading toward him. With the rain, Etchemin could not see the rower, but the latter seemed to have trouble controlling his boat. Seeing him heading toward the right, Etchemin rowed toward the left. But the canoe in front of him turned and also went to the left. With a powerful movement of his oar, Etchemin pointed the bow of his canoe toward the right. But the other canoe did the same. Etchemin felt anger rise within him. What was this guy doing? If he continued in this way, a collision would be unavoidable. Over the repeated course corrections, the two craft approached dangerously close to each other and Etchemin yelled with rage. Suddenly, he saw that the canoe in front of him was empty. There was no one on board. Etchemin understood the reason for these changes of direction. His anger vanished immediately. How could he be angry if it was just an empty canoe?

Recognizing the other person as an autonomous being is the premise of the notion of mutual respect. How can I respect the other person if I do not see him as a person in his own right? And how can I hope for him to respect me if I can't do the same?

The awareness of the other person as an autonomous being thwarts the desire to transform the other person into an object that is at my service to reach my objectives. It is the very essence of the verb "to manipulate," which literally means to hold and use something with one's hands, as a tool. A hammer, a saw, or a laptop computer do not have a will of their own. These are objects that I use for my personal aims. If the tool or object does not correspond entirely to what I need it to do, I can adapt it by adding accessories to it, transforming it in order to achieve my result. In conflict, we often find ourselves wanting to change the other person, to transform him so that he adopts my view of the world and modifies his behavior in the way that I expect him or her to act. My ego has transformed the other person into an object, carefully avoiding giving him the privilege that I gave myself, that is, to also be a separate being, another self. "I" does not want "You" to exist and turns the "You" into an object[60].

Recognizing the other person as an autonomous being, separate and endowed with his own will, is to see in him all the components that I recognize in myself. This awareness of the other as a person is the source of infinite lessons (see Premise 2) and opens the door to the relational dynamic of the following premise.

Premise 5 (P5): The Connection Nurtures Life

If I give up making the other person into an object, in other words, if I say goodbye to control over him or her, I run the risk of not getting everything that I want, or at least not as easily as I may wish.

I could consider this to be a defeat, a source of frustration, because my desire will not be fulfilled the way I wanted. By limiting my assessment to the narrow scope of my ego, I lose the wider perspective, that which makes me a being who belongs to a greater whole. The *Aiki* attitude invites us to create space for ourselves and become aware of the importance of the concept of connection. Connections to myself, to the other person, to my environment and, in a wider sense, to the universe. I am a *holon*, a term defined by Arthur Koestler and broadly adopted by Ken Wilber. A *holon* is an entity that is simultaneously a part of something and, by itself, a totality. Many authors denounce the fragmentation of our view of the world.[61] By distinguishing men from women, the mind from the body, myself from the other person, physics from chemistry, human from non-human, we have lost the global viewpoint, the ecological picture that highlights the connections between living things and their environment.

---

[60] We will return to this dynamic when we examine Aiki action and its principle in the section titled "The Quadrants of Kindness," beginning on page 239.
[61] I am talking principally about authors such as Ken Wilber, Fritjof Capra, and Edgar Morin.

If premise 4 made me see the *other* as a person, premise 5 connects me to him or her, but it does not stop there. It encompasses my environment, others, and the world. It is a form of ecological awareness, of interpersonal and intergenerational solidarity, taking the ecosystem into account in a global way.

Violation of These Premises

The failure to respect these premises inevitably leads to the following distortions:

Violation of Premise 1 "Being in the Flow"

Useless exhaustion that generates resentment at not recognizing the given effort, a desire for power and control that is doomed to failure.

Violation of Premise 2 "Awareness of My Condition As a Learning Being"

Loss of meaning, belief that things (and especially thoughts) are static, established once and for all, certainties and fundamentalism, belief in any form of absolute or subjective truth (my beliefs are my truth and describe how I believe the world to be), loss of the condition of being a learning child (*shoshin*, beginner's mind), misunderstanding of the fundamental processes of life, of the healing of living beings, of metabolism that is not just related to food, but also to the mind.

Violation of Premise 3 "Awareness of Being a Connected Individual"

Egoism, egocentricity, "me first," "my way or the highway," "not in my backyard (NIMBY)." Disconnect from others, with resulting affective loss of the nourishing aspect of connection; the illusion of the ego is dominant.

Violation of Premise 4 "Awareness That the Other Person Is Also a Being"

Manipulative behavior, not only to do harm, but also for the good of the other person (at least what we have decided is good for the other person); loss of confidence in the other person; resentment towards someone who does not act as I believe he must act; attempt to make the other person an object in order to control him better; and lack of control over more easily accepting not being satisfied (in the same way that I would not be angry against a wall that did not let me pass, while I will become angry if it is a person who stops me).

Violation of Premise 5 "Connection Nourishes Life"

Absence of a feeling of belonging; tied to the violation of Premise 3, it makes us perceive ourselves as unique beings, separate from the rest of the world, opening the door to shortsighted decisions, not taking into account consequences that do not affect us, or whose impact is far in the future, or which affect other people and other generations: spilling pollution into sewers, knowing that these products will pollute the rivers where, perhaps later, we will take a swim; consumption of products that are manufactured at low prices by vulnerable people (children, exploited people, etc.) in distant regions or countries; deforestation to create more pastures.

The Qualities of the *Aiki* Attitude

The qualities that allow us to better describe the *Aiki* attitude come from its fundamental premises.

Flexibility

Supple in its means, firm with respect to its objectives. This formula applies to the *Aiki* attitude. This fluidity is like that of water, which—when it becomes the wave of a tsunami—can smash solid buildings and which, in other circumstances, can slip into the tiniest cracks to go around the obstacles that are in its way.

When an action starts from your center, it opens itself up to all possibilities and unfolds itself according to what arises, without anticipation. In *randori*, the practitioner remains centered and does not anticipate the form of the next attack. When the attack comes, he slips into its energy. The technique that emerges from this has not been anticipated because it would not have been possible to take into account the reality of the moment. Anticipation is always outside of the flow, outside of the present time, and outside of what is truly happening. If a technique had been anticipated and executed, it would have been artificial, forced. During aikido classes, the *sensei* sets the form of the attack and the technique that is to be executed. This is because one must, of course, create the conditions that will allow the technique to be learned. One may compare this to a jazz musician who practices his scales before a jam session. A jazzman explains how people such as Toots Thielemans, the famous Belgian jazz musician—who played the harmonica—can produce solos that are so inventive and so right. Such brilliant musicians have already practiced for hours and hours. They have listened to thousands of jazz pieces and witnessed amazing solo performances. They have recorded millions of patterns and musical sequences (in music we talk about *riffs*). When they play, they have access to an incredible library of sequences and their true genius consists in truly listening to other musicians, immersing themselves in the rhythm, and entering into the notes. They then only need to gather the riffs that emerge in the musical flow, just like ripe fruit that is waiting to be picked. In aikido, *randori* is a martial "jazz session." The harmony that results from it calls to mind a dance more than a fight; this dance-like quality has been used against aikido by its detractors, but then again, does that really matter? The practitioner's goal is the reestablishment of harmony, the transformation of energy that arose to create chaos—in the meaning we understand from Greek mythology[62]. The aikidoka's intention is clear and limpid, and to succeed at it he makes himself available, ready to receive, to welcome what will transform. Acting from his center, which is a fixed point, he doesn't need to do anything but truly be there.

Respect

The feeling of being connected to the universe and therefore to another person, is difficult to explain with words. The paradoxical duality between the awareness of being unique and connected, an individual and part of a greater whole, is an experience that is beyond words. Premises 3, 4, and 5 are at the heart of this respect that throws open the door to kindness. In aikido practice, respect appears on different levels. There is, first of all, respect for the setting. Aikido is practiced in a place that is full of a strong symbolism: the *dojo*. The *dojo* is a unique learning space. When the aikidoka enters, he bows in the direction of the *kamiza*, the spot where the Founder's image is placed. This ritual transforms the space and makes it possible to practice combat techniques—which can all cause pain, injuries, and other traumas—while preserving the integrity of the people who are practicing. Next, there is the respect for the other person's personality, attitude, force or weakness, lightness or heaviness, stiffness or flexibility. Respect during practice manifests itself by not judging, by

---

[62] See Luc Ferry, *Apprendre à vivre 2, La Sagesse des mythes*.

becoming aware of everything that you project on the other person but that is actually a part of yourself, by the refusal to reduce the other person to the level of an object that is indispensable to your learning in the same way as a cyclist's bicycle or a soccer player's cleats. This respect leads to learning on another level: the exploration of the relational quality during practice. At every moment, thoughts, judgments, or comparisons arise and *Aiki* learning consists of acting toward them in the same way that I act toward my partner: openness, flexibility, centering. Each time that I fall into judgment, even reproach, and I hear myself saying, "He is resisting!"; "He doesn't work well!"; or "I should have chosen to work with someone else!" I lose my center and I am unbalanced[63].

Off the *tatami*, respect manifests itself in the acceptance of differences: difference of rhythm, of language, of age, of culture. The wish to experience a true relationship, even if it is fleeting, is the source of infinite learning. For example, let us look at a very common social ritual: the greeting.

In a professional setting, but also with our loved ones, a greeting is reduced to a sort of obligation, even a reflex. We all know the distracted greeting, with the mind already elsewhere, which is accompanied by a "how's it going?" that doesn't need a response. The opposite of respect is not contempt, it is indifference. The other person is only an object in our environment. It is true that we usually lack the time or we get lost in our work. We are are not really there and we behave like robots, distractedly shaking hands with a colleague without realizing that we have become the instruments of our activity. I am only a *human resource* serving the corporation, and the corporation is—in legal terms—the only "person" who is left. When I was working in a large company and someone asked "how's it going" in an automatic way, sometimes I had fun by answering "Me neither." Very often, this drew the person I was talking to out of his professional trance and it led him to talk about himself and about what he was experiencing. The application of respect in the *Aiki* sense can be experienced in daily life in various ways. The next time that you enter a meeting room, be aware of the space, of the spot where you are going

---

[63] Here we find the I-Thou thematic of relationships discussed by Martin Buber (See "Martin Buber's Reciprocity" on page 233).

to sit, of the place where the speaker will be, then size up each individual who is present in the room, one by one. Observe them as individuals, by their look, their attitude, the materials that they place on the table, etc. Each detail contributes to making them all unique and present. This is the first step on the path to respect.

Kindness

Kindness is the foundation of the *Aiki* attitude. It follows from Ueshiba's thinking, from Morin's definition of ethics,[64] and from the premises that I have just described. It is the manifestation of the awareness of our authentic self, this "egolessness" that is part of the link, of the connection, without, however forgetting my identity, that is to say, the fact that I am a person in my own right[65]. Kindness requires awareness of my individuality and commitment in an attitude of openness toward the other person. Kindness happens when I become clearly aware of who I am and accept the *other* as a person with whom I am in connection, from center to center.

Martial-ness

Beyond lovely principles and grand ideas, in a world where "every man for himself" is the rule, is it even thinkable to act with kindness? I often say this during *AikiCom* training: we do not live in a world of Care Bears![66] To want to live in peace and harmony does not immunize us against attacks, injustices, provocations, and other manipulations. It is for this reason that the martial dimension of *AikiCom* is so important. I have already brought up the notion of the warrior and I would also like to take a moment here to clarify some effects of this martial-ness. "Martial-ness" (*martialité* in French) is the characteristic of what is martial. While the etymology of the word refers to Mars, the Roman god of war, it is not so much war as combat that we must understand in its metaphorical dimension: the

---

[64] See Edgar Morin, *La méthode 6. Éthique.*
[65] The process of individuation of the human being, in the Jungian sense, is the act of becoming aware of being separate and different from others. This stage is indispensable in developing the *Aiki* attitude. This development happens through centering, which brings us close to our essential being without ever reaching it. If I succeeded in reaching it I would no longer be aware. Inevitably, there remains a distance between me and my center, between me and my essential being.
[66] Care Bears are stuffed animals known throughout the world. Francophone Canadians call them *Calinours* and other French speakers call them *Bisounours*.

mobilization of our energy to act, to change things. This struggle is the manifestation of negentropy (negative entropy), which characterizes our state of being alive with the capacity to create more order, more cooperation.

From the standpoint of *AikiCom* (or from the *AikiCom* point of view or from the *AikiCom* perspective), martial-ness does not cause violence; instead, it aims to control violence. It reminds us that we are not sheltered from dangers and it asks us to pay attention to what may happen. We are aware of our vulnerability and we are not trying to expose ourselves unnecessarily. The *Aiki* dynamic is separable from the notion of mobility. We do not remain in dangerous places and we put ourselves in a position to rediscover our potential for freedom. Martial-ness is the expression of our commitment to action.

We still must reconcile martial-ness and kindness, two apparently contradictory concepts that betray the dilemma that one can see in aikido. For some aikidokas, the act of seeing the person with whom they are practicing as a partner rather than as an adversary can make them lose touch with the necessary martial-ness. On the other hand, the excessive search for effectiveness in combat can make aikido practice lose all its spirit. The *Aiki* dynamic navigates between the reefs of naive innocence and extreme mistrust. It aims to participate, to co-create more peace by transforming conflictual energy into a dialogue that recognizes each in his personality and in his difference. With certain partners, this will be productive. With others, this will be in vain. It then falls to us to choose the environment in which we would like to evolve: in the development of more harmony and listening or in the exhaustion of a struggle against those who delight in, or are blocked by, conflicting, aggressive, or violent approaches. The strategy of martial kindness invites us to opt for *Ai* and *Ki*—harmony and energy—rather than to choose either to be victorious through power or to accept the bitterness of sympathetic powerlessness.

Beyond this practice of martial-ness, it is interesting to ask ourselves if we can hope to see cooperation emerge in a selfish world that has no central authority. This is the question that Robert Axelrod, a professor of political science, asked himself in his book *The Evolution of Cooperation*. Later in this book, we will examine how Axelrod showed that this is possible.

Chapter 3

Coming back to myself

We will now explore the basic models of *AikiCom*. First, we will describe the *Aiki* attitude, then in Chapter 4 we will explore how to act. The *Aiki* attitude is a way of being, of centering oneself and living in the present, which are the basic conditions for right action that comes from the self.

How often do we hear, "I acted on impulse, I wasn't myself"? Most of the time we live on automatic pilot, plunged in the past or sketching plans for the future. We will see how it is possible to come back to yourself at the moment when you need to. This isn't about suggesting some sort of permanent state of awareness or perpetual wisdom. *AikiCom* doesn't propose going through life isolated from the pressures of our hectic daily lives. On the contrary, it asks us to enter into life, but in a more balanced way, and thus to savor life, no matter what annoyances we run into all the time. The *Aiki* dynamic helps us to receive what happens to us and to bounce back with the energy of the events, whether they are agreeable or not, in order to make progress on our personal life path. To this dimension of *being* and of welcoming what happens to us, we ought to add the *acting* dimension. We will examine the foundations of right action, which will only happen if it comes from us, from our center. Otherwise, all that is left for us is to expose ourselves to the effects of the action without being at its source. On the following pages, I will focus on our interactions with other people, but also with ourselves. This is the case when we have to overcome interior conflicts or when we need to integrate, into our experience, events that are imposed upon us and that we cannot control. When we are interacting with a person or an event, we can influence the quality of the relationship that we establish with them. This connection must allow a dialogue, that is, a communication, an exchange of information. When I have an *Aiki* attitude, I am aware of the importance of listening, of perception. I am aware that communicating is not only expressing, it is also, especially, receiving, perceiving, and listening. In this way, I have the best information available about what I am experiencing. I can then fully exercise my freedom to choose the best possible action.

Centering

The Three Centers

Many approaches talk about the act of returning to oneself, of centering oneself. The most important thing is to agree on what is meant by these terms, and above all, to know how to do this. In our Western culture, our mind provides the dominant share of our perceived reality. Eastern approaches—but not only these—propose that we empty ourselves inside, that is to say to not let ourselves be carried away by the endless stream of our thoughts. In his book *The Power of Now,* Eckhart Tolle emphasizes the importance of returning to the present. Our mind carries us to the past or the future and separates us from the only moment that really counts: the present. Becoming aware of the present brings us back to the notion that Eugene Gendlin called the "felt sense.[67]" This perception of being comes unavoidably through our body, the seat of our feelings and of our emotions, but also of our thoughts. To broach this topic of returning to oneself, this "reintegration" of our body, I will propose to you a model that is constructed around three centers that correspond to our perceived reality and thus allows us to develop our ability to

---

[67] Eugene Gendlin, *Focusing*, 1978.

center ourselves. These three centers are the cognitive center, the emotional center, and the somatic center.

The Cognitive Center

First of all, let us begin with the cognitive center, in other words, our brain. The cognitive center is the center of our thought. Housed in our cranium, our brain handles multiple vital functions, of which we are more or less aware, but the ones that interest us here are the higher functions that allowed us human beings to think and develop our powers of awareness, anticipation, and memorization. The cognitive center can therefore refer to a specific part of the brain, the neocortex[68]. Descartes's famous "I think therefore I am" shows how much we tend to identify ourselves with our thoughts. However, we are far more than our thoughts. Moreover, our thoughts have the unfortunate tendency to lead us everywhere except into ourselves. In our thoughts, we can imagine ourselves in distant lands, doing various activities, with people who are either real or imaginary. Our mind stands out in particular through its ability to play with time. The past and the future are its favorite playing fields. So much so that it loses interest in the only moment that truly counts: the present. The brain is so entirely devoted to the anticipation of future events based on its memory of past actions, that we easily understand how it gets lost in the maze of time and tends to pull us out of reality, out of the here and now.

The Emotional Center

The fabulous human intelligence that allowed human beings to survive, indeed to put nature under our thumb, even though we did not run fast, did not jump high, and had neither powerful claws nor sharp fangs, shares the limelight with a new form of intelligence: emotional intelligence[69]. Although our emotions are handled in the limbic part of our brain (we often call this the mammalian brain), the fact that we feel it in our body, and principally in the torso, led me to place the

---

[68] Later in this book, we will see Paul MacLean's triune brain model and how it corresponds rather well to the three-center model.
[69] The notion of emotional intelligence came into popular speech after the success of Daniel Goleman's book entitled *Emotional Intelligence*. It gave rise to the term EQ, or Emotional Quotient, by analogy with the term IQ, Intelligence Quotient.

emotional center at the level of the heart or of the solar plexus[70]. The location can vary from one person to another. The important thing is to localize the place where we subjectively feel that we are "caught" by an emotion that sweeps over us. We should note that positioning the emotional center at chest level does not prevent us from feeling emotions throughout our body. Anger will thus cause tension in the jaw, frowning, accelerated heartbeat, cold sweats, or clenching of the fists. These are physical manifestations of our emotion. In the same way, our thoughts are not spared by our emotional experience. From Antonio Damasio's book *Descartes' Error,* we know that, in order for us to think correctly, emotions and thoughts make up an indispensable whole.

The Somatic Center

With the *hara,* we enter a radically different dimension. While the cognitive center and the emotional center are part of our Western human experience, the somatic center or *hara* opens a new dimension that is completely essential. Western philosophy tends to form our experience by defining it in terms of concepts. We must recognize that this does not always jibe with what we actually experience. There are experiences that words cannot describe. Being alive, and more generally "being," is terribly abstract while, in fact, experience is as concrete as can be. When words are not enough, when the best-developed arguments are contradicted by this sensation that we feel in the gut—and that keeps us from following what reason dictates, we are in contact with the third center, the somatic center, which is located in the belly.

To be interested in the somatic center is also to free oneself from the tyranny of our ego, which wants to exist at any cost by showing us how much we are different from everything else, from the world and from others. The ego thus makes us lose contact with our essential being, which gives us a feeling of loss inside that we try to fill by losing

---

[70] Chakras ("wheel" or "disk" in Sanskrit) are spiritual centers or energy junctions located in the body. The body has seven main chakras. In accordance with the principle of simplicity—Ockham's famous razor—which leads us to avoid unnecessary complexity, I chose a model with three centers, which is simpler than the one adopted by the "New Age" movement and the Eastern approaches that are behind it. The emotional center is therefore located near the chakras of the heart and the solar plexus.

ourselves in actions or in possessions. *Doing* and *having* make up for our difficulty with *being*. To become oneself is to go and meet our true being. As long as we do not discover our true nature, we are "pseudo-selves." The outside world drives us.

The *hara* is therefore the center of not doing, of not having. Meditation is in itself an activity that involves not acting. By returning to ourselves, without doing anything other than paying attention to our breathing, which reconnects us with the *hara*, we extract ourselves from the tumult of our thoughts and our activities. Paying attention to the present moment and nothing else: there is nothing more simple...and at the same time there is nothing more difficult.

The Enteric Brain

Advances in neuroscience have confirmed what people in the East have known for several centuries. Among these scientific confirmations, there is one that will certainly shock some of you: our belly houses a "second brain.[71]" Even though the idea seems rather trivial at first glance, by pushing our thinking a little further, it can become disturbing to admit that these unattractive organs that we call our guts or our entrails, with their tubular form that evokes something reptilian, with their contents and their odor, can be better capable of feeling than our heart is. It is interesting to note that in terms of vocabulary, the word "guts" brings to mind mainly our intestines while "entrails" includes the entirety of the organs that are contained in the abdomen, including the organs involved in gestation. On a literal level, the word "entrails" calls to mind the deepest, most intimate, most essential part of a person and even (by extension of meaning) of a question or of a thing. You should also note that the term "viscera" calls to mind the idea of the three brains because it designates the organs contained in the abdominal cavity (the somatic center), the thoracic (the emotional center), and the cranial (the cognitive center)[72].

The enteric brain, with more than one hundred million nerve cells, which is more than the number of nerve cells in our peripheral nerve

---

[71] According to the title of Michael D. Gershon's book *The Second Brain*, which highlights the importance of the nervous system in our abdominal organs, which is described as a second brain. Note that as early as 1903 Byron Robinson, an American doctor, published The Abdominal and Pelvic Brain.

[72] This comment refers to the meaning in French. In English, the term "viscera" is related mainly to the organs that are found in the trunk.

system, is the only organ of the human body that is capable of causing reflexes entirely separately from our brain.

Center of Gravity

The center of gravity of a body is "the point at which the entire weight of a body may be considered as concentrated so that if supported at this point the body would remain in equilibrium in any position[73]." In purely mechanical terms, the center of gravity of the human body is located in the *hara*.

In the martial arts, the notion of center of gravity is essential because its position with respect to our legs determines our balance. To master the adversary's center of gravity is to master one's own balance and thus be able to put him on the ground. Martial techniques teach us to take the most stable position possible, while providing optimal mobility. Having the center of gravity located at the pelvic level provides better stability. Quadrupeds have their center of gravity located higher because of their position on four feet.

It is by adopting a bipedal position that humans made the center of gravity descend to the pelvis. The transition from a quadrupedal mammalian state to a bipedal human state resulted in the differentiation between the somatic center and the emotional center.

Figure 2 : The Position of the Center of Gravity

Another interesting observation that I cannot resist sharing with you concerns the protection that the skeleton provides to the three centers.

The cognitive center is enveloped by the enclosed cranium; the emotional center by a "cage" made of the ribs, the sternum, and the spinal column; while the somatic center is open at the abdomen. Personally, it seems to me that the parallels between the enclosure of each of the three centers and their openness to perceptions of the world are particularly striking.

---

[73] Merriam-Webster's Collegiate Dictionary, Eleventh Edition, page 200.

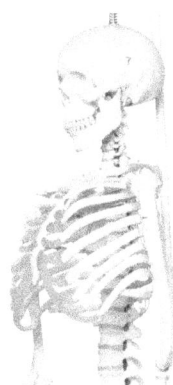

Figure 3 : The Skeleton Protecting the 3 Center

The Symbolism of the Hara

Because of its difference with respect to the cognitive center (our brain) and the emotional center, the somatic center, which is located in the belly or *hara,* is the seat of great symbolism. First of all, note that I am talking about the somatic center rather than the physical center. The term "somatic" comes from the Greek word σώμα (soma) which means "body", but calls to mind in this case the idea of a living, feeling body. It is the medium that allows us to perceive, to act, and to think. The term "soma" does not separate the body from the thought, it encompasses it, it in*corporate*s it.

The *hara* or the somatic center is the seat of the true self, also called the essential self. This essential self is connected, in a broad sense, to our humanity. If it is tied closely to who I am, it is also what ties me to the rest of the universe and, more particularly, to my *Humanity*. It makes me a Human being, with a capital H[74]. The *hara* is therefore the center of what is me and also of what is universal in me. It is what remains when I shed myself of my distinctive features, the characteristics that my ego puts forward to justify its existence and affirms loud and clear: "I am unique!" The *hara* therefore succeeds in reconciling "who I am" with "what I am connected to."

The practice of aikido movements contributes to giving us this *felt sense,* this physical sensation of the feeling of connection. First of all, connection with oneself, then connection with the other person. This

---

[74] Note the form of the capital letter H, well established in its verticality with its horizontal bar reminding us of the bridge between the sky and the earth.

is one of the powerful effects of centering: we create around us a sort of field of awareness that encompasses the other person, our environment, and even our entire universe. We will discuss this notion of a field further on in this book. The somatic center—by being the place through which my body enters into contact with what is universal in me—becomes a place of calm and intense depth. When my cognitive brain is saturated with information and flounders in confusion, I feel lost. When my emotional center is in the middle of the storm of my emotions, I feel tossed around and insecure. During these difficult moments, the *hara* becomes a refuge, a place of calm and security where I can take refuge in order to center myself, to become myself again. During my training sessions, I like to talk about the return to the somatic center through the metaphor of a soothing garden that one does not allow oneself to visit often enough.

Visualization Exercise

This is the transcript of a visualization exercise that you may wish to record so you can listen to it as you practice.
The *hara* is a tranquil, pleasant, flowery, calm garden. We love this garden, we appreciate it, but we must admit, we do not go there often.
Something holds us back, forbids us, prevents us from going in. Could it perhaps be a vague memory of paradise lost, of Eden from which God chased us when we took a big bite from the apple of the tree of knowledge?
Is it that by becoming aware—and by realizing at the same time that we were naked—that we left this garden to make our way through life by the sweat of our brow, trusting our rational mind to build our life?
We still do not dare enter this garden.
Just like children stealing apples from an orchard, we fear that the landlord will notice us and chase us away with a stick.
For we do not know, we no longer know that we have the right to enter, that if there is a landlord, this landlord is *us*.
But there is no landlord.
The *hara* is the space of being and not the space of having. Nor is it the space of doing.

So we circle around this garden without really going in, sometimes venturing to take a few steps in it to just as quickly rush to get out.

These moments of contact with our somatic center happen when we are admiring a work of art, a magnificent landscape, or a piece of music that transports us and seems to stop time, or they can happen quite simply by a look or a smile. To return to our center, to our *hara*, is to get back in touch with this place of infinite security. Numerous approaches open the door for us to return to ourselves. Meditation is one of them. By putting ourselves in a place of non-doing, we discover the uninterrupted flow of our thoughts like clouds in a blue sky. When the flow of these images, of these sounds, and of these sensations calms down a bit, we become aware that they spread out across a landscape, across the sky. This sky and this landscape provide the space that allows thoughts and emotions to develop, to follow one another, to transform themselves. This space is the *hara*, the somatic center. It is the movie screen that shows the dramatic film as a comedy and the suspense film as an intimate drama. Whatever images are projected onto the screen, it becomes white again at the end of the show, when the lights of awareness come on again. The problem is that the audience often gets up too quickly. They put on their coats and leave the theater while the credits have not even ended. To see the blank, white screen is frightening. It is better to dive back into action, into doing.

Life does not let you move through it while remaining in a permanent lotus position. We must take action, live, make plans, meet people. Under these conditions, it is difficult to create the conditions that let us remain in this state of welcoming of our inner experience. It is there that we see the full scope of the qualities of martial arts like aikido. It is difficult to be both in the "doing" and in the "being." We will see that this is not, in itself, a problem when we turn our attention to the question of centering.

What strikes those who explore this space of experience is the astonishment that comes from the fact that the more I go toward my center, the more I shed myself of my characteristics in order to touch the universal. The more I dig, the more it is empty. At the center, I get in touch with something greater that connects me with the environment that surrounds me. I am in nature and nature is within me.

> *I am just a fragment.*
> *Who knows where this fragment comes from.*
> *What am I? With this question humans travel through life.*
> *Why go so many places?*
> *Why tirelessly keep going until death?*
> *Why always look for new people, new experiences…?*
> *Because I want to know…. what I am*
> *I wanted to understand…. very deeply.*
> *Before becoming a fragment, you and me were one ?*
> *Before becoming a fragment, sky and me were one ?*
> *Before becoming a fragment, sea and me were one ?*
> *Awakened people said to me,*
> *Do not search outside, look in. Truth is inside of you.*
> *That's why I put a ladder inside to go in myself*
> *one step at a time.*
> *This is the beginning of butoh.*
> *(Hiroko Komiya and Atsushi Takenouchi, butoh dancers)*
> *extract of "Kakela", a poem by Atsushi Takenouchi*[75]

I am the *other*, the *other* is me. By centering, I connect myself with the universal needs that are shared by our humanity. Space is around me and it is in me. It is a sensation that is described by many authors as the experience of being a conduit, a point of connection. As a living being and as a human being, I can become aware of the marvel of being alive and aware. My cells are mainly composed of atoms of carbon, hydrogen, oxygen, and nitrogen. These atoms were used before me in other structures, living or not, and they will be again after I return to the earth. During this fleeting period between my birth and my death, I can become aware of being a momentary concentration of energy, the life energy that the Japanese call *ki* and the Chinese call *chi*. I use this energy to organize myself. As a living being, I structure myself to fight entropy, to prevent my cells and the atoms that make them up

---

[75] Original translation from Japanese found at:
http://www.karolfulillustration.com/tag/poster/ and
http://jinen-butoh.blogspot.be/2011/12/being-fragment-of-various-things.html

from spreading on the ground and scattering. My metabolism makes me a being connected to my environment, a discrete system that is set apart, among other things, by my skin, the outer, visible limit of my body. But it is still an open system: I breathe, I eat, I excrete, I exchange information.. My body is the visible part of my being, the part that is in intimate contact with the environment. This body is the seat of numerous processes: ingestion, respiration, digestion, production of heat, waste, thoughts, words. Excluding near death experiences, I can say that my body is the medium that allows me to experience my life. And the *hara* is the center of it, a center in connection with this awareness of living, this awareness of being alive.

And the other two centers participate in their own way in this experience of life. The mind creates a personal, subjective reality for us. Our perceptions are filtered, interpreted, connected, memorized. We create meaning, the meaning that we give to what we experience. These thoughts produce sensations that are grouped under the term of "emotions." But most of the time, it is what we have committed to memory that is at the root of these emotions. Perceptions are very often only the smallest share: not more than 20% to 30% of what we believe that we see, hear, or feel truly comes from the outside. The rest is fed by our memory. Two features are enough to remember a face, two sounds to piece together a word. The extraordinary abilities of our cognitive brain give us the awareness of being, the ability to think things, and we take a big bite from the apple of the tree of knowledge, still unaware of the fact that it will throw us out of a marvelous garden whose memory will remain in our *hara*.

The Three Centers and the Temporal Dimension

Greek mythology gives us a description of the birth of the world. In the beginning, there was Chaos, black space where nothing is identifiable. From Chaos emerges Gaia (the Earth), then Eros (Love). These deities are strictly speaking more energy than they are gods. Eros thus represents a form of vital energy that corresponds to the Japanese concept of *ki*. It is through Eros that all the deities are born. It is from the three deities that everything will be put in place to change from chaos to cosmos, to perfect order, beautiful organization, and *right* nature. Ueshiba evoked the cosmos in terms of universal harmony. Under the influence of Eros, the energy of life, Gaia gave birth to Uranus, the sky, but Uranus clings to Gaia and there is no space between the two deities. It wasn't until the intervention of their youngest son, Cronos, that they were separated. Cronos is the god of the passage of time. His action pushed Uranus to settle on high, in the sky. Thus, through Cronos's action, the space between the sky and the Earth was born. Greek mythology also tells us that Cronos, who originated the dynamic of time and space in the universe, was in turn dethroned by his son Zeus. The latter, aware that there is no victory without the help of others, was intelligent enough to establish an alliance that allowed the victory of the cosmos, or of the established order, over chaos. This mythical story, told by the poets of ancient Greece, illustrates in an exemplary way the challenge that we imitate on a human scale: to reestablish the interior harmony that was disturbed by the never-ending flow of our thoughts and the chaos caused by Cronos's creation, time.

Morihei Ueshiba tells us that the human being is "a bridge between the sky and the earth[76]" The ancient Greeks would say "between Gaia and Uranus." Our way of contributing to our interior harmony comes from our way of understanding the passage of time—a result of Cronos's action. This harmony opens the door for us to a new dimension of time, which is Xairos. Xairos is the time of the proper moment. In the Japanese martial arts, the equivalent of Xairos is the *de ai*, the moment when action begins.

As I mentioned above[77], when Morihei Ueshiba talks about reversal, he calls to mind two methods of practice. The first is concrete practice, the kind that one can see on the *tatamis* of *dojos*. It puts our body in movement, which is a part of a mechanical reality, a process of action-reaction: you attack me, I defend myself. Then, when the level increases, the practitioner can experience another level of practice: linear causality seems to disappear. Defense no longer arises as a consequence of the attack, it flows spontaneously. Events are no longer linked in a process of cause and effect, temporality is no longer the key dimension. We enter the world of synchronicity.

---

[76] I will return frequently to this metaphor when I discuss verticality (seepage 114).
[77] See "From the body to the mind, returning,"page 47.

But let us return for a moment to the practical concerns of everyday life and let us examine how our three centers understand time.

The Cognitive Center and Time

The cognitive center is the "organ" that allows us to understand the concept that we call time. It is not surprising that it manipulates it dexterously—to the point of forgetting the present moment!

The cognitive center evolved to optimize the process that allowed the survival of the human race: anticipation. This anticipation, built on the memory of the past, is the main concern of our mind, it is its main product. It is therefore understandable that our mind spends most of its time either in the past or the future. What is the present for the cognitive center? It is too brief to be exploited, but still sufficiently long to commit the event to memory so that it can be used in the future.

The Emotional Center and Time

If, like the cognitive center, the emotional center is influenced by the notion of time, it is nevertheless clearly more anchored in the present. A bad memory, a disturbing noise, or a word heard the previous evening can plunge us into an emotional state of fear, sadness, or anger that comes from the past event, but persists in the present, the time we're living in. In the same way, when a student thinks about taking an exam, a job seeker imagines a job interview, or a bashful lover knows that he will find his beloved, it is enough to create an intense state of tension or joy. Whether the reason for—or the object of—our emotion is located in the past or the future, the emotion itself is really a feeling that is experienced in the present. In order to remember a past sadness, we must recreate it in our body in the present and join with it. Otherwise, we can only talk about it, with all the powerlessness that words have to describe it.

The emotional center lives in the present and expresses the state that we are in, or perhaps we ought to say *the state in which we feel*. But it is also influenced by the past, by an effect of passivity. Our emotional states are complex electrochemical states. A fright or a stress causes hormonal discharges that influence our physical state for a period of time that can last from a few seconds to a few hours. This is how we can feel sad when the cause of this emotion has long since disappeared. If we add the power of our thoughts to our internal body chemistry, we can stretch this period of time to days, years, or even a lifetime.

On the other hand, the emotional center does not know the future. It is not possible for us to feel a future emotion. At best, we can feel an emotion through mental construction, through the anticipation of a future event. But this would still be an emotion in the present for a constructed thought, a representation of a future event.

Certain emotions depend on the way we understand time. Anxiety is thus an emotion that is related to a future event that one dreads, while regret is a form of sadness connected to a past event. However, whatever the characteristics of these emotions are, what we feel is always an experience in the present.

The Hara and Time

> *"At the still point of the turning world.*
> *Neither flesh nor fleshless;*
> *Neither from nor towards;*
> *at the still point, there the dance is,*
> *But neither arrest nor movement*
> *And do not call it fixity,*
> *Where past and future are gathered.*
> *Neither movement from nor towards,*
> *Neither ascent nor decline.*
> *Except for the point, the still point,*
> *There would be no dance,*
> *and there is only the dance."*
>
> *(From T.S. Eliot's Four Quartets)*

The body knows only one time, the present. I am, I live, I feel, I do. As T.S. Eliot writes, the center of a circular movement is immobile. The hub of the wheel does not turn. Movement originates in the center, but the center is not in movement. It is unchanging and outside of time. The somatic center—unlike the two other centers—is therefore surely in the present, in its fleetingness. Its elusive character connects to the timeless. If I ask myself what makes up my identity, I have a similar sensation. Most of the cells of my body are less than ten years old (the cells of our retina only live for ten days, those of our skeleton live for around ten years) and our physical appearance changes. Even though our brain gives us the sensation of a constant self-awareness, our thoughts follow one another and evolve. Our identity is therefore a completely subjective perception that our ego attempts to preserve with all its energy, but that cannot make us forget what connects us to the world and to others: our body is made of atoms of carbon, hydrogen, oxygen, and nitrogen that formerly made up other organisms or objects and our thoughts emerge from an ocean of thoughts, of *memes*[78], the elements of culture that are carried by our fellow creatures. We are therefore, whether our ego likes it or not, both different and similar, separate but connected.

The somatic center is the space of the ONE. It is not surprising that it is consequently the place where centering occurs. One single time, the present, one single place, here: the body is what connects us to the *here and now*. But the body needs the cognitive center to return there through the mechanism of attention. A sacred alliance of the being who is returning to himself, a union of water and fire, of the restless spirit and the physical body, of time and the moment, we live while attempting an unlikely full split. This existential gymnastics has a name: centering.

The Three Centers and the Triune Brain

At the end of the nineteen sixties, Paul MacLean popularized a three-layer model of the brain called "the triune brain." These layers, which appeared over the course of evolution, are different enough that we can call them distinct brains[79].

If we examine the three centers, we see that the cognitive center is connected to the most evolved part of our brain, the neocortex[80] which is our rational mind. We see that the emotional center is connected to the limbic part of our brain, which is also called the mammalian

---

[78] The term "meme" was proposed by Richard Dawkins. Formed from the association of the word gene and mimesis (imitation), it defines the distribution and replication of ideas in a way that is similar to the behavior of our genes.

[79] Advances in the neurosciences have since shown that this division of the brain into three distinct brains is relatively artificial. These parts of the brain function in a highly connected way and have a mutual influence on each other.

[80] We also find this most evolved layer of the brain, called the neocortex or mammalian brain, in the great apes.

brain[81], the seat of the emotions. The most important center in the martial approach, and moreover in most Eastern approaches is the *hara*, the somatic center, the vital center of the body, of the living body. This center is intimately connected with what we call the reptilian brain[82]. This is very much the most ancestral part of the brain. Tied to our instinct, it assures the survival of the individual and consequently of the species. For a long time, I was interested in the apparent contradiction between the reptilian center that is responsible for basic survival behaviors such as attack, flight, or immobility and the symbolic power of the *hara* in Eastern philosophy and spirituality. Morihei Ueshiba gives us the answer by recommending centering. Centering brings the person back to his center, where nothing is moving. It is the seat of non-action; according to Ueshiba it is the place where "the governor" resides. This governor, who is situated at the center, symbolizes the order that emerges from chaos, the principle of life that dominates entropy and its push for dispersal. When the governor is at the center, he *is* and it is enough for him to just *be*. If the governor acts, he gives up non-acting and loses his position at the center. He is no longer the governor. The *hara* is this center, the center of the individual, the place that connects us to the universe. However, it is an individual's center that connects the person to the species, to humanity.

If we come back for a moment to the concrete, to the reality of our modern world, we can wonder about the possibility of applying this approach, this philosophy, to our daily lives. It is there that the *Aiki* process becomes interesting.

While our modern world is dominated by the cognitive dimension, and therefore by the rational brain, the mind, *AikiCom* practice leads us back to an essential way of life by reconnecting us with our somatic center. *Aiki* work aims to reestablish and nourish a harmonious dynamic between the three centers, thus uniting the pragmatic, the logical, the reasoned, the temporal, and the aware self—which is dominated by the cognitive center—with the unchanging, the non-

---

[81] We also call it the paleomammalian brain or the limbic system.
[82] The reptilian brain is made up of the brain stem and the hypothalamus and generally handles all the functions that assure our survival (unconscious breathing, heartbeat, aggression, dominance, territoriality behaviors).

acting, and the essential self of the somatic center. This re-union happens through the emotional self, which colors and fills it with the sensation of being and feeling. This union of the three centers brings us back to our body, to our living body: the soma. The center of this living body is in the *hara*. We have already talked about how the *hara* is concerned with the survival instinct of the individual and the species as well as with the greater ideas of harmony and love—the materialization of life's forces of attraction and coherence.

Modern man is thus asked to reestablish connections through physical practice; we are asked to reestablish communication between the dominant, rational brain, the brain that is imposed upon by the necessities of modern life, and the instinctive brain, a brain whose existence we had almost forgotten, whose right to exist had been denied, but whose expression had nevertheless been indisputable, even inevitable. It is enough to see the behavior of many humans in situations of crisis, war, or catastrophe to understand that the somatic center—the seat of our instincts—can, if we do not listen to it, reveal itself by making us forget love and the meaning of life, which are characteristics of human beings. Returning to the somatic center allows us to reharmonize this instinctive dimension with the higher values that are associated with life. As long as the somatic center is denied, concealed, or driven back, it can only express itself unconsciously and instinctively.

By taking the somatic center into account and by recognizing its role, in perfect communication with the human being's two other centers, we recreate a new—or so often forgotten—dynamic, the search for a harmonious form that unites apparently contradictory interests: individuality and community.

In the aikido *dojo*, the martial artist rediscovers this harmony through physical practice. Learning with others in the absence of competition leads him, from the outset, to be a part of a cooperative mechanism. Individual progress blends harmoniously with the effort to respect the other person. Training allows each person to explore his ability to manage his instinctive abilities, which would otherwise plunge into fight, flight, or freeze[83]. Aiki training proposes a middle road between responding to violence with violence and letting yourself be pushed around. This is accomplished by reintegrating the three centers. Purely instinctive individual survival reflexes are transcended through martial kindness, which reconnects to the energy of life and gives a new meaning to the experience. One often forgets: in nature, the goal is not victory, the goal is survival.

Centering Oneself Is a Process

Centering oneself, returning to oneself, and focusing; these are all expressions that have entered common usage. But what do they mean exactly? What do we mean by "centering oneself"?

Centering is a process that consists of returning to your body, in the here and now. We very often lose ourselves in our thoughts and lose contact with our experience of reality. We are somewhere else in time and space. We frequently lose ourselves in our emotions, thus forgetting everything that does not feed this emotion. We then say that we are overtaken by emotion because it truly takes possession of us.

The pressure to which our environment subjects us, the constraints that are imposed upon us, the uncertainties, the challenges, so many external elements that lead us to action. Two options are available to us: react, that is to say, to act in response, or to take action starting from ourselves. The second option requires starting with a stable system of reference, a system whose origin is within us. When confusion and chaos reign around us, but also in us, we have to find something to lean on, the pivot from which the needle of our internal compass can orient itself to show the direction to take. Too often, we live in a fragmented, dissociated way. Our roles and life conditions push us to act in an uncoordinated way by modifying our priorities according to the situation. Too often, the urgency that is imposed from the outside dictates our behavior and makes what is important become secondary. By returning to our center, we can defragment and reintegrate ourselves. In the center of a circle, there is no movement. When the compass needle spins crazily to find north, the pivot remains

---

[83] The term "freeze" (paralysis) was added relatively recently to take into account a frequent reaction during intense stress situations that is similar to that of an animal that is paralyzed by the headlights of a vehicle.

immobile. Its presence is the indispensable element. Without an immobile center, the needle cannot find its direction. When I center myself, I get in touch with a natural state of integrity, a sort of fullness and presence. I am no longer a spectator in my life; I once again become an *actor* and I receive life's events with calm, in non-action, during the time we need in order to take one or several breaths. The centering happens through becoming aware of what I am currently experiencing. It is a physical experience that is both lived and felt. It is not possible, and undoubtedly not appropriate, to be permanently centered. We experience moments when we are truly ourselves, which alternate with moments when we are in action, in our thoughts, or in our emotions.

The main thing is to not be permanently centered, but to come back to our center when it is necessary and as often as it is necessary.

> *"I am not permanently centered. I simply notice more quickly when I am uncentered and I come back more quickly.*[84]*"*
> *(Morihei Ueshiba, Founder of aikido)*

Before we talk about centering, let us examine more closely the notion of the center as it applies to the human being. What is a center? *Webster's Dictionary* defines the center as "a point that is related to a geometrical figure in such a way that for any point on the figure there is another point on the figure such that a straight line joining the two points is bisected by the original point—called also center of symmetry.[85]" More simply, one could say that the center represents the middle of a figure or a body. These definitions are obvious if we are thinking about a circle, but for a person, locating the center is not so easy.

In the martial arts, and in aikido in particular, control of our balance is crucial. This balance is defined in a purely mechanical way by the position of the center of gravity, which, for the human body, is located

---

[84] This quote is attributed to Morihei Ueshiba, but we have not found a specific reference in the works that mention it.
[85] Merriam-Webster's Collegiate Dictionary, Eleventh Edition, Springfield: Merriam-Webster, Inc., 2005, page 200.

around the belly, which is called the *hara* in Japanese. In my aikido classes, I am in the habit of jokingly saying that the best position for your legs is under your body, that is to say, under your center of gravity[86]. The center of gravity is the point of the body upon which all forces are applied. It is from this point that the body goes into motion, even if our attention is drawn more by the movement of our legs and feet. Walking is a series of imbalances. We move our center of gravity forward by moving our feet to regain a new position of equilibrium before starting again with the other foot.

The *hara* is not only the seat of the center of gravity. In Eastern culture it has a strong symbolic meaning. We will talk about that later in this book, but first I would like to talk about the fact that other parts of our body could claim to be the "center of the human being."

Centering Yourself with the Three Centers

The discovery of our three centers allows us to better understand how to center ourselves. In a typical *Aiki* process, we do not try to dissect or criticize, but rather we try to take the best part and put it in the service of the whole. Let us examine what the role of the three centers may be in the process of centering.

The cognitive center can be seen as a projector. Its light is our attention. We can thus point it toward our somatic center, which is the center of our essential being, who we truly are. This ability of our mental state to direct our attention illustrates a basic principle in the area of psycho-corporal approaches: energy follows attention. By pointing our cognitive spotlight toward the somatic center or, to put it another way, by turning our attention to our *hara*, we create a new state; we return toward ourselves; we return home. This redirection of our attention is accompanied by becoming aware of our breathing, which opens the conduit that unites the three centers and thus facilitates the circulation of *ki*, the life energy that motivates us.

The somatic center is at the center of our body and does not need to *do* anything. It simply *is*. The sun is at the center of the solar system.

---

[86] Beginners in aikido often look for where to put their feet and which steps they need to take. They often take positions where their legs are too far apart. This statement brings them back to common sense. Place your feet so that you feel more stable by bringing your feet under your body.

It has nothing more to do but be there, at the center. Its position is determined by the planets, which revolve around it. This placement in the center endows it with its role as the structuring element of the solar system.

This process will inevitably exert an effect on the emotional center. The latter creates the context in which we center ourselves. If we are troubled, nervous, or angry, centering will certainly be necessary, but also more difficult than when we are relaxed and calm. Centering does not eliminate emotions, it brings us back to ourselves, to a timeless space where we can welcome them, distinguish them, and name them better. Emotional energy is a wild energy, an animal energy. Centering is necessary to "humanize" this energy. By naming it, we make it human. It becomes colored with meaning, but also with a direction in which to move us, not just emotionally but physically, from this shapeless space, from this chaotic agitation toward something new, through action, an action that starts from the center of our being.

Attentive readers will no doubt ask themselves: if the cognitive center is a projector, who is the person, or the part of us that points it at the *hara*?

It is in the amazing ability to create the sensation of having a free will that allows us to choose [87] how to turn our attention, and, in this case, to point it toward our somatic center, that lies the magic of our mind, the power of our brain.

Centering Exercise:

Become aware of being immersed in the bath of your emotional center. What emotions do you feel? How are you feeling them in your body? Where are these sensations located?
With your cognitive center, direct your attention toward your somatic center. You can help yourself by placing your hand on your stomach. Notice that turning your attention to your *hara* does not mean turning your gaze toward your abdomen. It is

---

[87] The decision-making mechanisms in our brain are organized in a hierarchical way, going from the most abstract choices (to go to the doctor after a meeting) in our prefrontal anterior cortex, behind our forehead, up to motor actions in the posterior regions (to ring the doctor's doorbell by pushing the button).

possible to direct your attention by continuing to look in front of yourself.

Take the time to become aware of your somatic center, which only has to *be*, but not *act*.

While keeping your attention on your *hara*, tune in to the change in the quality of your "emotional bath" while your breathing maintains a fluid circulation of energy by uniting your three centers.

I Am Multifaceted

If you ask the question, "Who are you?" the most common answer is, "I am Marie, Robert or James Dubois, or Mrs. Scott." In this case, who I am is defined by my name. Another common answer is: I am a sales representative, a civil servant, an engineer, a doctor, or a policeman. In this example, I am what I do or I am at least my role, my function, or my title. Parents will often say: I am a mother or father of one, two, or three children. They thus emphasize the importance that being a parent takes on for them. Others will stress their civil status: I am married, divorced, a widow, or a widower. We can also define ourselves according to our way of behaving (I am shy, absent-minded...), our dominant emotions (I am quick-tempered, depressed, cheerful, optimistic...) or even our age (I am an adult; I am 45 years old, but I feel like a fifteen-year-old). As we can see, the answer to "who I am" takes many forms according to the context in which the question is asked or according to the state of mind I am in.

Knowing who I am is no doubt a task that can take a lifetime, but we can already give an answer that is as obvious as it is full of implications: I am multifaceted!

The self is made up of many diverse faces, but they are complementary, overlapping in a spontaneous and fluid way and forming an undivided, indivisible whole.

This unbroken unit gives us the feeling of always being the same person in the same body, with the same gaze, even if we know that we are never the same as who we were yesterday and are even different from who we were a few minutes ago. The doctor who leaves a patient and gets in his car to go to his next appointment goes from his identity as a doctor to one as a driver, while spending a few moments in his role as husband.

So, while he is with his patient, he will be in a state of empathy, while painstakingly diagnosing and prescribing a treatment. When leaving his patient, he will answer a text from his wife asking him to not forget to bring back a loaf of bread for breakfast. Then he will become a driver who perhaps gets irritated at the next intersection when another driver refuses to yield to him. Our driver/doctor will then, well sheltered in the cabin of his car, utter several deeply felt insults at the bad driver who later this evening could end up being his patient.

We see in this example that the context defines the perception of who we are and these different identities bring with them a set of behaviors, beliefs, values, and emotions. It is as though we were different people. Of course, there are constants, behavioral patterns whose traces we find in all the roles that we play. The borders between our different identities are not impenetrable and between them circulates an energy that characterizes us and identifies us.

We are in a systemic logic, a logic where the links between each part of ourselves are more important than their identities. Each part of us is differentiated and remains in a living relationship with the others. They are interconnected. Our life energy, what the Japanese call *Ki*, circulates like a river between these various forms of ourselves and nourishes them. To be oneself then becomes a paradoxical process that both discriminates and harmonizes. It discriminates by preventing the homogenization of various facets of our composite identity and harmonizes in order to allow us to feel whole through the circulation of energy between these different aspects that make up our being. This energy protects us from disorder and from entropy, which is synonymous with death and decomposition. To be is therefore a subtle process of homogeneity within diversity and to become oneself is to become aware of the need to pacify these dimensions of our being, to get to know them instead of fighting them or being ashamed of them.

Our vital energy must be able to avoid excess, shortages, and overcompensation and circulate without being concentrated, getting stuck, or depriving certain experiential dimensions. If in our childhood we had painful or unpleasant experiences, we can feel threatened in our foundation as a living, real, whole being, and so we overcompensate by acting excessively in certain areas by hyperdeveloping dimensions that will offset the lifeless, devitalized part of us.

A Lively Discussion

In a disagreement with someone, we are far more "numerous" than we think. We try to present an image of ourselves and we do not always realize that the other person does not see this image of us. The other person sees another personality. We try to mask these entire sides of our personality, but we do not succeed in hiding them. We are very often like small children who put a hand in front of their eyes and, because they do not see you, believe that they have hidden themselves.

> Anthony and Nathalie are traveling. They have driven all day and they arrive at their stopover around 11PM. Both of them are tired. Nathalie is driving. When arriving at the hotel, Nathalie spots the entrance to the hotel parking lot. Nathalie maneuvers the car into the narrow entry of the parking lot. She has to make two attempts.
> Anthony says, "that won't make it" before Nathalie has the time to shift into reverse to begin the second attempt. While changing gears, she answers, "I know, I saw." Anthony perceives in Nathalie's nonverbal communication something that makes him think that she is irritated by this unnecessary remark and that she herself has seen that the first attempt was not working. Anthony gets angry to see that his remark was not welcome while his intention was to prevent a fender-bender that would have damaged the car. Nathalie does not welcome Anthony's reaction.
> The couple could have gotten into an argument or left well enough alone to avoid inflaming the situation, thereby leaving yet another conflict in their "bag" of unresolved disagreements. In the moments that follow the incident, each of them will go to his or her corner to think and to say, "I should not have reacted like that; I don't like how he/she reacted. I will make an effort to avoid inflaming the situation, but that leaves a bad taste in my mouth because I know that this reaction will return in some other circumstance and I will have to pack away the negative emotions that I am feeling when he or she reacts like that." Even though the intention to not inflame the situation is commendable, this behavior can give rise to a "bill" that

will grow longer and will inevitably be due later on, when it will have grown to the point where it cannot be paid. The third path consists of talking about this incident, either at the moment when it happens or later on when the tension has eased and the two partners are less tired from driving.

Centering Oneself as a Multifaceted Being

Daniel is 50 years old and he is in great shape. He plays a lot of sports, but not to excess, just to keep in good physical condition. He pays attention to his diet, devotes some time each day to meditation and has a fulfilling professional career in higher education where he teaches philosophy. He has been practicing aikido for almost ten years and his view of this martial art is imbued with Soto zen, which he practices in weekly sesshin[88] and on retreats when he is on vacation. Everything is going well and on the eve of his fiftieth birthday he decides to get a little checkup: blood test, medical exam, and stress test. The doctor—who is watching him while he is pedaling with more and more difficulty—suddenly stops him: the measuring device shows an anomaly in his cardiac rhythm. Further tests are ordered which reveal a cardiac problem that requires open heart surgery the following week. The news hits him like a bolt from the blue. How do you manage this news on an emotional level? Questions about life and death, which are a cruel reminder of our vulnerability, anxiety about the operation during which he will place his body and his life in the care of specialists, of other people, but not himself. Daniel calls upon all his resources, on the philosophy that transformed his way of thinking and giving meaning to things, and on zen meditation, which allows him to slow the machine that is racing in his head. With the news of the diagnosis, part of Daniel took control and became dominant. This part is the one that belongs to a man whose body must undergo a surgical procedure that certainly has been mastered on a technical level, but is nevertheless not free from risk.

This situation clearly illustrates how a significant event can throw us off center by grabbing onto a part of us and giving it control over a

---

[88] Zen meditation session.

large part of our life: our way of seeing things, of reminding ourselves of past experiences, of anticipating the future, of seeing and talking with our loved ones. Everything has changed. Daniel's reality has been completely changed by a simple statement. However, the risk was there before. Daniel could have had a heart attack while pedaling his bike, jogging with his son, or executing a technique in aikido. Reality remained the same, yet this diagnosis disrupted everything. Returning to oneself, centering oneself, consists in this case of making energy recirculate, of putting the part that has become dominant back in communication with all the other parts.

Centering then becomes a dance where Daniel puts himself in a state of awareness that favors alpha waves[89] and will use his mind to make his energy circulate between the different parts of himself. He will begin by putting his heart in connection with the other parts of his body: his heart with his shoulder, his heart with his foot. Then he will connect all the parts of his body between each other: his foot with his shoulders, his elbows, his hips, etc. His awareness of his body grows to encompass his entire body and no longer just his heart. Next he will put the parts of himself in contact with each other: teaching Daniel with sick Daniel, sick Daniel with Daniel the father of three sons, Daniel the father of three sons with Daniel the husband of Nathalie, the husband of Nathalie with the aikido practitioner, the friend of Steven and Joelle, the neighbor, the citizen, the philosopher, etc. He will continue by adding other dimensions of himself. Tender Daniel, powerful Daniel, sad Daniel, and joyous Daniel will all join together in the dance. Through a coming and going of the parts of himself, Daniel returns to himself because he is far more than a man whose heart is ill, and whose mind has been captured by a diagnosis. He cannot become disentangled without the strength of attention and without the support of his somatic center, which remains there,

---

[89] Our brain is made up of billions of cells that exchange information with each other. These exchanges are at the heart of electrical activity that can be observed by electroencephalography. This electrical activity presents rhythms that characterize our psychological states. So Beta waves are characteristic of an awakened state, but also, paradoxical sleep, during which dreams take place; the Alpha rhythm is present in the states of relaxation during which our two hemispheres function harmoniously together. There are also Delta rhythms, which appear during deep sleep states or unconsciousness; and Theta waves which appear during meditative states and drowsiness.

present, in its totality, ready to offer him a refuge of calm and security. This is the security of a connection to something greater, the deep connection with his loved ones, with the universal.

From this perspective of a multifaceted being, centering takes another form. It becomes a harmonization through the circulation of the energy of different parts that make up who I am. This process develops in the present and in my body, which remains the ultimate reference, the stable point of reference in this loose conglomeration that is my identity. Although my identities evolve and are influenced by my environment, there is a constant that will define me throughout time. I call this constant my *essential being*.

The essential being is the aspiration, the feeling of being called, drawn toward something that transcends all of life's constraints that I can live through. It is a founding principle. If we were talking about a business or an association, we would talk about its social purpose, the one for which its founders got together and the purpose that they wanted to achieve. When I talk about a calling, this does not mean a calling by an entity or a person outside of us. This calling, if it exists, is expressed by an internal voice. This voice is me and, at the same time, it is not me.

Because I am alive, I have lived through experiences, I live in a given context. This is what I call the existential self, the self I tend to identify myself with.

This existential self must struggle with the constraints of daily life, the resources at its disposal, the body at its disposal, the spirit that animates it. It could be content to live until death comes, but it is not content with that. Something calls it, a voice within it, a desire to go somewhere, to become. It is interesting to realize that "to become" is "to come to be" and "coming" calls to mind the place we come from[90]. To become who you are is to return to the essential being.

The essential being is the unifying principle of my being. Around this essential being there revolves a galaxy of parts, of identities that are more or less interconnected and more or less dense. At certain times, certain identities are more present. They block out the other

---

[90] In the original French, to become is "devenir," which can be transformed into "venir de" to come from.

identities, then join up with them again in the shadows when our awareness or the events decide to choose others. Certain parts of me are more attractive, more pleasant. We like to emphasize them. This is our good side, the one that we like to show in public. Other aspects are carefully run off, set aside, even forgotten. But they remain present nevertheless, on the lookout for the least occasion to reveal themselves.

An ignored part conserves its energy and the fact that it is set aside cuts it off from the overall flow of energy. This energy is sort of a time bomb when it is confined and kept on the margins of the system. When it emerges, its wild energy can overwhelm us. It plunges us into undesired states and makes us act differently than we would have wanted to.

> Julian is a young laborer. He has been working in a body shop for two months. He could have taken up other studies, but his low self esteem, inherited from a particularly difficult childhood, always made him doubt himself. In this way, he developed a personality that subtly combined rebelliousness with indifference. From failure to failure, he turned toward career paths where his strong physique allowed him to "forge his character." But now that he is in a professional environment, the rules that were in place when he left school are no longer in force. He feels watched, evaluated, and, against all expectations, he feels within himself a crushed personality, with its abilities buried, that he thought belonged to his past. This doubting part of himself remained buried without having received the attention that it needed in order to transform itself. It was only during the therapy that he began after the death of his mother that Julian took the time to welcome this neglected part of himself and could finally carry out the work of integration that will help him to get in better contact with his personal resources and develop his self-confidence[91].

---

[91] Aiki-Coaching tackles the question of change by integrating parts of our identity in an Ai-Ki process that is similar to the one that can be observed in randori in aikido. The attacker represents this neglected identity that shows itself aggressively. The aikidoka then uses his ability to move, to center, and to connect in order to receive the energy of the attack and transform it in order to turn his adversary into a partner.

It is during a period of crisis that we see the awakening of these identities that are conditioned by our past experiences. This is the case in situations of divorce, mourning, change of employment, intense disputes, etc. During these moments, we are disrupted by the flood of energy, which generates confusion and either vague or intense emotions. We then try to reestablish our equilibrium by reactivating attitudes that have been effective in the past and are imprinted in our body[92]. Even if these attitudes do not suit us, we accept them and adopt them because they seem useful to us in order to live through situations where our survival is threatened.

Centering leads us to get back into contact with ourselves, in our wholeness. Letting one part of our identity be dominant is inevitably a source of imbalance. Centering yourself therefore involves reactivating the most fluid circulation of energy possible in order to nourish the exchanges between our different identities. It is a reharmonization that integrates our diverse facets while retaining their richness. It does not exclude any part of ourselves any more than it fights them because struggle would only strengthen them and recognize them as separate entities. This is the very principle of *Ai-Ki*: to reharmonize energy by making it circulate, while welcoming difference as a source of richness that will contribute to increasing the flow of our overall life energy and will make our existential self evolve toward our essential self.

I center myself and I breathe. I feel that I am here, sitting in this chair, very comfortably ... I can feel my breathing circulate and come into contact with the different parts of myself that make me who I am: me-parent, me-lover, me-friend, me-quick-tempered, me-sad ... my breath circulates among all my identities and all my roles ... me-colleague, me-boss, me-customer ... I accept them all and I welcome them ... me-aggressive, me-jealous ... in the same way as the others ... me-tender, me-attentive-to-others ... like reunions among old friends

---

[92] These attitudes appear through characteristic postures, changes in respiration, tension in the arms and hands or in the face. They also appear mentally in an attitude that one may call intellectualization: a sort of mental diversion that consists of rationalizing the experience in order to escape emotions that could make us lose control or take on attitudes that we disapprove of.

... with all the tenderness in the world ... accepting their strengths and their weaknesses, which are only parts of the same whole.

This process can sometimes create the sensation of scattering, of making us dizzy, if we do not carry it out with awareness of our essential being, this dimension that encompasses and transcends all these distinctions. The essential being is materialized physically by our vertical axis, the axis of being that reunites our three centers: the cognitive, the emotional, and the somatic.

Verticality

> *"Standing amidst heaven and earth*
> *Connected to all things with ki,*
> *My mind is set*
> *On the path of echoing all things."*[93]
> Morihei Ueshiba, Founder of aikido

All that I believe, want, and desire, I desire with my body and my thoughts. From this come emotions that express the gap between the real and the ideal, that toward which I aspire. My actions, my thoughts, and my feelings express themselves in a whirlwind of energy that circulates through my three centers in connection, aligned and thus building the ***vertical axis of being.***

Verticality is a fundamental concept of *AikiCom*. It was born in aikido. Its founder, Morihei Ueshiba, never used the animal metaphors that are common in certain martial arts[94] such as kung fu or tai chi chuan.

Our ancestors stood up and took a vertical posture, thus distinguishing themselves from other animals and mainly from their cousins the apes[95]. This vertical position freed the forelimbs and allowed the development of the skull, but also contributed to moving the center of gravity of the body from the ribcage toward the abdomen.

---
[93] Morihei Ueshiba, *The Spirit of Aikido*, page 39.
[94] Note that this is the case in most modern Japanese martial arts. Most of the time, these martial arts originated in Chinese martial arts that often use animal metaphors. This is also the case with Burmese martial arts such as Thaing or Bando.
[95] Apes also took a bipedal posture, but did not make it their permanent way of locomotion. They continue to move as quadrupeds have and generally retained arboreal locomotion.

This verticality characterizes our humanity and our linguistic metaphors make numerous allusions to it:

I am feeling down, down-and-out. I am an upstanding young man. I hold my head high...

This verticality contributed to developing how we imagine the world. We have thus likened what is high to what is better or the most as in "I am on top," and what is low to what is bad or the least, as in "he has hit rock bottom." It is interesting to note how our posture has influenced our vocabulary and our expressions[96].

While verticality is the first quality of the axis of being, it cannot be compared to a perfectly vertical straight line. While perfect verticality can represent our essential being—a state we would like to strive for and which makes us want to grow—there is no perfection that is not accompanied by a sort of rigidity. With a spinal column as straight as a mast pointing to the sky, we could not take the shocks of life. Evolution has given us a spine that is naturally curved in the shape of an S, which gives us the flexibility we need. To this natural curve, more or less pronounced according to our build, we must add the memorization of past experiences that are imprinted on our body as well as the deformations that are imprinted on us by our more and more sedentary way of life. For the attentive observer, everyone's vertical posture is a book that tells us who we have become through our personal history and even our family history.

We all have an internal image of our verticality. This is not only an idea or an image, but also a physical sensation combined with a mental image. We tend to align ourselves toward this posture when things are going well for us and when we feel the living energy of our being within us.

In this vertical position, we are in the state of *being*. We do not *do* anything; it is the state of not-doing. Our skeleton has evolved so that we can hold ourselves upright and counter the force of gravity that pulls us toward the earth.

Stand up with your feet slightly hip-width apart. Imagine all your bones stacked up one upon the other beginning with the bones of your

---

[96] I refer here to the very interesting work of George Lakoff and Mark Johnson on metaphors: *Metaphors We Live By*, 1980.

feet, then your shinbones, your knees, your thighbone, your pelvis, your spine, your shoulders, your neck, then your skull. Feel how these bones support each other and how little tension it takes to stand straight, just enough to compensate for the fluctuations of our living body.

The axis of being is part of a vertical axis that both includes us and transcends us. This vertical axis is our Humanity. It unites the earth and the sky.

The Sky[97]

The sky is the world of abstraction, of virtuality. It is the world of ideas that was described by Plato in the allegory of the cave[98]. Words such as justice, equality, kindness, correctness, love, or hate are just so many abstractions that must be defined by each of us for them to take on meaning. This is what we do when we associate them with concrete equivalences, that is to say, descriptions of observable events:

> *When someone smiles at me, it shows friendship.*
> *Courtesy is saying hello when you see someone for the first time in the morning.*
> *Justice is when you are punished for insulting me.*

Throughout our lifetime, we create an encyclopedia of associations that make up our map of the world. This map is personal and highly subjective. While these associations are indispensable for giving meaning to our experience, some can be considered restrictive. They will be so when they prohibit or prevent me from acting as I would like to. It is therefore necessary to transform them in order to give us the freedom that we need. *AikiCom* teaches us how to keep our physical flexibility, but also our mental flexibility, in the service of our being. Each time that we freeze up because a person or a mental association takes hold of us, we lose our freedom of choice.

---

[97] In this translation, we sometimes refer to the sky, keeping in mind that O'Sensei had a more spiritual view that could be interpreted as Heaven.
[98] Plato, *The Allegory of the Cave*, Book VII of *The Republic*.

The Cognitive Center

Figure 4 : Cognitive Center: Creating Meaning

It is in our cognitive center that we create associations between abstract terms that are located up in the sky above us and concrete events that we experience. The more these associations are confirmed by our experiences, the more they are strengthened. Over the course of our experiences, these associations—our beliefs—will take on more and more weight and become self-realizing by activating perception filters within us. These filters highlight each event that confirms our beliefs and brushes aside the ones that do not match their patterns. A counter-experience is necessary to bring us out of our mental torpor and provoke us to call our beliefs into question in order to develop new ones[99].

The Emotional Center

As we continue our exploration of the vertical axis, beginning with the sky and then moving on to the cognitive center, we arrive at the emotional center, which gives life to our experience.

---

[99] Our mind abhors a vacuum and never stops automating its reactions in order to minimize its expense of energy. Our beliefs and the routine that they cause allow us to react more rapidly and economically, but draw us at the same time into more rigid and less adapted behaviors in changing environments.

Each moment and each event can call into question our map of the world[100]. Depending on whether our experience satisfies us or violates one of our values[101], we feel an emotion that is sometimes pleasant and sometimes unpleasant. So if I see a person shove someone else, my "harmony" or "respect" value will be shocked and I will feel bad. This disagreeable feeling will express itself in diverse ways according to my personal patterns: sadness, fear, anger, etc.

The emotional center thus gives color to the vertical axis; it gives it heart. It is the expression of our life instinct, of our vital energy.

The Somatic Center

The conjunction of the vertical axis with the somatic center is essential. It is the conjunction of myself as an individual with my characteristics as a human being. In Morihei Ueshiba's thinking, the somatic center—referred to in Japanese by the word *hara*—is both unique and universal. Rather than making ourselves withdraw into ourselves, it opens us up to the world. This center is therefore in a way both our center and a place that opens us up to the world. By becoming deeper, the specific becomes universal. It is at this point that we get in touch with our basic needs, "those that are essential to keeping us alive, those that we must meet in order to find a satisfying balance.[102]" These needs that we try to satisfy for ourselves and in our own way are universal needs that tie us to others in our humanity. Abraham Maslow categorized them in his famous hierarchy of needs.

---

[100] This map of the world can be seen as a network whose nodes are abstract words and representations of concrete experiences. In fact, there are classes of experience because it is impossible to memorize each individual experience. Over the course of our lives we have placed certain concrete experiences in a relationship with these abstract terms such as "values." We thus give meaning to experiences that we have lived through and they seem agreeable or disagreeable according to whether they go along with or contradict values that are important to us.
[101] The word "value" is used here in the NLP sense. It is a scale that allows us to evaluate to what extent an experience satisfies us.
[102] Translated from Thomas d'Ansembourg, *Cessez d'être gentil soyez vrai, être avec les autres en restant soi-même*, Éditions de l'Homme, 2001, page 36.

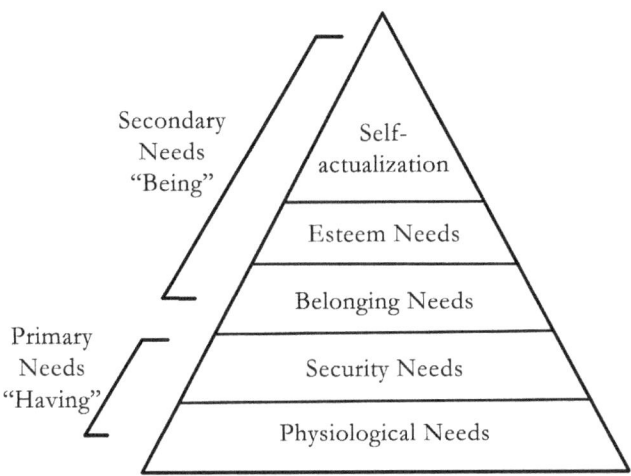

Figure 5 : Maslow's Hierarchy of Needs

Needs are the cornerstone of Marshall Rosenberg's nonviolent communication. It is by plunging into this level of needs that we succeed in moving beyond superficial dialogue—the kind that is produced by our thoughts with its succession of judgments and excessive talk—to move appropriately toward the *other*. In this way, by returning to the true center of our being, we return to ourselves and we open the door to the *other*.

"To go appropriately toward the *other*, we are led to go through ourselves; to meet the *other* in his well, we must first go down into our own. For me, this truly illustrates the fact that on the path toward the *other*, I cannot save time on the path toward myself.[103]"

The Earth

The end of the vertical axis is anchored in the earth. The ground is a concrete reality, a limit. The force of gravity continuously pulls us back to it. The earth represents what is concrete in our life. It is what we cannot escape, objective reality. I am here and now in my reality. I have the body that I have. I live in this country and not in another one, I have a family history that made me what I am now. I can wish to

---

[103] Translated from Thomas d'Ansembourg, *Cessez d'être gentil soyez vrai, être avec les autres en restant soi-même*, Éditions de l'Homme, 2001, page 161.

escape in dreams and imagine myself to be the hero of some fantastic story; unavoidably, I must wake up and return to reality and its limitations.

But the earth is also a reservoir of resources. Through its telluric energy, raw material, and nourishment of the plant world, the earth has always been symbolized by the nourishing mother, the source of richness and fertility.

Vertical Axis, Axis of Energy

Uniting the sky and the earth, the vertical axis must not be seen as a static or even rigid entity. It is an axis of energy, a conduit in which a continuous flow circulates, passing through the three centers and connecting the sky to the earth. Every discontinuity, every rupture or bottleneck brings a malfunction in one of the dimensions of our being. If I am connected to the sky and disconnected from the earth, I will be idealistic and not very anchored. I will be motivated by values, each of which is more beautiful than the next, but I will be unable to apply them in my life. And my fall will be harder because I risk melting my wings like Icarus[104].

This exclusive connection with the earth offers advantages that we make the most of during periods of reflection, when we try to give meaning to our experiences or when we brainstorm to make everything possible come our way[105].

Conversely, if I am anchored to the ground and lose contact with the sky and this condition continues, I will lead my life at ground level, preoccupied with assuring my material well-being, from day to day,

---

[104] Icarus and his father Daedalus, the creator of the Labyrinth, attempted to escape from Crete by means of wings that his father had constructed from feathers and wax. Icarus ignored his father's instructions not to fly too close to the sun, whereupon the wax in his wings melted and he fell into the sea (From wikipedia, Icarus, consulted December 21, 2015).

[105] In NLP, Robert Dilts defined Disney's strategy. This strategy passes through three phases. The first is that of the creator. In this phase, I deliberately disconnect myself from the earth to imagine everything that is possible without limitations. This is an illustration of the connection with the sky. In the second phase I reconnect myself with the earth and I become a film director to examine how to materialize the ideas that I came up with in the first phase. Finally, in the last phase I connect to the level of the cognitive and emotional centers to evaluate the relevance and feasibility of the solution that I have found.

with my nose to the grindstone and completely disconnected from my values.

With little enthusiasm and little satisfaction, I live my life without looking for meaning or having given up on finding it.

This is the strategy that I will adopt when I must suffer the effects of a hard blow, one of life's hardships: death, divorce, being fired, etc. I return to the essential and I try to ensure the satisfaction of my primary needs by drawing from the earth. I act by dividing time into brief moments: I live one step at a time while being careful not to fall. The pressure of external events seems strong to me; I endure and try to remain standing.

I can also identify ruptures or bottlenecks at other levels of this vertical axis.

Blocked circulation in the neck will disturb the harmonious circulation between the cognitive center and the emotional center. In this scenario, it is difficult to evaluate the options that we imagined in our mind's eye. Our feelings are weak and it is difficult to choose between one option or the other. Our motivation is weak because the emotional outcome is barely perceptible. People who tend to rationalize their experiences cut themselves off from their emotions to protect themselves and in this way they try to maintain control of the situation. Pushed to the extreme, this behavior makes us cold and calculating, walking computers, cut off from our feelings and even from our feeling of being alive because the rupture also cuts off the cognitive brain from the somatic center. The same constriction can have the opposite effect by cutting off the cognitive center from the other two centers. In this case, the person will define himself as impulsive, emotionally sensitive, acting without thinking, by instinct. The ultimate metaphor would therefore be that of a chicken that keeps running after you have cut off its head.

Blocked circulation between the emotional center and the somatic center is characteristic of life situations where we are cut off from our awareness of being; we don't live in the present moment. Our thoughts take us to the past and the future. We reflect, we feel, but above all we act. We get lost in *doing*. The somatic center is anesthetized, numb.

"I closed my eyes for a moment and ten years of my life went by."
(unknown author)

For people who remain for a long time in this condition – where the somatic center is numb – it takes a serious health problem to reconnect them with their body and their *being*.

> Philip is a busy manager; his professional career has been quite successful. He is concerned with details and he has put in countless hours to reach his objectives. When he had his first cardiac problem, his outlook on life was shaken. "Now I see life differently," he told me. "It will never be the same." Philip began to take care of his body, to do meditation and to take the time to simply be. He realizes that he has been chasing after successes that have certainly contributed to making him a "winner," but that he has strayed from his path. His retraining as a nature guide will give him the feeling of being reborn, of having found himself.

Breathing plays a key role in our perception of the vertical axis. It brings about the circulation of energy between the sky and the earth by passing through the three centers. Different exercises help us to improve our awareness of the axis of being. It is not a question of becoming this axis. We are beings who are fundamentally imperfect and therefore unavoidably different from our essential being, toward which we'd like to strive[106]. This exploration of the vertical axis is a process of awareness, an exploration of our being without being either relentless or disinterested; it is a personal evolutionary path that wakes us from the torpor of our anesthetized lifestyles.

To return to the topic of centering, we can look at it as a return to self that takes into account the dimension of *being*, that is, the vertical axis.

The vertical axis is more an experience than a concept. In *AikiCom* training, various exercises allow us to experience this axis through our body. The most striking exercise is based on a classic aikido movement called *tai sabaki*.

---

[106] Translator's note: In the original French version of this book, the author points out the similarity between the verb *tendre*, which means "to strive" in this context, and the word *tendresse*, tenderness, which is closer to the intent of the verb *tendre* than the word "tension."

Exercise 1 – Tai sabaki

Stand upright with your right leg forward. Both feet are roughly aligned on a front-back line (black footprints in the drawing below).
The movement consists of moving your left foot in front of the right foot (movement #1, grey footprint) then pivoting on both feet to make an about-turn with your body (movement #2, checkered footprints). Your right foot finds itself once again in front of your left foot. The movement ends by moving your right foot back, behind your left foot (movement #3). When you finish, you have made a complete about-turn in two steps.

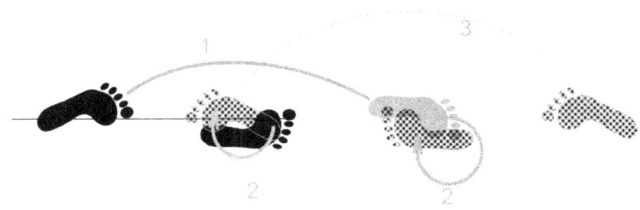

Figure 6 : Tai sabaki, step diagram

Other *AikiCom* exercises appeal to both visualization and breathing.

Exercise 2 – The cognitive Spotlight

In this exercise, we are going to use our mind's natural orientation ability. When you think about the floor beneath you, then about the book that you are holding in your hands, you are using your mind as a spotlight that lights up an element of your experience of the moment. You can use this ability to turn your attention to your somatic center by turning your cognitive spotlight toward your *hara*, your abdomen—more accurately to three inches below your navel. Breathe in through your nose and follow the path of the air passing through your throat, your lungs, and your emotional center to inflate your abdomen and connect

with your somatic center before reversing its course to go back up and be exhaled through your mouth. By following the path of the air that you inhale then exhale, you recreate the vertical space in a dynamic of exchange and reconnection.
This breathing exercise can be done in several ways.

Variation 1: Spiral Breathing

Imagine your inhalation as a wide spiral beginning in the earth and imagine your breath turning while moving up and narrowing to form a cone whose point coincides with your *hara*. Then exhale while reversing the direction of the spiral and widening it as you return to the earth.

Variation 2: The Double Spiral

In this second variant, you create the same spiral as in the preceding exercise but you breathe out while creating a spiral that rises to the sky while growing wider.

Coming into the World [107]

As soon as I have centered myself and become aware of my vertical axis, I can come into the world. I can take my place there. Although centering and verticality are the initial conditions for an aware life, this is not enough. As a living being, it is up to me to act, to influence, and to be radiant. This is what distinguishes the plant kingdom from the animal and human kingdom: action. A plant survives and develops in a favorable environment; an animal moves itself to find favorable areas where it will find the resources that are necessary for its survival.

As a person, I can be centered and still be cut off from the world, closed, and protected. I can also let my life energy go out from my center and be wasted, burning the candle at both ends, and having a blast. The explosion of energy may be impressive, but, without a doubt, it will not last long. The *Aiki* attitude consists of starting with

---

[107] In French, *venir au monde* is an expression that means "to be born."

centering, in verticality, and coming into the world, "to be born" in the sense of being "borne by life."

Exercise: Entering the World

Starting with my vertical axis—my axis of being—I will extend my awareness to envelop and include a space that is greater than me. This space is of course the place where I am physically located, but it is far greater than that. In this space I can include zones that are more or less distant from me. You will therefore use the word "field" (like the image of a magnetic field). For example, when I am at work, I can extend my awareness to encompass my immediate family, my children, and my spouse, even if they are not physically present. When I include them in my energy field, my *ki* field, I feel them close to me, with me. If they are not included in my field and I think about them, I will miss them and I will feel lonely.

Jean-Pierre is going through a divorce. He has two children and Michael, the younger one, is having a bad time with his parents' separation. He is suffering from anxiety over their separation. When he is with his father, he cannot take his eyes off of him without feeling irrepressible fear. One day when they were in town, Jean-Pierre parked his car next to a mailbox to drop an envelope in it. As soon as he turned off the engine, Michael, who was in the middle of a conversation with his brother, stopped talking and watched his father to make sure that he stayed in the car. Jean-Pierre then showed him the mailbox next to his window and told him that he was going to get out, mail the letter, and then immediately get back in the car. Nothing worked. Michael absolutely wanted to get out of the car with his father to walk the three feet that separated the car from the mailbox. This anxiety was a problem when Michael had to go to school. He had great difficulty seeing his father leave, even if he had complete confidence in his teacher, whom he liked a great deal. During a session, I suggested to Michael that he relax and join me in a guided imagery exercise in which I asked him to get into a basket suspended from a giant construction crane. From up there, he could see the countryside stretch out to the horizon and he could see his house, his school, and even his dad's office. The intent was to expand his field of presence to include the place where his father worked. This exercise helped Michael to better accept seeing his father leave in the morning when he was at school.

When I have extended my field of presence, I open myself up to what is around me. In contact with the feeling of my vertical axis and my center, I am "attentive to the outside" and in a state of openness. I am receptive, ready for the encounter, ready to live. My body is relaxed, without tension but without being limp. We are living beings. Systems analysts would say that we are open systems. We are in constant interaction with our environment., Life is basically an exchange between me and what is around me: air, food, drink, information, perception, action. The expression "open system" highlights these exchanges with the environment that keep us alive while preserving our uniqueness, our identity.

The Axis of Action

Centering and its complement, extension, put us in a state that I call "ready for action." I am centered, within my body, my emotions, and my thoughts and I am open to what is going on around me. I did not get here without a past. I know that behind me I have a series of experiences that made me, influenced me, and condition the state in which I now find myself. This past is behind me but I can feel its *presence*!

In this "space of the past," there are events, people, and memories that hold me back and others that push me, propel me, and make me want to move forward.

In front of me is the future, what is waiting for me, what I am going toward. My action comes about by the steps that I can take and that make me move forward. Suddenly, the space around me takes form. In my verticality, I am in a place where the front, the back, and the sides are undifferentiated. I am the sentinel, the observer. I see everything that is around me. I can turn around my vertical axis to see behind me, then turn again to see another angle. When I go into action and change from being a spectator to someone who is a spect-*actor*, my space takes on a structure and a direction.

This space is the subjective space, the space that I define myself—by myself and for myself. Wherever I go, my front-rear axis goes through me while passing through my *hara*. It is my direction. It carries out my intention. In front of me is my objective, the real one, not the one that I claim to pursue or that I believe I pursue. The orientation of my body and my being point toward the objective that I am pursuing with awareness (more or less). We have all had an experience where we acted, believing that we wanted something, then suddenly realized that in fact we were doing something other than what we wanted. We realize that we are moving toward an objective that is not the one that we have consciously chosen. Our subconscious seems to have the advantage and leads us toward a destiny that it has already chosen. Subconscious objectives can be the result of our personal, family, or even genetic history, scenarios that we have given ourselves and that confirm our deep-seated beliefs.

In aikido practice, I often see how practitioners, thinking that they are turning their energy in a given direction, move in a different direction. The *tori*[108] believes his *hara* is turned toward *uke's hara*, toward the center of the attacker. However, when you watch him you notice that his body is turned in a completely different direction. This is often the concrete manifestation of a lack of congruity and a dissociation between what someone is doing and what he thinks or wants to do. This incongruity makes the action less efficient. It turns the expression "doing several things at once[109]" into body language.

Orienting the Axis of Action

The axis of action shows what I am paying attention to. While I am now immersed in the world, I perceive what is happening around me. When I notice an event, an object, or a person who requires me to act, I naturally turn my body in that direction. This is the passage from *being* to taking action. We will talk more about this later on (see page 124).

---

[108] *Tori* is a term used in aikido to identify the one who makes the movement. See the glossary at the end of this book.
[109] The French expression used here is *courir plusieurs lièvres à la fois*. Literally, this is to hunt several hares at the same time.

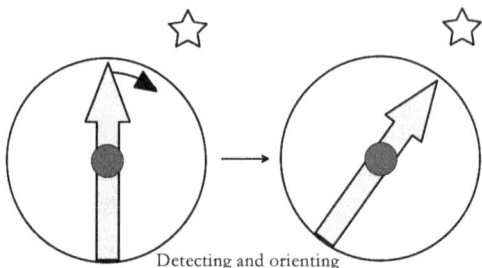

Figure 7 : Turning the Action toward the Objective

It is important to note that when I turn myself toward a point, an event, or an action, my attention is not totally absorbed.

I keep my gaze wide open and relaxed. I have not yet acted; I put myself in a position that makes me more capable of acting, with the most efficiency. I am ready and I can act without being surprised. Without being oriented toward this point, I may act in a reactive or impulsive way, hastily and therefore tensely. By turning my axis in the direction of my potential action, I can give myself the luxury of acting in a relaxed way and thus avoid resorting to the reflexive reactions of my reptilian brain.

As busy as we are pursuing our own goals, we very often go through life without going through this orientation process. Then this thought comes to us: "I didn't see it coming!" which reflects the attitude of someone who acts and moves forward without worrying about what is going on around him. The axis of action is added to the vertical axis of being, which is present in the world. The difference between a person who is lost in action and one who acts while remaining himself can be seen in the quality of his gaze. In the first case, his vision is rather narrow (tunnel vision), masking whatever is not the goal; in the other instance, his vision is oriented toward the goal but maintains a wide angle. Peripheral vision guarantees a certain relaxation in one's action and a readiness for any unforeseen event.

The Relationship Axis

To finish our exploration of our subjective physical space, we must talk about the lateral or transverse axis, which passes through us and connects our left to our right while passing through our somatic center. This axis is the only one that is not oriented. The left and the right are not distinguished from one another. What is important in this dimension is the relative distance with respect to the center.

This axis is the relationship axis. I am in the center and at my sides there are the other people in my life, beginning with the ones who are close to me, then progressively those who are more and more distant. On this axis, I can also put objects, organizations, and groups of people according to the role that they play in my life. Without the relationship axis, my existence takes on the form of a thin disk made up of my axes of being and action. What gives depth and consistency to my life is the lateral, social dimension. The more I feel surrounded by loved ones, the more dense and broad I feel. This contributes to giving me more stability. A disk that is placed on its edge is unstable if it is not rolling. My social network gives thickness to this disk and transforms it into a sphere; the closest people give more consistency and the farthest people have less impact. I am, of course, not talking about the actions of others on me, but about my interior representation of the role that others play in my way of being and acting. So a lone bachelor could "get around" in the world with a relative lack of concern. His "social disk" is narrow. When he is part of a couple and has children, his network of acquaintances thickens and the disk gets wider. He will live and act with the feeling of acting with close people next to him, people who give a certain depth to his life.

The Aikisphere

The three dimensions that I have just discussed—vertical, sagittal (front-rear), and lateral—define a three-dimensional space. This subjective and physical space gives us a grid to decode what we are experiencing. It can be visualized as a sphere whose center is our somatic center. It is the *Aikisphere*.

The *Aikisphere* is a model that we can use to explore our experience. It puts our body in a structured space that allows us to examine how our view of things and our behavior are suited to our objectives, our needs, and our values. In other words, it allows us to check that we are still aligned and centered in *acting* without losing ourselves in *doing*. We have all had the experience of working hard and at a certain point lifting up our head and saying to ourselves: "Why am I exhausting myself doing this? What goal am I pursuing? Is this my goal or someone else's? And if it is mine, is it still relevant?"

> *C'est le tango des forts en rien;*
> *Qui déclinent de chagrin;*
> *Et qui seront pharmaciens;*
> *Parce que papa ne l'était pas.*
> *(Jacques Brel, "Rosa[110]")*

The *Aikisphere* has gone through considerable development since its creation to become a powerful intervention tool for life coaches and support professionals. It is not the purpose of this book to give an exhaustive description and demonstrate all of its applications. This will be the subject of a separate workbook that will be published after this book.

The power of the *Aikisphere* can be measured by its physical dimension, which turns our body into a compass that points toward action. You will only appreciate its qualities by integrating it into your physical structure, that is, by applying it physically: by standing up and by getting in touch with your verticality, by breathing, and by orienting your body. When it is mobilized, your body becomes your guide and reconnects you to your inner wisdom. Generally, we make our decisions based on thoughtful reflection, by a level-headed evaluation of the pros and cons, of the risks and ways to control them. All this results in a process that comes from our cognitive center, our brain. Our map of the world that was created over the course of our experiences causes us to know the world in our own unique way.

No two persons share the same vision of the world. The question we have to ask is if our vision is the right one, if our map of the world helps us to make good decisions and to take the right actions. If we observe responses in our environment and even in our own experience, we have no choice but to notice that what is called "the good decision" or "the right decision" does not limit itself to reasoning, no matter how clear. When it is right, the impulse to act arises from the somatic center. It obviously feeds on our thoughts and our emotions, otherwise

---

[110] Loose translation: "It's the tango of those who are good at nothing, Who grow weak from sorrow, And who will become pharmacists, Because Daddy wasn't one."

it would only be an instinctive or impulsive reaction. The right decision emerges from our being as a general, physical sensation. It comes from our gut and cans thus contradict the good solutions that our mind comes up with. Have you ever said to yourself:

"This is what reason tells me to do, but it doesn't feel right!"

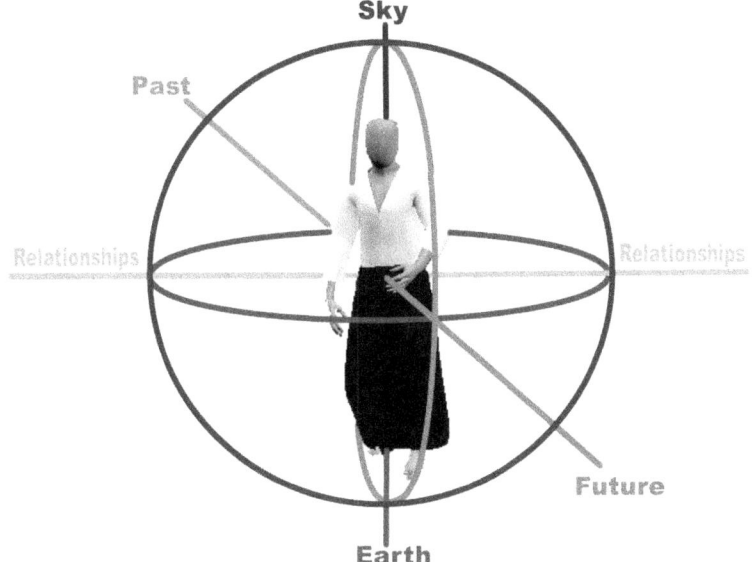

Figure 8 : The Aikisphere

The *Aikisphere* helps us to formalize this decision process. We'll examine the process starting from a life scenario in the next chapter[111]. Just like a compass needle pointing to the north, it turns us in the direction of the right action. The action then takes place in a clear, fluid manner. We feel that it is right and we are not surprised to see that events happen which help us. We meet the right person, someone sends us the e-mail that we were waiting for, we wake up with the solution to a problem that was bothering us. When we are in this state, we are a living example of the maxim: "The Lord helps those who help themselves."

---

[111] See Deciding and Acting with the Aikisphere page 121.

Being in the Moment and Outside of Time

In the chapter devoted to centering, we explored the relationship between time and the three centers. We saw how the cognitive center oscillates between past and future by only fleetingly passing through the present. We also saw how our emotional center lives in the present, but a present that is greatly influenced by the past and by the emotional inertia that sets off electrochemical processes in our body. Finally, we saw how our somatic center only exists in the present moment.

We also saw how the somatic center succeeds in reconciling the irreconcilable: the individual and the universal. It truly seems that it does so by uniting the present moment to the timeless[112]. It is the particular context of combat with an *Aiki* mind—that is, combat that is carried out with the intent of transforming it into "non-combat,"—which allows us to reach this state of presence.

In combat, it is essential to be present and attentive to what is happening. Otherwise, the consequence is immediate as the attacker lands his blow. If we do not react to what is happening, we are defeated. In aikido exercises known as *randori*—several partners attacking freeform—we experience a situation in which only the present moment counts. If the aikidoka lets himself be led by his thoughts—for example by trying to anticipate the attack that will come or by wanting to choose the technique that will be applied—he will quickly be overwhelmed and will not be able to respond to the attacks effectively. These exercises force us to join the flow of the attacks to become one with our partners. When the *randori* is well executed, the partners have the sensation that they no longer have a target. Time and space seem to have dissolved: there is no longer time or space. You are not sure if the attack preceded the defense technique or vice versa. Morihei Ueshiba spoke of letting the movement spring out within the action. This is what he called *reversal*.

---

[112] The atemporal (French: *atemporel*; i.e., without time) calls to mind what is not concerned with time while the timeless (French: *intemporel*) calls to mind what is not touched by time, that is to say, that is not subjected to its assaults and that is eternal. I would like to emphasize the timeless (French: *hors du temps*; i.e., outside of time) nature of the somatic center.

For Morihei Ueshiba, reversal[113] is the goal of *Aiki* practice. Training begins with physical practice. The body evolves in material reality and is, for this reason, subject to the laws of mechanics and causality: I react to an attack with a defense technique; if I unbalance my partner, he falls; if he steps forward, he can find a new position of balance. For the founder of aikido, the goal of training is not to always become more effective physically—a battle that is lost before it begins because we will eventually age and younger, more physically effective challengers will inevitably come along—but rather to carry out the reversal of the preeminence of the body over the mind. In Ueshiba's philosophy, the spirit lies outside of time. Without this passage of time, no event happens before another; the universe of the spirit is therefore an acausal universe, that is, without cause. In this space without time, it's all about synchronicity. What was an attack becomes the space for a meeting that unites us with our partner. We become one with him and the universe. We bathe in the flow of events that leaves the very notion of combat pointless. It is instead a dance, a dance of life.

The *Aiki* attitude is a progression toward the state of being in harmony, which comes from living in the moment, without judgment or anticipation, simply by being there, welcoming what comes.

All of this seems very nice and, above all, very esoteric. In real life, we can only live on the level where our training has brought us. We all struggle in this temporal and causal world, trying to anticipate what will happen to us next in order to retain a semblance of mastery. However, sometimes we experience certain moments when we are outside of a state of control, a state that makes us receptive to the unexpected. When we stop being in a state of expectation, new paths open themselves to us. They take the form of unexpected meetings, movie scenes that call out to us, music that brings us out of our torpor. Life plays with us and makes us begin a dance that Jean-François Vézina calls the "dance of chaos"[114], but which is quite simply the dance of life, freed from the strait jacket of control that we have imposed upon it in order to escape from the anguish of the unknown.

---

113 See "The Reversal of the Body-Mind Relationship," page 47.
114 Jean-François Vézina, *Danser avec le chaos, accueillez l'inattendu dans votre vie*, Éditions de l'Homme, 2012.

These precious moments of receptivity open up the doors to unexpected freedoms for us. They arise when we set our attention free. In moments of crisis and during important periods of transition in our lives, they can significantly change our life's trajectory. The *Aiki* attitude favors the unexpected appearance of these particular moments in two ways. The first follows from centering and verticality, which makes us feel the flow of life that we are bathing in and which connects us more intimately with the experience that we are going through. The second is tied to our union with the opposing energy, what we call *blending*. This energetic union synchronizes us with the *other* and our environment. We can then perceive synchronicities that would otherwise go unnoticed. To really understand this, we use the metaphor of a highway. If we stand on the side of a highway, we see vehicles pass by at high speed and we can only make out their shapes. If our gaze follows a particular vehicle, we can make out certain details, but it will soon be out of range. If, on the other hand, we are in a car driving on the same highway, we have a much better view of the vehicles that are moving at the same speed. We can then make out the details of the cars, watch the drivers and passengers, and even smile at them. By synchronizing our speed with that of the car next to us, we can grasp a great number of details and maybe even recognize someone we know, something that we would not have been able to do while standing on the side of the highway.

And it can be much worse.

There are people who have become masters at the art of going against the flow. They are the wrong-way drivers of the highway metaphor. Not only are they incapable of making out anything, but, on top of that, they turn opportunities into threats. They expend an extraordinary amount of energy trying to make progress while living in an environment that they consider to be hostile.

The blending that characterizes *Aiki* practice puts us in the flow of life. Rather than trying to arm wrestle with life, we refine our perceptions in order to live through experiences while seizing the opportunities that they present to us. We are then in a state that is outside of time, or at least we have this strange sensation that time has slowed down. The vehicles that go down the highway at the same speed as we do seem immobile.

There is no causality: this car is not here because I am, it is here because it is here. There is neither need nor expectation; I go along, that's all.

The highway metaphor brings us another lesson. While I keep my vehicle at cruising speed, I feel neither acceleration nor deceleration. It is the same for my verticality. The vertical axis is the axis of being, in which there is no need to do anything at all. Verticality is not a state where I desire nothing. I can want to go ahead on my path, define my goals, and reach them. Without a goal or an objective, or without a desire to reach them, I am more like a vegetable or a plant. This can often confuse us when we talk about states of fulfillment in Buddhism. For some, this evokes a certain sort of passivity. It is nothing of the sort. We can live in a state of fulfillment while maintaining a life impulse that puts us in motion, that touches us (in the sense of moving us emotionally). The important thing is to not lose our balance and our verticality by leaning forward, thus creating a feeling of unbalancing frustration from not yet having reached our desired goal. Fulfillment encompasses the delicious sensation of being in movement, all the while remaining balanced in the present. This is what we feel at cruising speed. We are not nailed to our seat with our nose on the steering wheel. We roll along with the satisfaction of moving forward while taking into account the rules that are in force, the speed limits, the current meteorological conditions, the traffic density, etc.

The verticality of the *Aiki* attitude is not an immobile verticality. We experience it by the very fact that we are alive and therefore in movement, like gyroscopes that constantly turn and that, through their movement, create their ability to remain on their axis.

Chapter 4

Taking Action

"So, now what do I do?"

Living in an aware state implies giving ourselves choices. Otherwise, we put ourselves in a reactive position and our only option is to endure what happens to us. We re-act by dipping into our reserve of programmed behaviors. This reserve has been created over the course of our lives. It is very often during our first experiences, when we are children, that behavioral patterns are established. In the face of an attack, or a refusal, a child gets angry. He attacks or curls up on himself and cries, hoping, with his cries, to attract the attention of his protecting parents. Over time, this reaction becomes more refined, but it will remain fundamentally similar to the first experience we had as a child. In attack situations—I mean situations that we experience as being attacks— we react by choosing one of the fundamental physiological responses that are common to any animal that feels threatened: attack, flight, or paralysis. These are the 3 Fs: Fight, Flight, or Freeze. Our human body has integrated these fundamental modes of action in response to any peril that could threaten our existence, our survival. As soon as a threat is perceived, our body switches to survival mode: respiration increases, hormones are secreted, blood flows toward our muscles.

We switch to reptilian mode[115]. It is useless in these moments to hope to modify our way of seeing things, of thinking, or of creating options for ourselves. Our neocortex is inhibited by the reptilian brain for obvious personal safety reasons: when the threat comes upon us, whether it is a car coming at full speed or a bear that comes out of its cave to attack us, it is too late to think. You must act. This survival process is very useful when we have to face an immediate physical danger, but it becomes a problem when we see the least conflict, or the least pressure, as an attack. Neurologically, we have not adapted to the numerous sources of psychological stress that we must face in our modern lives. Our neurological system reacts in the same way that it would if, while strolling through the woods, we came face-to-face with a threatening bear. Our body reacts according to a program that has been written into our biology. It is the result of tens of thousands of years of evolution. Although this way of reacting is useful to avoid a speeding car that is bearing down on us, it is less useful in a conflict with a colleague, our partner, or even a stranger who wants to take the last parking space from us in the supermarket parking lot.

The Geometry of Conflict

It is interesting to examine conflict from the point of view of geometry, or more precisely, mechanics. As autonomous beings we try to satisfy our needs or our desires and to do this we try to control our environment. At the same time, all the people around us do the same to satisfy their own needs and desires. We can represent these different intentions as forces that are encountering each other. By representing those forces by arrows, we can categorize the different geometrical shapes that can be taken by these encounters. These shapes are snapshots that illustrate the basic geometry of conflict. During the conflict. these shapes will evolve. Let's not forget that we are talking about human beings and not machines or passive objects. The mechanical metaphor that we are using here is, of course, simplistic, but it is not without interest.

---

[115] The term "reptilian" alludes to the model of the triune brain developed by Paul MacLean, mentioned above on page 115.

Non-meeting, Parallel Paths

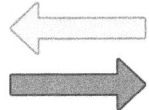

The two people are driven by opposing intents but are positioned at a distance. Their trajectories are parallel and therefore they never meet. There will therefore never be conflict. There are couples that have become masters at the art of creating parallel paths and could live their entire lives without ever arguing, but also without meeting each other.

> Joseph has been married to Juliette for over twenty years. Juliette is a nurse who works at night in a large regional hospital. Joseph is an executive in an international company located about fifty miles from home. He is a member of a band and plays with the group almost every weekend. Juliette is a volunteer in an aid organization that helps the needy and she devotes most of her time to it on weekends, when she is not working at the hospital. They have each found a balance that satisfies them, but if you add up the time that they spend together it barely adds up to more than a few hours a week. It is difficult to argue under these conditions.

Frontal Opposition

The two people are driven by opposite intents and they meet head-on. The end result is inevitable: it is the stronger who will win.

> "Anthony, give me that!" "No!" Marie will take by force the electronic game that her son Antoine has been playing with for more than an hour.
> "Mr. Ducart, I will have to take the day off next Monday." "Out of the question, Serge. I need you in the workshop." This refusal will bring Serge to plan an appointment with his doctor that will make him unavailable for work. Meanwhile, his boss will not hesitate to send someone to his home to verify that he is absent for a medical reason.

Scene in a parking lot: "Sir, I arrived at this space before you. I moved aside to allow that lady to leave her spot easily and you have taken the space from me even though you saw that I was already there!" "So what! I'm here and I'm staying here!"

These situations are obviously exaggerations, but they are nevertheless not rare. The force relationship is a dead end: either I win, leaving the other person frustrated and wanting revenge, or I lose and I will try to ease my frustration later by modifying the force relationship. I may even turn it on a third person who has nothing to do with the conflict. The energy of the conflict thus renews itself in future situations that feed the chain of negative behaviors, which has a strong chance of falling back on me later on. In one-time encounters, that is to say, unexpected encounters that are unlikely to recur, we can be tempted to win when we judge that the probability of revenge is low. On the other hand, in recurrent relationships, it is clear that we can expect a backlash at some point, which will certainly harm the atmosphere of the relationship.

The Standard Conflict

This shape is without a doubt the most common for an encounter. Within it, this encounter contains the ingredients of both the conflict's escalation and its resolution. If we break down the opposing energies, we can make out two dimensions: the frontal conflict and the possible resolution:

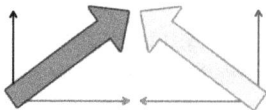

The vertical arrows show the dimension of the possible agreement while the horizontal arrows show the frontal opposition. The two arrows that show the opposing forces therefore contain both the possibility of head-on conflict and of possible agreement. This illustrates the choice that we are given in the vast majority of cases: to transform conflict or escalate it.

> *Nathalie wants to go out to take her mind off things. James is tired and he would prefer a quiet evening in front of the TV.*

The opposing forces could be represented as follows:

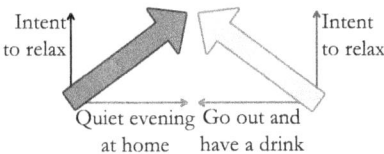

The outcome of the discussion will depend on James and Nathalie's choice to emphasize either the common intent to relax or the following opposition:

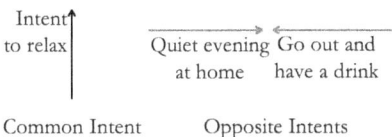

It bears repeating, these geometric shapes are simplified and reality is often far more complex. In most conflicts, however, we are faced with the two dimensions of both agreement relationships and force relationships. We thus have a choice once again and this makes us the one who *acts* rather than feeling like a victim of the other person's will, against which we must either struggle or give in.

Facts and Emotions

When we communicate with others, we transmit ideas through the words and phrases that we utter, but we also communicate on another level that we could call the emotional channel.

> Marie is 45 years old. She is the mother of two children, Michael and Sylvia, who are 13 and 15 years old, respectively. The scene takes place on a Saturday morning. Marie has already put a load in the dryer, which was running all night, and she has started another one. She is in the middle of putting yesterday evening's glasses in the dishwasher while thinking about the agenda for the day that awaits her. She would like to order curtains before driving her

daughter to a birthday party. Sylvia, who has been watching cartoons, begins to get hungry. She asks: "Mom, how about I go get some rolls?" Marie quickly adds things up. By the time Sylvia finishes her cartoon, chooses her clothes, gets dressed, and makes the round trip to the bakery, it will be almost 10 AM and she will not have enough time to do what she had planned with her morning. While she is finishing tidying up the kitchen, she feels exasperated by this prospect and answers in an irritated tone: "No, that won't work, there's bread in the house." Sylvia, who is very sensitive to the exasperation that showed in her mother's tone of voice, answers: "Oh, that's okay, that's okay, I was just asking to make you happy!"

If we look at the situation on the verbal level, we can understand Sylvia's offer to go get rolls, to which Marie responds with factual information: it isn't necessary: "We have what we need in the house." This is the dimension of words, the verbal dialogue. But the most important thing seems to happen on the emotional level, in nonverbal communication. Marie expresses her exasperation through this channel and that's what Sylvia responds to. Imperceptibly, the morning's tone has been set and Sylvia will accompany her mother on her shopping trip, sulking and waiting patiently for the moment when she can get back together with her friends at the birthday party.

The nonverbal channel is directly charged with emotions. Etymologically, the word "emotion" comes from the Old French word *esmovoir*, from the Latin word *movēre*, to move, to put in movement.[116]. Nonverbal communication is charged with energy, an energy that sets us in motion. The verbal channel is factual. It transmits concepts and words that must be interpreted in order to be metabolized into emotional energy. They could be compared with complex sugars and simple sugars in our diet. The latter are directly assimilated into the blood and this will make only one circuit of the body while the former will need to be broken down. *AikiCom* is interested in the energetic dimension (*ki*) of communication and as such leads us to be aware of this communication on two levels. In this dialogue, Marie and Sylvia seem to be exchanging information only on the verbal level

---

[116] *Webster's Eleventh Collegiate Dictionary*, page 408.

while the true communication is happening on the nonverbal level. While unaware of this—that is, while sticking to the exchange of words—they charge the climate of the relationship with an energy that might find a trigger to express itself later on. It will be set off by something totally innocuous, and lead to a dispute. Later on, each of them will wonder how things could have taken such a turn. It is also possible that the energy will dissipate simply by having breakfast in peace.

An alternative would be to become aware of the exchange on the nonverbal level. When Marie expresses her exasperation, it is not directed specifically at Sylvia. In fact, Marie would need more time in order to do everything that she wants to do. At the same time, she wants to please her daughter by driving her to the birthday party and already knows that the weekend will be too short. This is what is making her feel exasperated. As for Sylvia, she can feel that this exasperation is being aimed directly at her (after all, it is to her that Marie is speaking) and she can feel anger building up inside her when she gets such a negative response to her generous offer to go get some rolls.

To illustrate this scenario, let's imagine a person who is walking in the middle of the street. A car is heading toward him and has not yet seen him. The driver has no intention of injuring anyone, but if the person remains in the road, that is what will happen. Logically, all the pedestrian needs to do is to return to the sidewalk and thus find safety from the dangerous path of the vehicle. Otherwise, the pedestrian risks being injured by the driver who is simply driving his vehicle—which is in movement (motion, emotion)—and has no intention of injuring anyone at all.

If Sylvia becomes aware of the fact that the exasperation being expressed by her mother is not aimed directly at her, that her mother is like the driver of a vehicle, she can stand on the side of the road and let the vehicle (Marie's emotional energy) go by. By doing this, she gives her mother's emotion the space to be expressed and perhaps for the resolution that she needs. This is the power of communication when it is done correctly (in reciprocal empathy), which permits the other person to do a better job of clearing up the emotional feelings that weigh on him.

The act of withdrawing from the direction of the emotion is sometimes enough, but sometimes the failure to take into account what has been expressed on the nonverbal level produces anger or frustration because you do not feel like you have been understood. In this situation, there has been no demand, and we can completely understand that Sylvia has decided to ignore the nonverbal message which, after all, was not directed at her.

> Manu is preparing coffee with a new electric coffee maker. Knowing that Sabine has already used it, he asks her how many teaspoons of coffee she uses. Sabine answers in an irritated tone of voice: "It's like we did with the other coffee maker. I don't see why you're asking this question!" Manu is faced with a choice: either he ignores the tone with which Sabine has answered him or he reacts to it, dropping the initial discussion concerning the coffee measurement to tackle a subject that is more important for him: the harmony between the two of them. By choosing to react to the nonverbal level of Sabine's response, he is once again faced with a choice: either he stays on the path of the emotional energy that Sabine has expressed and takes it head-on, which will not fail to make her angry and incite her to respond aggressively, or he moves away from the emotional trajectory and connects to Sabine in order to reposition the discussion in a new direction: "My dear, I was asking you the question because I wanted to make some good coffee so we could have a nice breakfast together. When I saw you putting the cups away irritably, it seemed to me that you were annoyed. If you want, we can talk about what is aggravating you and obviously has nothing to do with the measurement of the coffee. I would like more than anything for us to spend a good weekend together. So, if you agree, we can separate the question of the coffee from everything else. Tell me how many spoonfuls you put in yesterday because it seemed so good. Then we can take the time to talk at the table. Is that okay with you?"

We Are More Sensitive to Differences than to Similarities

A well-known scientific experiment shows that we are more sensitive to differences than to similarities, which are synonymous with the *status quo*. When things are the same, we have a tendency to notice them less. The famous anthropologist Gregory Bateson defined information as being the difference that makes the difference[117]. If I write the word "happiness" with chalk on a blackboard, I create information through the contrast between the white chalk and the black board. If I erase the word on the blackboard, where did the information go? Is it hidden in the eraser? The information has disappeared through the act of erasing this difference between the black and white of the board and the chalk.

Let's return to the experiment itself. If we toss a frog in a saucepan containing very hot water, the frog immediately leaps out because of the heat. If we take this same frog and put it in a saucepan of cold water, it will accept staying there. If we heat the water in the saucepan very slowly, degree by degree, the frog will not move, gradually getting used to the temperature of the water. It will end up being scalded to death when the water becomes too hot, without even trying to escape.

When we are living on automatic pilot, we can be surprised by the healthy expression of someone else's will. As living beings, we are more sensitive to differences than to similarities, which very often leads us to perceive the seed of what could grow into a conflict by first detecting the conflictual dimension against which we can be tempted to react in a quasi-automatic way through confrontation. The *Aiki* attitude leads us to use the trigger of a difference to center ourselves and not fall into the trap of confrontation, which leads to a tug-of-war. The important thing is to not stay in a position where we feel attacked because we will then justify eventually launching a counterattack. This is the *raison d'être* of the first movement that *AikiCom* tells us to make when we return to ourselves through centering: get off the line of danger.

Perceiving

Life would be exhausting if we had to be attentive to everything that went on around us, always and all the time. Our brain consumes a great deal of energy and constantly tries to automatize our actions so

---

[117] Gregory Bateson, *Steps to an Ecology of Mind* (1972), Chapter "Form, Substance and Difference" (p. 459).

that we do not exhaust our energy reserves. In this way we often live with our automatic pilot switched on. This leaves room for our mind to wander.

Perceiving a change, a movement, a sound, or a vibration will bring us out of our automatic mode. Our attention is drawn by something. Does this disruption demand a reaction? If yes, what reaction? And when?

When Should We React?

We are flooded with information and with auditory, visual, or kinesthetic perceptions. Some will attract our attention more than others[118].

Very often, we notice them, but we do not take them into account for a variety of reasons.

Robert returns home after a long day. His mind is still burdened by all kinds of red tape at work. He notices the distant kiss his wife gives him, but doesn't think twice about it. No doubt that is his interpretation. Over the course of the evening he notices that Marie's responses are brief and a bit abrupt, but he decides to ignore them, not wanting to start a discussion that would quickly turn to their relationship, their life, and in short, to the sort of endless discussion that Marie loves. Later in the evening, all it takes is a trivial question about their plans for the next day for Marie to burst into sobs, expressing her feeling that she doesn't count for anything and that he doesn't notice her. By choosing to avoid asking Marie how she was doing, Robert let the dissatisfaction build until he had a real crisis that was as inescapable as it was difficult to resolve.

We often do not react to unpleasant behavior because it is not unpleasant enough to disturb the good atmosphere of our relationship or for fear that our reaction will set off an argument.

> Jean-Pierre is divorced. He only sees his children every other
> weekend. His son Quentin loves video games and spends most of
> his free time playing them. On Saturdays, Jean-Pierre is too happy

---

[118] In my book *Au-delà de la magie*, I spend more time looking at the neurological mechanisms that make certain stimuli cause a change in attention.

to see him again and doesn't dare mention it. He wants Quentin to feel good with him and he wants the transition to go easily. He chomps at the bit each time he goes through the living room and sees his son absorbed with his face in the screen. Jean-Pierre goes along with him and uses humor, tossing out a joke or two to make Quentin understand that he ought to stop, but his son continues to hang onto his joystick. At the end of the day Jean-Pierre can't hold himself back and blows up. Quentin looks at him, taken aback, and responds to his father with a "but why didn't you say anything to me?" that ends up knocking him out.

In Jean-Pierre's case, seeing his son waste his time playing video games goes against his own educational and cultural values. He is sorry that his son does not read more, that he does not go out to play with the neighbors' children, and that he does not have fun the way he himself did at the same age, before video games took over. But he will put off his reaction out of fear of spoiling the rare moments that he spends with him. However, by reacting earlier, he could have clarified things without everything becoming so dramatic. This is what Quentin's reaction seems to confirm.

Another reason to not react resides in the fact that we doubt our ability to say things without resorting to anger or extremes. We all too often choose to launch a volley of criticism instead of starting with ourselves, with our feelings and needs as, for example, non-violent communication[119] recommends.

It is still important to say a word about crises. Crises are paroxysms, that is, moments when emotions are intensified and powerful. They require a great deal of expertise to avoid escalating violence and reacting excessively. The crisis very often arises when we have not taken into account the warning signs for what was going to happen. Because of a lack of time, out of fear of acting, because of laziness, or from lack of concern, we believe that time will take care of reestablishing the normal course of things. When we notice that this is not the case and that, on the contrary, the situation has gotten worse, there is a crisis. It puts us on the ropes and leads us to say or do things

---

[119] See the four components of NVC: the observation, the feeling, the need that is either satisfied or not, and the request.

that we would not have said or done at another time. It often leaves behind it a bitter taste in our mouths. During these moments, it is necessary more than ever to recenter ourselves and think about strategies we can apply in order to return to a condition where dialogue can be restored. Crises are difficult and intense moments, but they are also opportunities for those who don't have the possibility of living in the moment and being connected to what is going on around them. We only have to act before things take a turn that forces us to make radical changes instead of making continuous improvement, as is recommended in *kaizen*, a management approach known as the "little steps" method.

How Should We React?

Events that some would consider to be trivial make us react disproportionately when they remind us of past experiences that went badly for us.

> Steven is pacing up and down outside the meeting room where he has to present the project that he has been working on for several weeks to the board of directors. He has been preparing for this meeting for three days, but several minutes before the presentation he is feeling worse and worse. While entering the room and seeing the participants taking their places, he pretends to have an emergency and hands the presentation off to his colleague. This presentation reminds him too much of the speech that he had to give in his first year of high school, where he had been the laughingstock of his class.

In a transactional analysis, an emotion that awakens an analogous situation from our past is called a "rubber band emotion." In these situations we very often react in a way that is inappropriate and certainly excessive. *AikiCom* work focuses on acting in the present moment. Reminiscences about the past limit our freedom. In *randori*, which simulates a real combat situation, I try to be entirely available to respond to the closest attacker to me. If I think of the one who will come after him or if I recall a past battle, or if the attacker reminds me of someone else because of his physical appearance, I risk jumping into a fight against a phantom. My emotional state and my thoughts tie me to the past and make me lose my availability and my leeway to manage the current situation. There is a clear difference between being possessed by the events of my past and acting in the present by drawing from experience that I have gained during these very same events. In the first case, I relive the event. It seizes me and deforms my present reality. It deprives me of a part of the freedom that is necessary in order for me to orient my action. In the second case, I have turned the event into an experience. This "digestion" of what I have experienced enriches my background and my knowledge. The action has become flesh and blood, it has become a part of me. From now on, I will never be what I was before. Experience is the breeding ground in which action develops.

However, it remains clear that life does not spare us from misfortunes. Nobody is sheltered from the bad experiences that remain in our stomach and are not "digested."

Sometimes the event is significant enough for us to be aware of it. Disappointment, sadness, and fear, or any other emotion that it causes, will be so difficult or painful that we will not try to put it aside, forget it, or immerse it in the reservoir of past experiences. Unfortunately, there is a great risk of seeing it resurface at an inappropriate moment.

Sometimes the event is harmless, almost imperceptible, like a bite of food that is swallowed without taking the time to taste it. This bite is not a problem in itself. It only becomes one when it is followed by another, then another, then another.

We have all experienced going through a series of small incidents that are unimportant when they are seen as isolated events but which, when they are seen lined up end-to-end, bring about reactions that very often stun the people around us.

> The first time, I did not react, it wasn't worth the trouble. The second time I raised an eyebrow, but I acted like it was nothing. The third time, I felt annoyed, but I took it upon myself to say nothing. The fourth time, she couldn't finish what she was saying and I lashed out. She fell silent and, completely stupefied, asked me: "What's come over you?"

At a certain point, an incident as trivial as the ones we've just talked about can be the "last straw." The reaction will be a response to the overall buildup, not to the final incident.

AikiCom is a physical practice that connects us to the energetic dimension of our being. The *ki* of *AikiCom* reminds us of this. Through our attitudes, our movements, and our tensions, it is our *ki*, our life energy, that expresses itself. The physical exercises of *AikiCom* are not just a metaphor or a set of bodily movements. They aim at creating conditions where our energy will be able to find the material it needs to express itself, just as it does in each moment of our life. While redirecting our attention, we can truly enter into communication with ourselves. *Ki* expresses the least conditioned part of us. In situations where we react disproportionately, we witness the expression of our vital energy. It is no longer about a given situation or a particular context. We live through the expression of our being, which is created over the course of our experiences and opens the door to what will emerge. The physical dimension of *AikiCom* brings us back to what we are feeling in the moment, how we get ready to react if we give free rein to the repetition of past patterns. The exploration of our physical feelings recenters us in the present in the dimension of our vertical axis. Memories of the past then emerge, which give meaning to what we are experiencing. This is the case in situations where we react disproportionately. This is not about letting yourself be distracted from the present by these memories, but instead to integrate the past that we have created so that the right action will emerge in the present. The action comes from ourselves, from our somatic center, which only exists in the present. We then become part of the flow of life that circulates in us and our action is only our personal contribution to what emerges. We are then aligned in our *Aikisphere* toward the right action, whatever it may be.

Aiki-coaching is nothing more than a form of support in this personal development process that reconnects us through our body to the energetic dimension of our being, and from there it orients us toward action.

> Phillip is going to go in for the final interview that will possibly open the door for him to the job that he has coveted for so long. He stands upright, in his verticality, and welcomes his thoughts and

emotions with calm. His hands are clammy, his legs feel ready to give out, and he is afraid of not passing this final test. This fear is reasonable given the stakes of this interview. He experiences it and welcomes it as the healthy expression of what he is going through. Memories of similar interviews that did not turn out as he had hoped also come up in his mind. Becoming aware of these thoughts brings him back to his centering. He deliberately leaves these memories behind him. They do not belong with what he is experiencing here and now. Phillip turns his attention to his breathing and keeps the orientation of his Aikisphere turned toward the office where he will enter. Before, the mere recollection of past interviews would have been enough to turn his attention away and waste his energy. The Aikisphere reorients him in the direction that counts there, at that moment.

To Whom Do We React? The Enemy Within

We saw above[120] that we are essentially made up of many parts. Among these numerous parts of ourselves, there are some that we hold back.

Edward is a very active man. In his professional life, as in his private life, he never stops working. It is only in the evening that he collapses on his sofa, completely exhausted, and falls asleep, unable to keep his eyes open. His son Antoine is fifteen years old and seems to take pleasure in an idleness that is equaled only by his father's frantic activity. When Edward returns home and sees his son like this, he is overwhelmed by an anger that is difficult to contain and that often ends with an outburst, followed by sending Antoine to his room for the rest of the evening. Edward has never let himself take time for himself and the sight of his son not doing anything (at least that is how Edward judges what his son is doing) awakens the part of him that dreams of doing the same thing.

Certain behaviors annoy us more than anything. They have an ability to awaken in us those parts of ourselves that we have buried or those attitudes that we have not allowed ourselves to experience. When

---

[120] See the "I Am Multifaceted" chapter, page 126.

they emerge, we feel angry or sad or sometimes even ashamed without really knowing why. The classic reflex in these situations is to look for an enemy to fight outside ourselves. Edward sees, in his son, a child who allows himself what Edward himself has never been able to. He is angry with himself, but projects this bitterness on Antoine.

> Roger is an artist. He lives alone and he is convinced that his messiness is an essential condition of his creativity. The day when he met Sophie, who is also an artist, it was love at first sight. They agree about everything. They decide very quickly to live together. But very soon Sophie's messiness irritates him. He can no longer find his things in this new kind of messiness, which leads to frequent arguments. While talking with her after a particularly intense argument, Roger realizes, through Sophie's sloppiness, that it is his own messiness that irritates him. He sees how unpleasant what he called "his creative side" could be. Gaining this awareness gave him the energy to change his behavior and his habits.

The presence of the *other* brings about the emergence of these awakened parts, which results in the externalization of an inner battle. We open up a new front. The battle is lost before it begins because we are mistaken about our adversary. This sort of misunderstanding happens frequently to a couple in a close relationship. Certain couples remind us of battlefields more than fields of love and tenderness Living together, the day to day and the intimate moments increases the opportunities to awaken these parts of ourselves that we have left to lie fallow. When this happens, very intense emotions of fear, passion, and anger sometimes reveal themselves. We feel surprised at how vulnerable we are to the person who is closest to us, which brings out aspects of ourselves that we wanted to hide. We have the sensation that something is not right within us. This sensation is intensified by the voice of our inner critic, who reinforces a feeling of worthlessness. We then switch to a defensive mode and try to neutralize the source of the threat by displacing it onto our partner. We externalize the inner battle.

We want the other person to see our true nature, our intrinsic beauty, but the problem is that it is sometimes difficult for us to appreciate the innate beauty that is inside us. The image that we have of ourselves is a false identity, a facade that we would like everyone to admire. Even if that happens, it does not satisfy us. We want our partner to see this intrinsic beauty within us, which goes beyond any concept of good or bad. As long as our partner sees our beautiful facade, everything seems to go well. But as our intimacy deepens, we begin to notice cracks in the facade. What we wanted to keep secret reveals itself in broad daylight, thus creating a trail of unpleasant emotions. And our defensive reactions have a paradoxical tendency to accentuate the negative aspects that we want to cover up. A person who is afraid of being abandoned will thus become aggressive and bring about the abandonment that he fears. A person who believes that his needs will never be met conceals them, thus assuring that they will never be filled and he will criticize his partner for this. We thus create our own hardship, but we attribute it to the other person. As long as this process repeats itself, we cannot make progress.

> James wants to control everything. When he was a child, his parents were overprotective and he developed a real aversion to feeling powerless when facing a difficult situation. To avoid this feeling of powerlessness, he pretended to be someone who has control over everything.
> However, life gives us numerous occasions to feel powerless, to not control a situation, and a couple is a beautiful example of this. Maintaining this image of control gets pretty tiring. When James finds himself lacking control, he goes into rages that frighten even him.

The solution to avoid setting off on a crusade outside of ourselves and making our partner the source of the threat is to invert the self-rejection process. By rejecting a negative emotion that emerges from deep inside of us, we transform it into an alien, a stranger. We give it its own strength, a status as an enemy. Never having learned to welcome these negative feelings with self-empathy, we sound the alert, sharpen our weapons and above all, we lead the combat outside of ourselves, that is, with our partner.

A solution to get us out of this infernal and exhausting loop is to take responsibility for our experience.

Rather than accusing the other person of being responsible for my emotion ("Why do you make me feel so bad?") and trying to change him, we transform our view of our experience by taking responsibility for it, that is, by owning up to the response that we give him.

The encounter with the *other* thus becomes an opportunity for growth[121], to work on what Jung called "our shadow."

Exercise: Taking Responsibility for Your Experience

Taking responsibility happens in several steps.
Turning our attention to what we are experiencing and questioning ourselves rather than judging ourselves or believing that we have already understood everything.
Accepting, that is to say, recognizing and identifying: "Yes, what I am going through now, that's it! I feel like I'm on the defensive, wounded, angry,..." We generally prefer to react even before we have accepted what we are going through.
Allowing the experience that we are going through to happen without sinking into it and without taking action. This is about creating a space so that we may be able to experience what we have to experience, keeping these emotions in a space that is aware, soft, and tender, not strained, not tense, and without judgment.
Opening ourselves up to what we are experiencing and maintaining an open presence that gives us more room and gives us access to our resources, the ones that will allow us to transform the situation. This opening allows us to get away from oppositional thinking: good side / bad side, good / bad, me / the other person. It's surprising to see how, in this state of openness, simple solutions can emerge in this state of openness.

Remark:

We often tend to identify ourselves with our emotions. These emotional states are frequently accompanied by stories that we tell ourselves about the emotion. The model of the three centers is particularly useful in order to avoid identifying ourselves with our

---

[121] This unique opportunity cannot take place except under certain conditions that we will discuss later.

emotion (to avoid falling into it) and to recognize the stories that we tell ourselves.

Awareness of our emotional center helps us distinguish who we are (somatic center) from the emotion that we are feeling. We can then create the space that the emotion needs in order for it to be experienced without letting ourselves be absorbed by it.

Rationalizations are produced in our cognitive center to give meaning and to justify what we are experiencing.

Awareness of our somatic center creates space. The role of breathing is crucial here to create the necessary space and to reduce pressure by favoring the circulation of our vital energy. Most of the time, our emotions subside when we give them a space where their energy can be expressed and they can reconnect themselves with our *ki*. Conversely, confining them to an enclosed and rigid space tends to increase their intensity.

This space of solutions is the *Aikisphere*, which encompasses all the dimensions of my being (vertical axis), the temporal dimension (sagittal or front-rear axis), and my personal dimensions (transverse axis).

In aikido practice, we discover how we reinforce our opponent's strength when we oppose it. *Aiki* techniques put us in a state in which we can act in a different way and we can center and orient ourselves toward the *other* in order to welcome the energy of the attack. My opponent then becomes a partner—a partner in my personal development. The attack provides the energy that makes this transformation possible. Without it, nothing happens. With it, everything can happen. If I am not ready, not present, and not centered, the attack can injure me. If I have an *Aiki* attitude, it becomes an opportunity, a gift given to us by life. I am talking about the attack in the context of aikido practice. Of course, it is clearly more difficult to see an attack as a gift during a mugging! The priority is to first get out of the bad situation and disarm the aggression of the attacker. Regular aikido practice helps us to increase our self-confidence and not let ourselves be overcome by the threat or the danger. Aside from blatant acts of aggression, which are fortunately rare, we end up far more frequently seeing our conflicts with our relatives, colleagues, and friends as attacks of this kind. We then resort to survival reflexes, such as attacking, rather than seeing, within the conflict, the magnificent opportunity for growth.

React to What?

> Marianne is exasperated. She sees the condition in which her son Julian has left the living room after his "TV time" evening the previous night: shoes, blanket, dirty dish, half-empty glasses, table out of place, crumbs from chips and peanuts on the carpet, missing remote controls. It's too much. Julian defends himself weakly, arguing that she is exaggerating, that it will take him five minutes to clean up and that there is no reason to make a big deal out of it, which ends up increasing his mother's irritation. He moves from words to action and begins to clean up the mess, but Marianne still has a feeling of dissatisfaction that she does not understand. After all, she could be delighted that her son has reacted by cleaning up the living room. Marianne does not realize that what is irritating her is not so much the fact that the living room has been messy, but the fact that the situation has been repeated regularly for several weeks. What she has had a hard time accepting is the repetition, the behavioral pattern taken by her son, which amounts to leaving the living room in a mess and then cleaning it up when his mother comments on it.

When we fall into this sort of emotion it is important to distinguish three levels of cause: a single event, a repeated pattern of events, and the relationship itself.

If it is a single event, very often the act of taking corrective measures can be enough to ease the situation. If the events are part of a repeated pattern of behavior, the mere act of correcting the situation will usually not be enough. It will be necessary to take the pattern into account and begin a dialogue to put an end to it. In Marianne's example, it may be necessary to talk about the fact that Julian systematically doesn't bother to clean up the living room after his TV time and his mother must express her dissatisfaction in order for him to react. The specific event is, by itself, harmless; what is irritating is the repetition. Finally, if the pattern continues, we move to a higher level: the relationship. While Julian is perfectly aware that his mother is irritated because he leaves the living room in a mess each time that he watches TV until late in the evening—and that he continues repeating this scenario—it is at the relationship level that the dispute arises: What is the relationship at work, are the roles recognized by each of them, and is there respect for all the parties involved? In the current example, does Julian care about what his mother is asking him to do? Perhaps it will be necessary for his father to convey the message; perhaps he is systematically rejecting any form of authority from his mother or pretending to ignore her moods under the pretext that from his adolescent point of view these are simply exaggerations. In this case, as we see, we are far from being concerned with some occasional messiness; Marianne and Julian will have to approach the subject differently and the discussion may have to take place in the presence of Daniel, Julian's father.

As we can see, when we go from a state that could be considered neutral to a state that requires an action or initiative, in addition to the act of recentering ourselves, it is essential for us to orient ourselves in the direction of the potential action, that is, to turn ourselves toward the center of the problem, of what is bothering us or threatening us. In interpersonal communication, we turn ourselves toward the other person and connect ourselves with his center[122]; we enter into true communication with the person who is in front of us. It is the same when we are debating a question or a problem. It is useless to talk about something other than the problem or to beat around the bush. The right action will be the one that goes to the heart of the problem. This requires first identifying the center of the question so that our actions can go in the right direction and our energy will not be squandered through disorganized movements. We identify the object of the dispute and we turn our center in that direction, which allows us to avoid exhausting ourselves. We will then act with the right intensity, which very often will soften the conflictual atmosphere.

> Nathalie is irritated. After a particularly exhausting day of work, she has used what little energy she has left tidying up the house and starting off the weekend on the right foot. When Nathan returns from school with his muddy shoes and tosses his schoolbag right in

---

[122] See "Connecting Yourself, Linking Yourself" on page 179.

the middle of the hall, it's too much. Nathalie explodes. And it is definitely an explosion because it goes in all directions. Nathalie criticizes not only the mud stains on the floor and the neglected schoolbag, but she opens Pandora's box and lets loose everything that she has in her heart and that has piled up during the week: the bad report card, the repeated lateness, the morning oversights that made her late several times this week, etc. Nathan does not understand this flood of yelling and blame. Although he is able to understand the fact that he had gotten the house dirty with his shoes and that his schoolbag could have been put directly in his room, he finds it totally unjustified that it could set off a crisis that is so out of proportion. He runs off and closes himself up in his room, leaving his mother worn out, exhausted, and frustrated at not having been understood.

Nathalie's "enough is enough" reaction is completely understandable, but it does not let her get the result that she had hoped for. She finds herself in a combat situation facing multiple opponents: her negligent son who comes home, messes up the hall, and dumps his schoolbag; her fatigue from the week; the morning lateness; her son's bad grades; etc. Anger has put her outside of herself, out of her center, and has not let her turn her action toward her son and his sloppiness. Left alone, she will take the time to welcome her anger, her sadness, and her fatigue while getting back in touch with her verticality and her center. Later, she will be able to go find her son in his room and start a calmer discussion about what has happened and about the need to reexamine some things that have gone badly during the week.

Getting off the Line of Danger

> *"Don't simply look at the opponent's eyes, because they will absorb your mind. Don't just look at the opponent's sword, because it will take away your ki. Don't just look at your opponent, because his ki will control you. Martial arts training is the training of the magnetic power in yourself to absorb the other as he is."*[123]

---

[123] Kisshōmaru Ueshiba quoting Morihei Ueshiba in *The Spirit of Aikido*, page 77.

Morihei Ueshiba

Nowadays, there are numerous approaches that lead us to empathy, comprehension, and active listening. This is surely the manifestation of a growing need for better communication between people. But there is an essential point that we must not forget: when I feel threatened, I cannot show empathy for him. I cannot show empathy or listen to the other person and I try above all to save myself.

When we feel threatened, our survival reflexes—what I call our reptilian reflexes—are activated and momentarily "unplug" our neocortex, that is, our ability to think, to reason. We should note that all it takes is to feel attacked for us to switch to this state. It is the interpretation that I give to an action, a word, or an event that counts, not the action, word, or event itself. In the context of a physical attack, a person commits an act with the intention of wounding or even killing. When we perceive the blow and it is clear that it will hit us, we switch to our survival reflexes: protection, counterattack, or paralyzing fear. At this moment, there is no space to begin any sort of dialogue with the other person. He is no longer there. All that exists is the blow, the striking hand, the stick, or the knife that is heading toward me. In less extreme situations, for example in conflicts that lead to verbal violence, hurtful words, murderous words, and insults that hit us with a "knockout blow," all have the same effect. As I have already said, the action, the word, and the event themselves do not matter; what matters is the interpretation that I give them.

The same words will be seen by some as harmless while others will see them as an attack. The context and our personal history play a great role in this. So, there are harmless words that can open old wounds, unbeknownst to the person who spoke them. If we cannot ignore the responsibility of the person who is speaking to us, we should take the responsibility for our own interpretation of what was expressed. The immediate positive effect of this is that we go from being a victim to being an active participant.

Practicing *AikiCom* exercises teaches us to notice with more subtlety, and more quickly, the moments when we switch to our reptilian survival behaviors. The sooner we notice when a word, an action, or an event activates our reptilian brain (which inhibits our ability to reason), the sooner we have a chance to be able to adapt our behaviors and keep our freedom of choice. Otherwise, our body initiates hormonal mechanisms that will make us switch to physiological states that help us to either defend ourselves or attack. The **event → interpretation of the event → activation of reptilian reflexes** sequence happens very quickly. *AikiCom* practice allows us to intervene at the moment when this third step is activated by identifying the physical tension that accompanies it. This tension alerts us, so that we can make an essential *AikiCom* movement: getting off the line of danger.

The aikidoka who sees a hand coming to strike him does not remain in place, nor does he try to block it; he makes a slight movement to get off the line of danger[124]. In all situations where we perceive a threat, we can do the same. Of course, this movement can be metaphorical and not just physical. We move internally, from the center, and we can feel the energy of the attack whistle past us toward the mental space where we were and then disappear behind us. In *AikiCom* training sessions, the participants are asked to practice an exercise that begins with physical[125] attacks. Then they carry out the same exercise with words. In this way, the act of getting off the line of danger progressively becomes imprinted in the body, allowing us to choose how to act rather than reacting through self-defense reflexes. What is pernicious in our first "instinctive" reaction to the attack is that it brings us a justification for carrying out a violent action, whether in word or deed. After all, he's the one who started it and "I" have every right to counterattack. How many conflicts and attacks start out with this feeling of a "legitimate" reaction, of "legitimate" revenge? Mechanistic reasoning builds on the logic of linear causality: I do this to you because you did that to me and you did that to me because you are blaming me for some other past actions. This chain of actions that are tied together in a causal way takes away our free will and our responsibility through the meaning that we give to our experience. The *Aiki* attitude brings us back to ourselves in our choice and our

---

[124] Aikidoka refer to this as the "line of attack."
[125] The attack consists of a hand strike that aims at hitting the head. This attack is made at a speed that is adapted in order to create a sensation of energy coming toward you, not to learn how to defend yourself.

responsibility. I act from myself. The action starts in my center instead of in the other person's action.

By getting off the line of danger, I move away from linear causality and I return to myself. The other person's action does not guide my choices and, moreover, my movement allows me to reconnect myself with the other person. I am not hypnotized by the attack that I avoided; I see him (or her)—the person who initiated it—and I orient myself to connect my center to his center. I can then see his true nature. He is no longer just an attacker. This person again becomes an individual with his own personal history, needs, and values. I can then try to reestablish dialogue with him. The question that then comes to my mind is: "How can a person of sound mind like him be led to act in this way?"

Getting Out of Trench Warfare

Getting off the line of danger is a way to regain our ability to move and prevents me from ending up in trench warfare, where the two opposing parties become deadlocked. Once the positions freeze, each one reinforces his defenses and tries to take the next blow stoically before responding in kind. There is a certain pride in taking a good punch, in showing that you are resisting. Plus, this strengthens us in our feeling of being in the right. In a war of position, the smallest withdrawal is seen as a defeat. The participants are closed up in a zero sum game: if you win, I lose, or vice versa. Through my movement, I transform the situation and I avoid being trapped in trench warfare.

Rendering the Attack Useless

Because of my movement, the attack is not successful. The attacker strikes where I no longer am. The attack doesn't reach its target. This is the very principle pursued in *Aiki* practice. Once the attack has been defused, we can take the path of transformation. By using the energy of the attack, I initiate a movement that contributes to giving new meaning to the action, an indispensable step in satisfying what I call the *need for impact*.

The Need for Impact

The attacker who strikes has an intention: to hit us. If we move, his strike ends up in emptiness. If I do not manage this critical moment, the person who has tried to hit me will become frustrated. This is the need for impact.

We have all been in a situation where we express something very important to someone, then we notice that the person is listening with only one ear, doesn't react, or talks about something entirely different. This situation produces a feeling of intense frustration, of not being heard, and of not having an impact on the other person[126].

Not Withdrawing, Going Toward the Attacker

A frequent reaction when facing an attack is to back up. If I merely want to avoid the blow by backing up or, more generally, by gaining some distance, I very often only postpone the problem because I give the attacker the opportunity to attack again. If it is not certain that my opponent will attack again, it is still probable that my backing up will be seen by him as an opportunity to win. Backing up creates an opportunity for the other person to advance and repeat the scene until I have my back against the wall with no other possibility to get some distance, thus leading me to switch to my reptilian survival mechanisms, with no solution but to attack.

Starting the Wheel of Transformation

Getting off the line of danger is far more than a sidestep that aims to avoid being struck by the attack. It is the movement that initiates the transformation process.

Let's take another look at the course of events. First of all, the aikidoka is the target of the attack. The energy of the strike is headed for him. This energy is powerful and will result in an injury, even death, if he stays there. By getting off the line of danger, the aikidoka redirects the energy of the attack, changing it from radial (directed to

---

[126] I recommend reading *Stop! You're Driving Me Crazy* by Dr. Georges R. Bach and Ronald Deutsch, Putnam, 1979.

his center, like the spoke of a wheel) into tangential, which will give the wheel a circular motion.

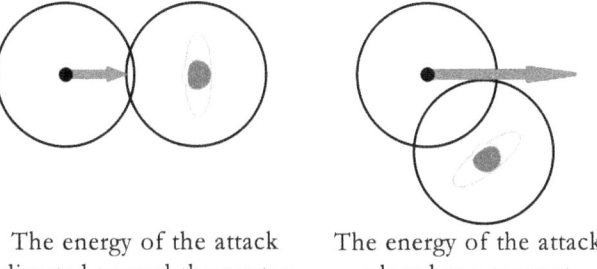

The energy of the attack directed toward the center

The energy of the attack placed at a tangent

Figure 9 : Moving the Energy to the Tangent

The aikidoka has put himself at the center of movement. The center of a wheel is the only point that is immobile, and the energy of the attack is placed on the tangent that is created by rotation around the center.

Summary

When I am attacked, I do not stay in the same place; I move so that I will not be hit. I do not back up because that would give the attacker the opportunity to attack again. Instead, I turn my *Aikisphere* in his direction and I establish contact with him. In this way, I avoid driving him to the frustration that can result from not reaching me. Out of danger, centered, aligned toward the other person's center, I create a totally new situation. I am no longer exposed to the attack. I have put myself in a place where I have choices and feel present. In this approach, my attacker has become my partner.

Connecting Yourself, Linking Yourself

Establishing Contact

Once I have avoided the blow by moving in a way that gets me closer to my partner, I will establish a connection with him. Centered, in my verticality, I turn my *Aikisphere* toward the other person's center and I remain open and relaxed, that is, *not tense*. The other person's action does not make me rigid; it opens me up to the encounter. In *Aiki* practice, getting off the line of danger gives me the opportunity to connect and communicate with the other person rather than to resort to combat.

The Link Maintains Security

When I avoid the attack, I also try to establish a connection with my partner. This connection will be indispensable for the rest of my action, but right now it permits me to create a space where there is mutual security.

The act of being connected to another person creates a sort of mutual assurance. As long as we are in contact, we feel safer. Otherwise, if one of the two breaks contact, he puts the other in an unsafe position. He does not realize that once the satisfaction of making the first move has passed, he will find himself in the same unsafe position. In the end, the two of them will find themselves in a situation of great uncertainty, continuously waiting for a new action on the part of the other person or thinking about the next action that he himself could initiate. In situations of intense conflict, when the communication becomes bitter and the only goal of the people in conflict is to win, when one dialogue turns into two monologues, they both become fed up. The partners have such a strong feeling of not being heard, the other person's words seem so absurd, and our own are so obvious that it appears totally useless and pointless to continue to talk to each other. In fact, they had not been talking to each other for a long time already.

> James and Francine come for my advice. They are about to get a divorce. They both agree on one point: it is impossible for them to communicate. For James, the image that characterizes their mode of communication is two people in two different hallways of a building. Each one tries to say something to the other, but they do not hear each other and have the very unpleasant impression that they are talking to a wall. For Francine, their way of talking to each other is a bit like two people who are each speaking a language that the other does not understand. No matter how much they articulate and slow down their speech, the words do not get through to the other and they end up abandoning their attempts to talk. James and

Francine both speak English, but it is as if the words meant something else. It's a dead end.

Connection Before Action

Connection is the precondition for action when your goal is restoring harmony. Before, I was alone. Now, we are two. We make up a system and this system needs a certain form of cohesion in order to survive. The connection opens up a channel of communication between the two partners who make up the system. In aikido practice, this connection is physical, but in our daily interactions it takes on multiple forms. Sometimes it will be visual and sometimes it will be verbal or physical. Connection exists as soon as the two partners are each aware of the presence of the other. At a meeting, I am connected to the other participants by my gaze and by my words. The presence of a table, the placement of people around the table, and the projection of transparencies on a screen will all influence the connection. In a meeting, people can be physically present, but absent from the system: sending texts, reading documents, or simply thinking about other things. If I am leading the meeting, I will try to keep all the participants in the necessary state of presence to reach the goal we have set. The meeting agenda is a powerful link that brings their minds together by imposing the sequence of topics that are to be covered. In the private sphere, with children and particularly with teenagers, it can be difficult to establish and maintain a connection. It is a question of rhythm, biorhythm, and language, but above all of taking into account the other person's reality. The proliferation of means of electronic communication brings up the crucial question of our connection with other people, but especially the quality of our connection. Social networks increase the number of connections, but they are unavoidably more superficial, disjointed, and impersonal. Just look at the birthday wishes that are exchanged on networks like Facebook. This is the app that reminds us of a date that we very often do not know because we have never asked our friend to give it to us. On their wall we add a "Happy Birthday" that is as dispassionate as those added by everyone else. In most cases, for the person in question, what really counts is the number of messages received rather than the individual messages. This somewhat satirized view highlights how watered down the notion of connection can be. True connections, those in which we are truly there and present for the other person are drowning in quantity, in a rhythm of life that favors "interpersonal channel surfing." It is difficult under these conditions to truly be oneself in connection with someone else. We need only observe the manner by which people exchange morning greetings at work, but worse yet at home with those who share our daily life. However, all it takes is a bit of awareness, a few seconds of centering and attention to the other person, to create or recreate the interpersonal quality that is more and more often lacking and makes us feel alone even when we're with others. Effective leaders have this sort of natural disposition that allows them to have these strong connections, even if they do not last long. This quality of connection can be seen in someone's gaze, it is felt in a handshake, it is felt in the warmth of his tone of voice, and in the way they ask, "How's it going?" that gives the feeling that the other person is truly interested in us, at least for a moment.

The quality of the connection will be determined largely by the initial conditions of the encounter, that is, by the state of mind in which I approach the other person. A true connection develops without any presuppositions. It happens in the moment, open to all possibilities.

The Right Tension, the Right Perception

Working with a partner is not simply blind action. We both make up a system that interacts closely. The slightest variation can require adapting or even changing the action.

Exercise: How Many Grabs?

A grabs *B*'s wrist and *B* concentrates his attention on the sensations that he feels from this grab of his wrist. *A* varies his grab by trying a series of different intentions: fixed grab; grab aimed at making *B*'s arm move up; arm grab to pull *B* towards him, to push him away, and to make him back up; grab to make his wrist turn, etc.

Each of these intentions will change the reaction that *B* must make to respond to the grab. As we can see, a simple wrist grab can in fact reveal different "attacks." *B* can identify the type of grab and respond to it in a suitable way by taking on the correct tension of his arm. Or, he can be led to react ineffectively and use too much or too little force.

Aikido practice leads us to develop better management of our muscle tone and thus improve our sensitivity. We often tend to imagine muscle tone in a binary way: tight or relaxed. However, there is an infinite variability between these two extremes. Furthermore, we can also discover how to adopt a differentiated tone, for example, to keep the arm relaxed and the body in a powerful stance or the left arm firm while the right arm is relaxed.

We are often tempted to respond to someone with the same level of energy that he has. If a person grabs your wrist roughly, you will be tempted to make your arm rigid in the same way. By doing this, you put yourself under the other person's will. His strong grab has caused muscular tension in your arm, but very often also in the rest of your body. Tension brings tension. You thus become a link in a causal chain, a reaction to his action. You have lost your ability to take the initiative. The result is immediate: you give the other person the chance to control you.

If I grab a stick at its end and I move it around, the stiffness of the wood transmits the movement to the entire piece of wood. If I do the same with a rope, the movement will only be transmitted to the other end if the rope is taut. The tension in the rope, just like the stiffness of the stick, extends control, while relaxation only guarantees control of the end that is grabbed. It is the same when someone grabs my arm. If I relax my arm, he will only control the wrist he is holding. Since this grab is meant to control me, I will regain my freedom of movement by relaxing and extending my arm, which nullifies the attempt to control me with a grab.

Exercise: Tension and Control (2 People A and B)

A and *B* face each other. With his right arm, partner *B* grabs *A*'s left arm roughly.
A is attentive to the tension that springs from this grab, tension in his arm, but also in his entire body.
While *B* maintains a firm hold of *A*'s wrist, *A* increases the muscular tension in his entire body to become stiff like a piece of

> wood. B shakes A's wrist and observes how his movement influences all of A's body. He controls him from head to toe. B maintains the grab, but A relaxes his arm completely (as though his arm were asleep). B shakes A's wrist and observes the fact that A's relaxed arm disconnects the control that he had through A's body. B isn't holding anything more than A's wrist, while earlier he had the impression of holding all of A.

Let's keep looking at the scenario of an arm that is grabbed roughly. By making my arm rigid, not only do I give my partner better control of my arm and my entire body, but on top of that, this stiffness deprives me of the correct and sensitive perception that I will greatly need in order to react. Managing muscle tone allows me to be present in the relationship, connected with the other person, without imposing myself or giving in. This muscle tone is not invariable. On the contrary, it evolves and varies according to the circumstances. This is a basic principle of the physical dimension of *Aiki* work. I do not leave myself open to the grab, I recover my freedom of action and my sensitivity to take the proper initiative that will unblock the situation.

On the verbal level, the effect will be the same. The advantage of working with an arm grab is to bring to light any tensions or contractions. On the mental and emotional levels, they are less obvious or apparent, but are still just as present. If I am the object of a verbal attack, my first reaction could be to tighten up. This tightness will be felt throughout my body and my mind will be frozen by words and the way they are said (volume, intensity, rhythm, etc.). In this instant—and this instant can last a long time—my attention is paralyzed by the tension and I lose my freedom of action. On the contrary, if I relax myself, I regain my freedom to move and also my freedom to think and to ask myself what led this person to say what he said, the actions that led him to this point, the need that he is trying to satisfy by saying it, etc.[127]

---

[127] We will discuss this technique below.

Deciding and Acting with the *Aikisphere*

Let's look at a concrete situation to illustrate how the Aikisphere can help to act with the Aiki attitude.

> You have to make a decision to phone or send an e-mail to someone with whom you have a disagreement. Let's call him Charles. Charles has just sent you an aggressive e-mail about a comment that you made during the evening of your high school reunion. Reading this e-mail has an emotional effect on you and hits you like a bolt out of the blue. From the first lines, you feel a drastic change. This is far from the relationship that you had been working on. You see the e-mail and you see Charles's face, you even hear him reading the e-mail, and you begin to feel bad. You read the e-mail from beginning to end. You even read it a second time, then a third time. Charles criticizes you for having put him at the foot of the table and having deliberately tried to isolate him, that you hate him and that this has been going on since you were fifteen years old. You are stunned. Why so much aggression? There is not even a hint of a request for clarification; this e-mail is like a prison sentence that cannot be appealed. You are aware of Charles's impulsive nature. You had forgotten about it because it had been so long since you had seen each other. Under other circumstances, you could smile and say, "That darn Charles! Always the same." But it is you who are being condemned in such a direct and brutal way. Your first reaction could be to click on the "reply" button and tell him what you are thinking. But you know that this would only set off a series of messages that would only make the situation worse. It is also unacceptable to you to not respond. Your compass is going crazy. You want to ask for advice, to share your emotions, but you know that this would not help you much. Your compass is more and more lost...
>
> ...awareness of your emotional state, of your lack of balance. You were comfortable, calm, and focused. Then all of a sudden this e-mail unbalanced you, as though Charles had come and shoved you. In the current situation, you have a little time to reflect. Charles is not there physically and nothing requires you to react right away. The situation is ideal for you to work on yourself and apply the

Aikisphere compass. Just the word *Aikisphere* is enough to remind you of the first step: centering and verticality.

You begin to exhale deeply and become aware of your position. Your back moves away from the back of the chair and you reconnect with your verticality while you turn your attention to your breathing. The emotion you are feeling is intense and it compresses your ribcage. The pot is boiling inside you and you wish that Charles were in the room, perhaps to grab him. This is an expression of the anger that is simmering within you. You continue to breathe and that helps you to become aware of these emotions. Breathing creates a place for them, they are less oppressed, but they remain strong. The verticality of your torso seems to make it easier for you to reconnect with your three centers. First the emotional center, so intensely present. Then the cognitive center. You seem to hear a small voice inside you that contributes to increasing your anger. This voice comes from the past, from the time when you were at school with Charles and when you had to chomp at the bit because Charles's explosions were so vicious. You didn't feel strong enough to respond to them. So you chose to either flee or be silent. Meanwhile, you grew up, gained self-assurance, and learned to no longer be pushed around. This e-mail takes you back to a time that you thought was gone and you hear a little voice that shouts at you: "Are you really going to let yourself be pushed around like in high school?" "Haven't you learned anything, or is it only skin-deep?" So many statements take over and feed your anger. Continuing to breathe, you become aware that the e-mail has become of secondary importance and that this voice has become the main cause of your anger. Inhale, breathe. Progressively, the air drops deeper, to the level of your *hara*. Your abdomen fills and makes a feeling of calm emerge. It is strange how it is possible to feel both this anger and, at the same time, this calm that seems to envelop it. It seems so vast while your anger is so concentrated. A few more breaths and you feel like you have returned to yourself. The flow of energy among your three centers has been reestablished. The anger is still there, the small voice is still present, the e-mail continues to fill the screen in front of you, but the situation has changed. You have returned and you are no longer angry, even though you still feel the tension caused by the anger.

You are no longer the 15-year-old who is controlled by Charles's shouting. You are no longer possessed by this e-mail that has returned to its place on the flat screen. You are yourself: adult, human, alive. You feel life inside you through your breathing. The anger that pulses inside your ribcage is the marvelous manifestation of being alive, feeling, thinking, and present. Already, you are no longer unbalanced and, in your verticality, you have found your stability again. You still need to decide about the sequence of events. This is where the *Aikisphere* comes into play. You are alone in your office and you can allow yourself the luxury of continuing the exercise while standing rather than sitting in your chair. Your verticality is at the center of the sphere. You take the *Aiki* attitude, with your left leg slightly forward; you can easily make a circular movement that checks your verticality. Now the question is to find out in which direction the needle will move. You continue to explore your vertical axis while turning your attention toward the sky. What is important for you at this moment in your life? Which values count under these circumstances? Words emerge: respect, priority, responsibility, evolution. These words are connected to your experience. The experience of having evolved, of no longer being a fifteen-year-old, of having learned how to manage these kinds of provocations. You are also aware of being a responsible adult, but also a professional who needs to meet deadlines. You are aware that life passes by so quickly that it is better to set aside your time for things that really count, for people who nurture us and who love us. But at the same time, it is important to live in respect, respect for oneself and respect for others. Your breathing leads you to not get lost in these thoughts and brings you back to your somatic center and then to the earth. What are your current responsibilities and your professional obligations that have you sitting in front of your computer instead of running with your dog or reading that novel that someone recommended to you? What limits you in your choices concerning Charles? Can you go find him, call him, send him an e-mail? Is he reachable? Your mind makes round trips between the earth and the sky, between obligations and what is important.

The *Aikisphere* compass oscillates and begins to find its direction. Return to the somatic center during an exhalation that connects you with your lateral axis, the relationship axis. Your arms spread spontaneously to get back into contact with the space to your left and your right. You are there, but who else is next to you? In the present case, you feel strangely lonely. Within you, a feeling emerges of other high school classmates, but you put them pretty far out on the relationship axis. There is certainly a problem that needs to be resolved between you and Charles. Standing in your office, you feel that your body is turning naturally toward the screen. The compass seems to be orienting itself in the direction of the action, perhaps a response to the e-mail. You check to see if that suits you while turning in a different direction, but that doesn't feel right. You turn back to your screen. That's the right direction! Behind you, you have the sensation of your past experiences. Some of them make you want to retaliate with the same harshness, but the feeling of your verticality restabilizes you in the here and now. The future takes shape. The screen is in front of you and you feel that you will answer; it remains to be seen if that must be done now. For this, the answer is clearly "no." Within you, you feel the axis of action that is unfolding in front of you and you feel that the moment for answering is farther away, undoubtedly more toward the end of the day. Meanwhile, the anger has been transformed. You do not know exactly when its energy dissipated, but it is no longer there. You have become yourself again and you are even surprised to have some compassion for Charles. The e-mail that is displayed on the screen suddenly seems to no longer concern you, as much as it has to do with Charles talking about Charles. You smile faintly, go back to your seat and close the e-mail window, leaving your report showing on the screen. The affair is settled and you know that in a little while you will write a response to him in which you will express to him that you do not agree with the tone of his e-mail and that you are ready to discuss what upset him, but only in mutual respect.

The presentation of this *Aikisphere* process may seem either long or shallow to you, and it is...as long as you have not tried it physically. With a little training, this process shows itself to be extremely useful and effective in activating the "physical checklist" in us that balances our emotional and mental processes. In practice—and with a little training—this process may take from just a few seconds to a few minutes. When the stakes are higher, we can repeat this process several times during the same day or over the course of several days.

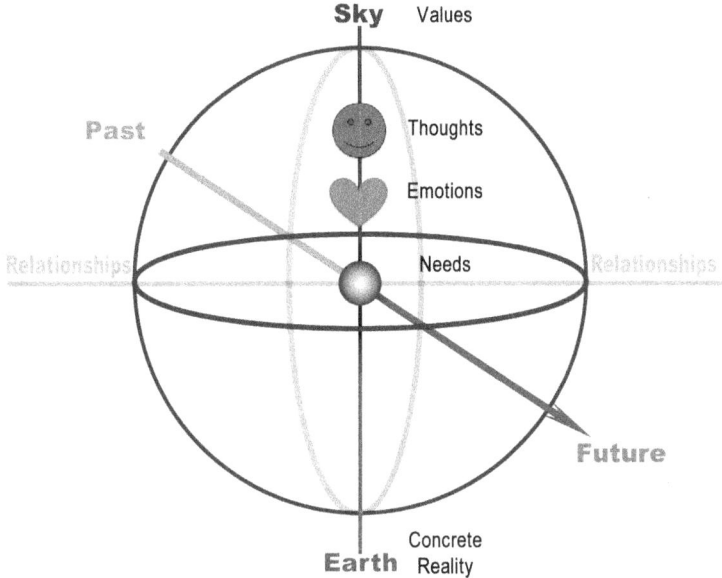

Figure 10 : Aikisphere as a compass for the Aiki attitude

Let's go over the sequence:

The Start of the Process: The Trigger

1. When an event takes place that requires action.

Step 1: Centering and Verticality

2. Returning to oneself through centering and verticality while turning our attention to our breathing. (It is recommended to begin with a deep exhalation that helps us to release a huge amount of tension.)
3. Breathing while listening to our emotional and mental centers.
4. Breathing moves downward until it comes into contact with our somatic center, which creates a space of calm that helps us to welcome our emotions and our thoughts.

Step 2: Exploration of My Vertical Axis

5. When breathing has reestablished the circulation of energy between the three centers, I turn my attention toward the sky or the earth (in the order that you prefer).
6. Contact with the sky reconnects me with my values and with what is important for me in the present.
7. Contact with the earth reconnects me with my present obligations, what I can or cannot do, what I must or must not do.

Step 3: Exploration of My Relationship Axis

8. I reconnect myself with my relationship axis and I become aware of the people who are around me and whose presence will influence my choice of action.
9. The preceding steps follow one another while I remain aware of my breathing and my feelings. I avoid the trap of letting myself be controlled by my thoughts; I accept them without losing myself in them.

Step 4: Exploration of My Axis of Action

10. Vertical alignment and my awareness of my relationship axis have helped to reharmonize me; I can let go of the desire to control my mental center and let my body turn itself in the direction of the right action.
11. My axis of action takes shape in my experience; my body turns itself in the direction of the action I will carry out, toward my objective.
12. While turning my attention to the rear part of my axis of action (in my back), I can become aware of the resources or blockages that result from my past experiences, from what keeps me from acting or, conversely, what pushes me to action. This step can require quite a bit of work, which is sometimes difficult to carry out without outside help.
13. Finally, my attention turns toward the front, toward my action. The closer it is to me, the more I will feel that I must act right now. If the action is farther away toward the front, I will not have to act right away. The action may often be complex and require me to develop a plan of action that is broken down into steps. Here we enter the realm of action strategies that are geared toward reaching the goal that we have set for ourselves.

I cannot say it enough: This process is carried out through your body. Practicing *Aiki*Com exercises helps you to optimize the approach. Most of us are not used to listening to our bodies like this. We tend tend to ignore what our body tells us because we are not sure of what we sense and because we have gotten in the habit of trusting only our mind.

However, with a bit of practice—and the development is similar to that of someone who is learning about meditation—we detect, more and more subtly, the signals that guide us. These signals do not come from out of nowhere. They do not come from some higher intelligence outside of us. They emerge of their own accord, from the experience of being alive, whole and aligned. This process does not ignore the mind, it incorporates it and harmonizes it. It opens the door for us toward the appropriate action. We know the direction, even if we do not yet know how we are going to do it. The Aiki fundamentals options of action will help us during the action phase.

Dialogue in the Present Moment

AikiCom is anchored in the reality of martial combat. This reality leads us to remain in the present. If I anticipate what will happen, I project scenarios and by doing so I risk being surprised if the action does not take the path that I had imagined. In aikido, during a *randori*, several *uke* come at me and attack freely. As *tori*, I execute a technique that is adapted to the attack and ends by a throw or a pin of the attacker. During these moments, everything happens very quickly. If I have the foolish idea to anticipate the attack or to choose the technique that I will execute, there will be a good chance that I will be surprised and that the technique will not be as effective as it would have been if I had let it emerge based on the attack. All it takes is a movement that is a little more circular, a kick instead of a punch, a slight variation in the timing and I find myself in a position that is no longer centered, since I am focused on trying to force the technique that I had anticipated. *Randori* offers a unique opportunity for me to confront myself in the present, to test how returning to centering—in the *hara*—allows me to come back to the moment, to free myself from the tension of a state of mind in which I am continuously trying to anticipate, to project myself into a future that I do not yet know and that will probably not happen. The *samurai* entered combat with the full acceptance of the fact that they would possibly not come out alive. The main thing was to make it through the combat well, accomplishing what they had devoted their lives to: combat training. Of course, we are not *samurai*, but their experience opens a path for us to live in harmony with ourselves, in the present, and to act in harmony with our life choices. As a result of always trying to project myself into the future, I miss what I am experiencing now. It is through my alignment in my *Aikisphere* that I determine the right action. This flows naturally and becomes a part of the flow of events. Of course, we should not delude ourselves. This apparent effortlessness comes from mastery. It is the result of diligent and disciplined training and a clear commitment to practice consistently. The choices in each moment come from intuition. They are felt rather than thought out. Intuition is not the sort of knowledge or wisdom that comes from out of nowhere. It is the result of work, practice, and *discipline*, a word that is not very popular these days.

Shoshin: Beginner's Mind

Not only do I have to avoid anticipating—by choosing the next action before the conditions that would justify it have come about—but I must also get rid of everything that I believe I know, my prejudices, my locked-in views of life that can be recognized by the excessive use of the verb "to be" and by generalizations: "It's always like that."; "With him, it's always the same thing."; "She's ticked off."; "He is still going to say that it isn't right." The human brain has developed an extraordinary ability to anticipate that can sometimes save our life, but very often locks us into repetitive behavioral patterns by trying to repeat, in the present moment, solutions that worked in the past. A newborn child learns that by crying he can bring his mother, who will bring him food or will console him. This effective solution will not work in all of life's circumstances. A young student who breaks into tears because she has ended up with the exam question that she had feared the most, expresses her sadness and hopes to possibly touch the parental side of her teacher, and encourage him or her to offer consolation.

The nine-year-old boy who decides once and for all that "carrots aren't good" will not be able to realize that his sense of taste can evolve and that, all things considered, they aren't so bad after all.

When my children were young, I introduced them to the *shoshin* state of mind as it can be applied to food. I repeated to them throughout our meals that while growing up our sense of taste changes and I was curious to know at each meal what had changed in their way of appreciating—or not—certain foods. The only solution to learn this was to taste the foods that had been classified as "not good" at each meal and to change their opinion, retaining the right to award the "not good" label...until the next meal when the same food would be offered. This ritual was repeated day after day, week after week, then month after month. And each discovery of a food that was "not too bad after all" became a chance to celebrate and to become aware that they were growing up. They had integrated the *shoshin* state of mind through food.

The beginner's mind is characterized by a sort of mental receptivity, of a curiosity that rids me, at least for a moment, of everything that can block the flow of energy in me, in my relationship to another person or as a result of the event that I am experiencing.

This state can also be expressed as the act of accepting letting yourself be surprised, not knowing—or wanting to know—what will happen.

Necessary Vulnerability

In this openness to the moment, in this acceptance of not knowing, we take the risk of vulnerability. This vulnerability is the inseparable complement of the notion of commitment. We do not go through life timidly, nor do we stay on the edge of the pool: we plunge in. This commitment is unavoidably accompanied by a certain vulnerability. I cannot commit myself by staying at a distance or by taking shelter behind thick walls. Nature has made us living beings, presenting our flesh and skin—fragile tissues—to the world while the harder parts, our bones, are inside our body. This is the exact opposite of the strategy that has been adopted by crustaceans, in general, and lobsters in particular. Psychology frequently uses the image of armor protecting the individual. For example, the book *Paroles pour Adolescents, le Complexe du Homard*, by Françoise Dolto and her daughter Catherine, talks about the vulnerability of teenagers by comparing this period of their lives to that of a lobster changing its shell, which leaves it temporarily vulnerable to predators. We should also keep in mind the concept of armor as it was initially defined by Wilhelm Reich[128]. This concept is the inspiration for the method for releasing body tension created by Marie Lise Labonté ("**Méthode de Libération des Cuirasses**," **MLC**[129]). The armor of a knight or a *samurai* and the castle rampart behind which the knight takes shelter are protection that aims to protect us against attack (but only from certain weapons). However, they also offer serious drawbacks. Not only do they limit our freedom of movement, but they also prevent us from perceiving and from feeling. MLC takes the same path by explaining how, by means of inhibitions, emotions, and repressed thoughts, we construct for ourselves a sort of armor that is embodied through muscular tension, which limits our sensitivity to sensations that arise. How many people decide, after a painful breakup, to never again commit to a romantic relationship, in order to avoid sustaining new injuries? Don't they know that they are thus depriving themselves of living, of feeling alive? The *Aiki* attitude advocates living without armor, flexibly joining the flow of life.

Of course we are then more vulnerable and we are no longer protected from injury. But we are confident about our ability to heal from these injuries, even if they leave a scar. And then, even if we accept the vulnerability inherent in being alive, we need not be martyrs. Of course we risk being injured, but not by leaving ourselves open to injury for no reason.

It is interesting to see that a human being, by standing up on his hind legs, puts the most vulnerable parts of his body in danger. It is partly for this reason[130] that aikido advocates taking a *hanmi no kamae* stance that can be translated as half-body stance (*hanmi* is made of the word *han*, half, and *mi*, body, while *no kamae* means stance[131]). *AikiCom* has adopted the same principle by taking a stance in which you face the other person without naively being open to a possible

---

[128] Wikipedia, Wilhelm Reich, consulted December 21, 2015.
[129] *Cuirasse*=armor.
[130] Another reason resides in the fact that this stance initiates rotational movement at the level of the pelvis and the *hara*.
[131] *Kammae* means to prepare oneself, to put yourself on guard. The word comes from *kamaeru*, which can be translated as: to make, to construct, to prepare, to wait with intensity, to be sharp and on the alert.

attack. I open myself to the other person; I take the risk while keeping an attitude of attentive receptivity. If something happens, I can face it.

The Aiki Fundamental Options of Action

After centering ourselves; after getting back in touch with our verticality; extending our energy to perceive our environment, then turning our *Aikisphere* in the direction of the action; after getting off the line of danger and entering into connection with the Other, center to center, we have arrived at the transformational stage. The opposing energies are connected. Now we can enter into the active phase of transformation[132].

In a confrontation, forces enter into collision and oppose one another. Conflict escalates and finishes with the victory of the stronger and the defeat of the weaker.

Aikido proposes circular techniques that keep us from falling into this dynamic. The energies at work are mixed and unified; we use the verb "to blend" to express this mixture, this fusion of energies. This is the dynamic that we see where one river flows into another. The waters from the smaller river increase the flow of the larger river, which flows toward the sea. This inescapable characteristic gives meaning to action. The turbulence that is caused by the meeting of the waters evolves to reach a sort of order and harmony. The larger river welcomes the water of the smaller river effortlessly. It simply flows out; that's all. Also note that the larger river, which is welcoming the smaller one, does not fade away; it remains present. It's the same in an *Aiki* confrontation. The aikidoka acts from his center and, while he seeks to reestablish harmony, he does not disappear. He does not fade away to leave the field open to the attacker. Circular movements do not make him disappear. They put him at the heart of change.

Taking action, in the *Aiki* meaning of the term, lies within commitment, a commitment that is not without risk and leads us unavoidably to the question of vulnerability that we discussed above. I cannot commit myself while remaining at a distance. When the attack happens, I am already connected to the Other. My movement begins

---

[132] It is important to emphasize that this happens at the energetic level and not at the level of content or form—even if the energetic level influences the form as much as the content.

at the same time as my attacker's. This is at least what I strive for through my training. As we have already discussed, the act of getting off the line of danger has nothing to do with escape. It is quite the opposite. The movement that is initiated to avoid the shock of energies is a movement that allows me to apply a fundamental principle of aikido that is called *irimi*. *Irimi* could be translated as "to penetrate the flesh," "to get to the heart of the matter," or "to get to the point." This principle leads us to turn toward the center of the partner who is attacking us. Our reaction to an attack is therefore a movement that protects us and allows us to connect to the Other, from center to center. The *Aikisphere* has moved and is turned toward the Other. In doing so, I have gone from "one" (I am alone) to "two" (you and I), which automatically gives rise to "three" (you and I, and the relationship that I establish among us).

The *irimi* principle initiates the first fundamental *Aiki* option, which is the triangle. If I choose this option, I can act with incisive power. I have the ability to injure and it is from that point that the *Aiki* attitude is fully revealed: I choose not to harm. I deliberately enter into a constructive approach that encompasses the attacker, who has become my partner. To do this, I must become an agent for the transformation of the energies involved. According to Anaxagoras of Clazomenes[133], nothing is created or destroyed, but things that already exist combine, then separate again. The founder of aikido also took up this maxim and turned it into movement by going from the principle of *irimi* to the *tenkan*, a circular movement that introduces to us the second fundamental *Aiki* option. The attack that does not reach me—because I have gotten off the line of danger—feeds the circular movement that gives our partner a new experiential framework. It will lead to a state of balance, embodied by the shape of the square, the last *Aiki* option, which we will study in more detail below.

---

[133] "Anaxagoras of Clazomenae [..] says that principles are infinite in number; for he says, almost all the things that are homogeneous are generated and destroyed (as water or fire is) only by aggregation and segregation, and are not in any other sense generated or destroyed, but remain eternally." (Aristotle, *Metaphysics. Book I*). This maxim was taken up by Lavoisier in the very popular expression: "In nature nothing is created, nothing is lost, everything changes." (Antoine Lavoisier, *Traité élémentaire de chimie*).

These three shapes—the triangle, the circle, and the square—follow each other in *Aiki* movement. They are always present. Their application in real life shows the need to adjust one or more of these shapes—with more or less intensity or presence—according to the circumstances: this is the strategy of the three Aiki fundamental options of action.

> *"The body should be triangular, the mind circular. The triangle represents the generation of energy and is the most stable physical posture. The circle symbolizes serenity and perfection, the source of unlimited techniques. The square stands for solidity, the basis of applied control.*[134]*"*
>
> Morihei Ueshiba

In the *AikiCom* approach, the three simple geometric shapes of the triangle, the circle, and the square symbolize the three Aiki fundamental options of action. These options express energetic modes of action.

The Triangle

In *Aiki* training, the triangle is called *"Iku-musubi."* It is the root of vitality and it symbolizes both initiative and the animal kingdom. Ueshiba described it by the term *"masakatsu"* (true victory). The triangle is life, movement, and the flow of *Ki*. Technically, the triangle is considered to be the key for entering. It is therefore linked to the concept of *irimi*. In aikido, the fundamental defensive stance is the *hanmi no kamae* stance, which is sometimes also called *sankaku* (three angles). This position is the key for entering into the movement. The triangle allows us to take the initiative within the action, through movement, but not just any movement: a movement that respects the laws of the universe[135]. When it is done in this spirit, it naturally leads to the circle, which is called *"Taru Musubi."*

Embodying the Triangle

The triangle is a pointed shape that symbolizes the act of gathering our energy and focusing it in order to produce an energetic action. The

---

[134] http://www.azquotes.com/quote/770710.
[135] In modern terms, we can call it ecology.

triangle injects energy into the interaction. In *Aiki* practice, it takes form through the *hanmi* stance. I put myself on guard with my right foot forward and I place my right hand in front of me and align it on an imaginary line that starts in my *hara*, my belly, and goes toward my partner's center. To create this triangular form, I bend my wrist slightly to align my hand with this line and unite our two centers.

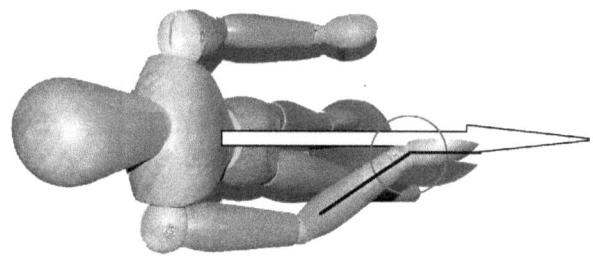

Figure 11 : Taking a triangle stance

In this position, my hand becomes the point of the triangle. In aikido we talk about the *te-katana* or the hand-sword. This hand-sword is a weapon that concentrates all my energy of action like a laser beam. This position is a position of power. It gathers all my energy in one unique direction.

The Triangle in Daily Life

We take the shape of a triangle when we must inject energy into an interaction. We need the triangle when we want to say "That's enough!" The action is powerful, firm, penetrating, even incisive. By being centered, the triangle does not expend too much energy, just what is necessary to contribute to making the situation develop. I therefore clearly distinguish the "That's enough!" of the off-centered triangle—which betrays the fact that I am already "beside myself"—from the "That's enough!" that allows someone who is centered to clearly set the boundary that should not be crossed.

Figure 12 : The Triangle

The triangle is not an offensive shape, it is assertive. If we associate the triangle with aggressiveness, this can only be through the meaning that biology gives to the notion of aggressiveness, which is different from what is commonly understood by the concept[136]. In fact, Konrad Lorenz defines aggressiveness as a natural instinct that is tied to all the other vital needs, a vital element that does not give in to violence or power struggles. It has more to do with a vital energy that is often expressed in various cultures through codified rites that are meant to avoid showing pointless or harmful aggressiveness. Henri Laborit defines aggressiveness as:

> *"The quantity of energy that can increase entropy (disorder, agitation) of a system, in other words to destroy its structure more or less rapidly. The structure is thus defined as the entirety of the existing relationships between the elements of a whole. Aggressiveness is thus the characteristic of a means that can apply this energy to an organized whole.*[137]*"*

This definition is interesting because it illustrates the attack just as much as the "triangle" response to the attack. The intention in the case of an attack is to cause a significant disruption in the *person* who is being attacked while the "triangle" intervention aims to initiate a significant transformation of the *attack*, to take down its structure in order to lead to a situation that is radically different and centered on

---

[136] It is interesting to examine the etymology of the word "aggressiveness." Aggression comes from the Latin *adgredi*, which means to go toward, to walk forward (*gradus* means "step" and *ad* means "toward.").

[137] Henri Laborit, *L'agressivité détournée. Introduction à une biologie du comportement social.* Éditions de Poche, 1970.

harmony and cooperation. The triangle is necessary in order to initiate this transformation.

When a situation does not suit us, we can hunker down and endure it or muster our energy and leave. Sometimes it takes more courage to leave than to stay. This courage mobilizes our energy to stop being idle and get moving. Whether it is to go meet the other person or to leave him, the triangle opens the door to initiative, to the movement that brings about change when the system seems paralyzed. In a discussion that gets bogged down, a "triangle" strike can sometimes be necessary to get the exchange going again: "Okay, I see that we agree on this point, let's keep it in mind and move on to the next point." At a family reunion or gathering of friends, when it's late in the evening, it often happens that some participants want to leave, but don't dare make a move out of fear of "spoiling the mood." The triangle allows the most dynamic one to take the initiative to leave: "Well, it's getting late. I've had a great time with you, but tomorrow is another day and I have to get up early." In general, this declaration is enough to inspire the others, giving them the energy to get up and leave. Leaving with the help of the triangle is a choice, a commitment. This is nothing like a retreat. Leaving is not fleeing.

The triangle induces a sort of determination, of commitment to action. By focusing my energy in a single direction, I am more powerful in that direction because it is my choice, but I also know that this choice makes me weaker in all the other directions. I made a choice and I act fully in that direction. The triangle is the opposite of fragmentation, distraction, or hopping around. In its centered shape, it allows you to be assertive, to express what you are feeling by taking the risk of possibly displeasing someone.

> A few years ago, I was participating in a seminar on personal development. The leader of the seminar was very nice and he was attentive to each of the participants, but the content of the seminar was especially disappointing. At the end of the seminar, all the participants gathered together and formed a circle. Each spoke in turn, beginning with Nathalie who was at the left of the trainer. Nathalie set the tone and couldn't stop praising him for the two days we had spent together. Then each participant spoke, praising the trainer with a stream of superlatives that continued to amaze me,

given that I was especially dissatisfied. Moreover, I had had the chance to talk with two participants, Marie and Joanne. They both shared the same point of view: the seminar was certainly very pleasant because of the social qualities of the trainer and the group cohesion, but the content and the instruction were disappointing. The two days had consisted of a bunch of miscellaneous exercises, without a common thread.

When it was time for Joanne, who was ahead of me in the talking circle, to speak, I was astonished to hear that she was delighted and had learned a lot! I just didn't understand, or actually I was beginning to understand. Caught in the long string of praise, it was difficult for her to get out of this dynamic and speak from her heart. The question here is not to know if the people who were satisfied really were, or if the dissatisfied people, including me, were being overly critical, but rather to explore the difficulty we sometimes have in expressing what we feel, independently from what the others expressed before us. When it was my turn, I had taken the time to center myself. I especially needed to get in touch with my triangle energy so that what I was truly feeling could emerge from me and break the chain of praise. Fully anchored to the ground, with my right foot forward—thus showing, discretely, the hanmi position that allowed me to stay in contact with my "triangle" dimension—I expressed myself from my center. My tone of voice was calm, even though I was feeling a slight trembling in my body. I expressed that, although I appreciated the trainer's personality and skills, it was important for me to express my dissatisfaction concerning the content of the training. I used the image of a gourmet restaurant where you are welcomed very pleasantly, but where they only serve you a soft-boiled egg. "The egg was delicious, the chef was nice, but I do not go to a gourmet restaurant to eat a soft-boiled egg." The trainer welcomed my feedback and took a few seconds before thanking me for this sincere opinion. Afterwards, several participants came looking for me to thank me. They had not had the energy to say what I had expressed and wanted to thank me for having the courage to do it.

The triangle, like all the other shapes, does not offer only advantages. It also has its dark side, its negative aspects. This is the case when it is not centered. A triangle that is off center and badly balanced will present its cutting, wounding side. This is the case when we lose ourselves in the emotion of anger, for example. The triangle will then be more pointed and its center will be shifted toward the point. The intent is to wound, to destroy. In this unbalanced state, we have no other choice but to hope to win because we are lost in action. In aikido practice, a person who loses himself in the attack loses all his balance, to the point of falling, if the target of his attack slips away at the moment where he had hoped to hit it.

The off-center triangle is the characteristic shape of people who are angry or aggressive. It can be found in excessively authoritarian, arrogant, or hostile behaviors. The triangle that is too pointed is the perspective of fundamentalist attitudes, of those who do not see more than the direction that seems the most valid to them. A person who is stuck in the triangle shape will be a hardliner, a radical, an extremist, even a fanatic.

Centered Triangle	Off-Center, Excessive Triangle
I am ready	anger, aggressiveness
energy, fighting spirit, dynamic, penetrating, having a definite goal, action, conquest, rhetoric, verbal jousting, competition/surpassing oneself	fundamentalist, dictator, hostile, arrogant, piercing, incisive, single point of view, competition pushed to the extreme, extremist attitude (death)

Like the two other Aiki fundamental options of action, the triangle taken alone—that is, without being nourished by the energy of the two other shapes—easily becomes excessive. It is by centering that we succeed in getting the best out of it.

During *AikiCom* training, some people confuse the triangle with aggressiveness, which is expressed with a certain degree of violence. This is the caricature of the triangle, the dark side of its force. The triangle is the shape that allows the flow of our personal energy. It nourishes the relationship and gives it some rhythm. It is the shape that allows us to stop being passive or saying, "like before," or "like the others," or "like always." Without a triangle, nothing is created. The triangle displaces the "C" of the word "reaCtion" and puts it in front of the word to give us "Creation." In this spirit, the triangle makes itself curious, enthusiastic, dynamic, a beautiful life energy that is brought into the relationship and into the world.

The Circle

Following the triangle, which initiated the movement, the circle is the shape of transformation. Arising from the meeting of complementary forces (fire and water, *yin* and *yang*) and of their union, it thus establishes the return to Unity, to the undifferentiated ONE, from which they came to form the unified *ki*. The circle represents the fluid dimension, the basis of completeness (in Japanese the term *taru musubi* is used). The circle thus symbolizes unification and the plant kingdom. The founder of aikido tied it to the *Agatsu* principle (victory over self).

Embodying the Circle

The circle is embodied by the movement that we call *Tai sabaki* (see page 101) in aikido. It is a movement around the vertical axis. When practiced with a partner who is attacking, this movement allows us to draw him into a circular movement by taking advantage of the energy of the attack. When we do *tai sabaki,* we turn around our vertical axis. We become the center of movement and our partner sees his force—which is at first turned toward our center—become displaced so that it becomes a tangent of the circle. Practicing this movement teaches us a lot of things about ourselves. We sometimes have the impression that we are straight and very vertical when in fact we are leaning forward (oriented in action toward the future), or toward the back (apprehension, something keeps us from moving forward). When doing *tai sabaki,* the slightest flaw has immediate consequences: if I am not vertical, my rotation will be slower and unbalanced. My steps will be heavy. If I am, on the other hand, very settled in my verticality, I will feel the rotation happen naturally, flowingly.

The Circle in Daily Life

The circle is the ultimate shape that allows us to transform conflict in a positive way. Circularity diverts aggressive energy to send it in a new direction. The circle welcomes and transforms.

The circle leads us to swim in the direction of the current, to feel the direction of the flow while making necessary adjustments in order to go in the desired direction. The helmsman of a sailboat does this when he uses the wind to make progress toward his destination. To ignore the wind would be nonsense, even if it didn't blow in the right direction. The helmsman uses the force of the wind to reach his destination. Instead of confronting it when it is blowing toward him, he will tack while still keeping his heading. Good helmsmen show flexibility and feel the wind. With each tacking movement, they get the maximum benefit from the force of the elements.

Figure 13 : The Circle

The circle is the movement of dialogue, of listening. In verbal language, it corresponds to active listening. The person who is expressing himself feels like he is being listened to. His partner listens and changes the wording while imperceptibly transforming it and looking for the best solution. This can be done by replacing a word with a similar word, even though it may be noticeably different, by emphasizing one word over another, by modifying the inflection of a sentence to turn an assertion into a question, etc.

> *"I've had enough! With you, it's always the same thing!"*
> *"You've had enough, with me it's **always** the same thing?"*

"No, not always, of course, but too often."

These reframing techniques are also an application[138] of the circle.

"James is really disagreeable. He never smiles."
"Is someone who smiles always nice?"
or
"Don't you know any disagreeable people who smile?"

The off-center circle leads to what I call the *weather vane effect*. In this case, the person does not give a specific opinion or changes it all the time. He is vague, absent, and gives the impression of not being there. This is the negative side of some salesmen who recommend an article of clothing and find that everything looks good on you as long as you buy it. If you say that something doesn't please you, they change their opinion, agree with you fully, and recommend something else to you until you frown once again, which leads them to suggest something else to you.

It can be touching to see young couples discussing what they are going to do with their evening. Each one, wanting to please the other, hesitates to express what he or she really wants and asks the other what he or she wants. The other, wanting to do the same, does not dare express himself or herself, not having received information about the preferences of his or her partner. They thus find themselves in a situation where neither partner is ready to suggest something that might please the other because the other has not expressed his or her desire. If neither of them comes forward, they run the risk of ending this discussion with the very same feeling of frustration that each wanted to avoid for the other.

"Tell me, my dear, what do you want?
— And you, what do you want?"
— Oh no, but it's as you wish, what would please you?
— Everything's fine as long as I'm with you. What do you want?"

---

[138] Provided that the reframing is not too direct, in which case it is more like a triangle, as in: "There is nothing good in this file!" "Who are you to say that it has no value?"

The Centered Circle	The Off-center, Distorted Circle
joining energy, seeking harmony, synergy, transforming without confronting flexibility, flowing, accepting force rather than fighting it, seeing all aspects of the question, contributing to the exchange, favoring dialogue, communication, accentuating complementarity rather than difference	instability, inconsistency, being a "weather vane," irresponsibility, evasion, always agreeing with everyone, taking the side of the last one who spoke, taking no position, beating around the bush, scheming, chameleon, easily influenced, unstable

The Square

The square is the final shape in the *Aiki* movement series. It symbolizes the return to a new state of balance when the cycle (circular movement) is finished. The flowing circle is solidified. The square embodies a sort of achievement, fulfillment, or satisfaction. It symbolizes the mineral world. It is nourished by the force of the earth unified with the sky by Mankind in accordance with the laws of the universe. The founder of aikido called the square "*Katsuhayabi*," which can be translated as "victory at the speed of light." If we have mastery over ourselves (*Agatsu*) and we act in perfect harmony with the fundamental principles that govern the universe (mostly the principles that govern ethical interactions), we have the power of the universe at our disposal and victory is immediate: there is no more fighting.

On the systemic level, the square symbolizes the return to a new state of equilibrium. At the beginning of the movement, the system was in an initial state of equilibrium that was disrupted by the attack. The energy of this disruption threw the system out of its state of equilibrium and the *Aiki* movement led it to a new stable state, preferably a more harmonious one. The system's equilibrium states are not necessarily static, immobile states. These are states that absorb slight disruptions and carry out corrective movements that assure the system's homeostasis[139]. If the system is subjected to a disruption that is too strong, it will be knocked out of its state of equilibrium to enter into an unstable state that can either lead it to a new state of equilibrium or destroy it.

Figure 14 : Homeostasis and Change

In the drawing above, we see that a light push will make the ball move, but it will remain in the trough. If the push is stronger, the ball will leave the trough and will roll toward another recess. If the push is even more forceful, the ball can be destroyed.

Aiki movement is a little like a maze game where you put a marble and try to guide it toward the final hole. The player guides the marble by a series of circular movements and avoids the holes in order to arrive at the goal. "

---

[139] Homeostasis is the property of systems that, through a retroactive mechanism, maintain themselves in a state of equilibrium. The classic example is a central heating system. A thermostat constantly measures the temperature and turns on the heat when the temperature drops or turns it off when the desired temperature is reached.

Figure 15 : Maze

Embodying the Square

In aikido practice, the square is embodied by a pin, when the *aikidoka* controls *uke* and leads him to the ground by going to his knees. Technically, the square is the key to controlling someone through immobilization.

In *AikiCom* practice, the square is experienced physically by placing ourselves in a standing, stable position and turning our attention to the quality of our contact with the ground. Your right foot is forward as in the *hanmi no kamae* stance, but your arms are placed parallel to your body as if your hands were resting on two large balls on the ground on either side of you. Your knees are slightly bent to accentuate the stable position.

Figure 16 : Taking a square stance

The square is not a way of fleeing from interaction. If I choose not to react, this decision must often be accompanied by a commitment (personal or expressed to the other person) to put the situation back on the table. If not, we fill our ever-growing "bag" of unresolved incidents.

It may be helpful to remember that immobility does not mean absence of movement. To remain standing, I make countless micromovements and microcorrections to keep myself vertical. Complete immobility is death. As long as I am alive, there is movement.

The square leads us to "do nothing," which is different from not doing anything. Far from "doing nothing" in the sense of *putting up with* something, this is "doing nothing" in an active way. In the square shape, there is always a notion of stability. When I listen to someone who is beside himself and who is shouting angrily at me—for example, someone who has lost someone close—I can receive his energy in an actively positive way, that is, by being fully there, present, and listening. This is radically different from just *being* there, with your body, while your mind wanders elsewhere. To receive the other person's emotion, I must be stable. Otherwise, I will be unbalanced and I risk getting caught up in his emotion. Lacking stability, I can be pulled with him into the ocean of his feelings.

The square is used to decrease the ambient energetic charge. When the exchange happens with great intensity, it can be necessary to choose this shape, which calms the energy just a little. This will be the case especially when we must face someone who is angry. We must make a distinction between the "square" choice that we make when facing a person who is angry (to offer him stable listening), and the sort of calm that we display that contrasts too much with what the person is experiencing and that often has the effect of increasing the person's anger.

The square is the shape of all attitudes of empathy, true listening (not the kind where we are already preparing our next response) or when we rephrase what we have just heard in order to give the other person the deep feeling of having been heard. This is also agreement on a non-verbal level, which encourages the other person to express himself further. This is useful if the energy of the exchange is great enough to feed it—and possibly end up exhausting or emptying it—to go to the very limit of what must be said and to arrive at true silence, a silence that speaks, a silence that communicates just like the "immobile movement" that is symbolized by the square.

> Delay
> Disregard an absurd attack
> Let aggressive energy exhaust itself
> Solid, Stable
> Take a stance
> Security
> Anchor, Root
> Foundation

Figure 17 : The Square

At its extreme, when it is off center, the square is the shape that is experienced by someone who is discouraged, depressed, or unmotivated. It is the shape of the absence of energy, the shape of giving up.

In short, the square is an energetic shape that is particularly appropriate in the following situations:

- If, at the moment when conflict breaks out, I do not feel like I am in an appropriate internal state, if I feel tired, or in a state of health that is not optimal, or an emotional state that does not let me be in full possession of my resources.
- If the emotional intensity is too strong. If the person in front of me is angry and visibly beside himself, I have every interest in letting him express his anger while making sure to remain very stable so that I do not let myself be knocked over by the flood of energy. When this flood of energy has "dried out," I can start the exchange over again on a healthier base.
- Under the effects of alcohol, coffee, or medicine, etc.
- If the place or the moment are inappropriate: people who are present, circumstances, etc.
- If I clearly do not have the time to carry on a discussion.
- If I perceive that the situation that I am experiencing touches something strong or deep within me, or that reminds me of incidents and inner crises that have not been resolved, or have been poorly resolved.

Decoding and Choice Grid

The Aiki fundamental options of action can be used as a decoding grid to better understand how exchanges take place, but they also constitute a framework within which we choose how we want to act. Through practice, you will discover the power and simplicity of this model.

The Three Shapes Are Present Within Us

It is essential to really understand that the three shapes are always in us. Of course, we all have our preferences. These depend on context, on our energy, and on our temperament. A proactive person, full of energy, ambitious, who wants to move forward, will naturally be inclined to use, and even *ab*use, the triangle, while a discouraged person will prefer the square and the diplomat will prefer the circle.

Let's not forget that these shapes interest us only in terms of energy. It is energy that I will inject (triangle) into the interaction and it is energy that will transform (circle) the interaction or calm it (square). This management of energy will be carried out through our words (the content of the discussion, what we want to say), our tone of voice, or our physical posture.

The structure of *Aikido* techniques is a sequence of the three forms in this order : triangle → circle → square. Every *Aikido* movement contains this sequence, even if one or several of these shapes may appear less prominent at a given moment.

The sequence of shapes determines the transformation process of a system that is balanced at first and is subject to a disturbance (triangle) whose energy is then transformed (circle) to lead the system to a new state of equilibrium and stabilize it in a new state (square). The energetic equilibrium between the various shapes allows us to avoid an excess of each of them.

Too much triangle can damage the system and too little will not disturb the balance of the system. The circle transforms the energy of the triangle and would turn endlessly if it were not followed by the square, which does not remain eternally idle because it is eventually followed by a triangle. With this sequence, we find a continuous cycle of change that passes through points of stability that are only temporary. This is an application of the notion of impermanence that is so precious to Buddhists. There is no final shape. Each of them leads to the next.

> Lou is nine years old. His behavior is what we would generally describe as sullen. His sister Lea likes to take advantage of this character trait. When she wants to get rid of her brother, she doesn't hesitate to provoke him, knowing that Lou will fall into her trap until the moment when one of their parents asks Lou to calm down. Convinced that he is in the right, Lou feels like the victim of an injustice and without finding the words to say it, shuts himself in his room, only to come out several hours later, if nobody comes to get him before then. When he switches to this state, Lou falls into a square energy state that immobilizes him. All alone, he has a hard time getting out of it. He needs some triangle to breathe the necessary energy into him that will allow him to recover emotionally and mentally in his movement.

AikiCom: Testing through Conflict

Randori

To understand how *AikiCom* can help us to transform our life, we must return to its source, the martial combat of aikido.

An aikido practitioner trains to face combat situations. His training is carried out in a secure environment, the *dojo*, and while respecting *reishiki*, the set of rules that deal with respect and the smooth running of training sessions. While an aikido class is always conducted in the same way—the instructor presents a technique and the students then practice it with a partner—*jiyu waza* is free practice in which students can test the fluidity of their execution of movements as they come. When there are several attackers, we call it *randori*. The aikidoka will execute defense techniques according to the attack, its speed, or the proximity of the attackers. An experienced aikidoka does not choose the technique that he will execute. The technique emerges by itself; it flows from the moment. The angle of an elbow, the height of a strike, a foot that is farther forward than the other, so many countless clues that lead to the right movement. An aware mind could never process so many parameters in so little time. Because there is no imposed form, *randori* reveals the integration of aikido principles within the practitioner. A well-executed *randori* becomes a harmonious martial ballet. Poorly executed, it can transform into mimicry of violent and aggressive combat.

The main lesson of *randori* is to make us discover how we can maintain control of ourselves and develop our flow in order to absorb the series of attacks, one after the other, while staying centered and moving in a way that keeps us from ever being surprised.

When an aikidoka gets up to stand in the center of the *tatami* before a *randori*, he first takes on the *Aiki* attitude by centering himself and coming back to his verticality. This position puts him in an observational attitude with a wide field of view. He can thus have a more global view of his environment and size up the attackers who have taken their places around him. Then comes the moment of the first attack. Either it will flow spontaneously or it will be provoked by the aikidoka, by approaching one of the attackers so he can force him into action. In this case, it becomes difficult to know who really initiated the movement. The blending of energy is already at work. Attack, movement, unbalancing, throw. New movement, new attack, unbalancing and throwing, putting the aikidoka in a new position facing the next attacker. The people taking part in the *randori* quickly form a nebula of energy where there is no longer a distinction between cause and effect, and where energy leads movement. The aikidoka is an orchestra conductor. He is not pressured by the attacks, he receives them. He assures harmony, sets the tempo, and chooses the next entry. Through centering and verticality, he remains present in the action. Through movement, he creates the conditions that put him in contact with "the universe" surrounding him, and in this way he also connects with the energy of the attackers. His movements are circular and his breathing blends with them. Very quickly, time no longer exists. In any case, it no longer exists as *Xronos*, time that passes, clock time. All that is left is *Kairos*, the right time, the present moment that calls for the right movement. In aikido, the term *de-ai* calls to mind this very moment. In Kyudo, the Japanese martial art of archery, we talk about *hanari* (or *hanare*), the moment when the archer has drawn his bow and feels that he can no longer hold back the energy of the arrow. He does not decide to release the arrow; he feels that the time is ripe. It is now. Afterwards, it will be too late. *Randori* is a series of *hanari*. Time and space join together to the point where the aikidoka feels the attack coming from behind him without having seen it. He pivots from the hips and his hand goes exactly where his attacker's hand does. Neither magic nor miracle, it's all about the harmony that is manifested by the synchronicity of the movements of each of them and their integration in the flow of the overall movement.

The *Aiki* attitude is present at every moment during the *randori*. Before the attack, it puts us in a state of receptivity that keeps us from being surprised, a state of vigilance without tension that makes us perceive without flinching. Verticality assures a 360° presence (or almost). No preference, no anticipated choice. Plunged into *sho shin,* the beginner's mind, ready for discovery.

When the attack is launched—but I could also say when the moment of the encounter happens, this moment when we naturally go toward the other person or he comes toward us—we turn ourselves in the direction of the action. The space is no longer neutral; it is "turned toward." The energy is focused, even though we still have an awareness of the environment.

Just before the encounter, when the strike reveals all its threat and risk of injury—even death—we avoid switching to our reptilian survival reflexes by moving ourselves off the line of danger. We are no longer there, where we were. The attack now heads toward emptiness. This moment is fleeting because the attacker will quickly notice our absence. Before he recovers and starts a new attack, we have already moved and the absence of tension has made our movement so flowing that the attacker hardly notices it, or notices it too late. By avoiding the attack with a rough movement, we would attract far more attention from the other person, leading to a more rapid counterattack. Instead, we make the movement in a continuous way, like water avoiding a rock in the river. It is certainly not a movement of retreat or withdrawal. On the contrary, it "penetrates the flesh" and goes to the heart of things, thus applying the *irimi* principle. The movement did not aim to retreat, which would allow a new attack. It goes toward the center of the attack and the attacker. Going to meet him. Going toward him to enter into connection, to join together. At this moment, the attacker is already no longer an attacker, but a partner, our accomplice in regaining harmony.

As long as the connection has not been established, the situation will remain dangerous, threatening, and uncertain. Nobody knows who will attack first or how he will attack. This uncertainty is a source of tension and opens the door to our reptilian survival behaviors. Our connection to the other person creates a space that favors change. It joins us together, secures us, and embodies this system that is formed by the two of us.

Until now, we have been talking about several principles of the *Aiki* attitude: presence, verticality, observation, choice of direction, intervention by going off the line of danger, and finally connection of our center to that of the attacker, through the principle of *irimi*. The attacker becomes our partner in a connection that will allow us to redirect the energy, to guide it, and to transform it.

Aiki technique begins by causing an imbalance that will put the partner-attacker out of his state of equilibrium. If the attacker remains stable, he will stay in his position, "stuck" in his role of attacker. To bring about a change, we create a situation that is uncomfortable enough to lead the other person to discover something new, a new attitude, by showing him the uselessness of his attack. This attitude is that of cooperation, of kindness.

Here is a broad outline of the *Aiki* attitude and its fulfillment in action:
- Centering and verticality
- Presence in the world (perception, observation, vigilance without tension)
- Turning in the direction of the action
- Getting off the line of danger
- Connecting with the center (*irimi* principle)
- Causing an imbalance that will bring the attacker out of his state of equilibrium (condition for transformation)
- Transformation through the blending of energies, to lead the other person to a new experience (attack is useless, kindness is the path of a new experience)

In the *Aiki* process, we do not try to change the other person. We create an experience that lets him see the alternatives to the attack, by revealing its ineffectiveness. Our partner keeps his freedom to choose, but has experienced that something else is possible and that we are open to dialogue, to cooperation. Wanting to change the other person amounts to denying him the right to fully be a person, with his three centers and his verticality, an autonomous being. We enter the domain of manipulation. Premise Number 4 leads us to mutual respect. In concrete situations of conflict, this can be quite a challenge.

The aikidoka's stability is not rooted in immobility. His combat is far from being a war of position or trench warfare. Aikido develops the skill of being stable within mobility. A moving target is more difficult to hit. The aikido master becomes unreachable, untouchable, but nevertheless very present. By throwing the first attacker, the aikidoka creates a shield that will disturb the coming attacks and his circular movements will let him get imperceptibly close to the next attacker before he even feels ready to attack. *Randori* ends when the attackers give up their attack. The battle has lost its meaning and stops, without there being a winner or loser.

Randoris, as they are performed in aikido dojos, illustrate how life is when it is lived in the *Aiki* attitude. This is what we could call the *randori of life*. Let's look at how we can apply the principles of *randori* to a series of circumstances that are clearly more connected to our daily life.

Physical Aggression

In a situation that degenerates until it comes to blows, the *Aiki* attitude leads us to first center ourselves, to get back in touch with our verticality in a way that increases our presence and shows the person in front of us that we are there. We reveal ourselves to be a person rather than an object or a target. It has nothing to do with an aggressive or confrontational presence. We simply try to say, "I am here." Convinced that the battle is in vain, we have already begun to transform the aggressiveness, the violence, into something different.

Into what? We do not yet know. Everything depends on the situation. It is astonishing to see how much the act of taking on the *Aiki* attitude sometimes helps us to avoid a fight without doing anything else. A person who is present in his body and in the moment can discourage certain attackers who prefer to choose a victim who is more distracted, vague, or busy. Sometimes, there is something instinctive in the behavior of an attacker, who will not be tempted to fight unless he has judged that he has a chance to win. When faced with a person who is turning confidently toward him, many attackers will have doubts and will possibly look for an easier target.

If the fight must still take place, it will be a repetition of movements that have been executed during randoris: centering, verticality, getting off the line of danger, connection, unbalancing, then throwing or pinning.

The Verbal Attack

The second case is that of the verbal attack. This is not about responding to a strike or an arm grab, but rather to a verbal attack, a hurtful word, an insult, or a particularly painful criticism. This sort of attack is clearly more frequent than physical attacks. They cause psychological, moral, or emotional wounds that are sometimes as painful as physical injuries—and often more long-lasting. Harassment has become a scourge in the workplace and sometimes causes irreparable harm. A couple living in a close relationship also offers a field of combat for particularly biting words that cause numerous emotional scars that can remain for years.

AikiCom leads us to work with a verbal attack in the same way we do with a physical attack. When I was talking about centering, I emphasized the impossibility and uselessness of being permanently centered. Living in the *Aiki* attitude does not transform us into disciplined ascetics who control, at every moment, everything that happens inside us while moving through the world on the lookout for a surprise attack. When we live, we speak, act, think, and feel. Then comes an event, an incident, a word, or an attitude that attracts our attention and draws us out of our daily routine, out of the predictable flow of life. At that moment, I have a choice to either pay attention to it or set it aside, along with the deluge of sensorial stimuli that engulf us.

Let's take the situation where you are in a discussion with James, a work colleague. You calmly converse about the weather and the latest television program, then the conversation comes back to professional goings-on and in particular about a proposal that you are finishing and getting ready to propose to the board of directors. In the middle of a harmless sentence, your attention is drawn by James's tone of voice. Something has obviously changed in him. While you were both lighthearted and calm at the beginning of the discussion, you become aware that he has progressively steered the discussion toward your proposal. You know that he is also preparing one and that they are both in competition. The board of directors will not free up the necessary funds to back both proposals at the same time. You know it and James knows it too. As long as you are working on your proposal, you do not worry any more than usual about the possible resistance or criticism that one of your colleagues might express. The corporate culture in your company has always favored this competition between employees that pushes each one to surpass himself to submit successful and promising proposals. But there, at that moment, having arrived at this point of the discussion, you have felt a change. The mood has changed a little bit. You have the choice to act as though nothing is wrong and continue the discussion or to use this perception to return to the *Aiki* attitude.

By not reacting, it is possible for the discussion to follow its course without leading to an incident, but it is also quite possible that you will be surprised by a verbal attack, a criticism that throws you off balance. You therefore choose to return to yourself, the first step in the process that leads you back to the *Aiki* attitude. First, a deep exhalation that puts you back in touch with your somatic center at the *hara*, then an inhalation that revives the communication between your somatic center, your emotional center, and your cognitive center. Visualization of the vertical flow, which arises from the somatic center and lifts up toward the sky, the seat of (my) values, of what is important to me and which, coming from the abdomen, descends toward the earth, stabilizes me, and connects me to the concrete reality from which I cannot escape, as gravity constantly reminds us. In a few seconds, after several breaths, I have gotten back in touch with my verticality. I am present, here and now, ready for what can happen. I already perceive, with a different acuity, the emotional change in James that I had vaguely felt. It is strong or significant enough for me to decide to turn myself toward him. Through a slight movement, my body turns more clearly toward James. This movement is amplified by the turning of my mental energy, my attention, toward him. Before, I was with him, in a friendly discussion, simply present, but nothing more. A part of my attention was on my cup of coffee and I was aware of the movement of people walking in the hallway, the color of the walls, my thoughts about the day's events. My mind was wandering freely from the words of our discussion to the movements around us. By getting back in touch with my center and my verticality and by turning myself toward James, my mental landscape and my presence have changed. Without truly realizing it, I get in touch with James. My sensory antennas are open and turned toward him, but not only toward him. My attention has turned, but it is not focused, just like my gaze that is not fixed on James, but encompasses him in a wide, panoramic view. This wide view stimulates my peripheral vision rather than my focused vision. This makes me more sensitive to the smallest variations. I am there, ready, available, and attentive without being tense. If I feel muscular tension, I decide to relax it. I feel stable and anchored to the ground but still mobile. I am ready. If James continues the discussion and I see that it is only a false alarm, I will have benefited from this moment to recenter myself, which is entirely beneficial for me. If James leads the discussion in a more aggressive direction, I am ready to act from my center, without being surprised.

Suddenly, James opens fire: "Hey, about this, I think it's too bad that you're devoting so much energy to your proposal while you know for a fact that it has fewer chances than mine.

Everyone knows that you want to benefit from your good relationship with the president to push your proposal through and sink mine!"

It's an all-out attack, direct and rapid, and it would have taken me by surprise if I had not already recentered myself.

Just like a physical attack, a verbal attack can hit and wound, drawing us into our reptilian survival reflexes. Although we are obviously not in the same situation as a hunter who is surprised to see an enormous grizzly coming out of the bushes to attack him, our reaction is nevertheless the same, or at least it is similar. The blow that is received, even if it is only psychological, has the same effect as the slash of a claw. According to my perception of the situation and my temperament, I will react by choosing one of the only three possible choices that my reptilian brain knows: attack, flight, or paralysis. We all have patterns that we prefer. If I have the impression that I am not in a position of strength (this will be the case if James is higher than me in the company hierarchy, for example), I will probably choose flight. I will change the subject of the conversation or I will make up an excuse and pretend to have another obligation so that I can disappear into my office. If I perceive that I have the resources to respond to the attack, in other words if I feel suitably armed, I will tend to counterattack, thus falling into a spiral of violence and aggressiveness. In a professional context like the one that I'm talking about, social mechanisms will inhibit these aggressive attitudes. I therefore risk finding myself back in the third reptilian option: paralysis, prevented by social conventions from using my "weapons," and knocked out without having had the opportunity to react or even to flee.

Fortunately, having returned to the *Aiki* attitude, I can receive this attack in a radically different way.

At the moment when James launches his attack, I make a mental movement, identical to the one that I would make to avoid a physical attack. I get off the line of danger. In concrete terms, I hear his words, I understand his statements, but I perceive them as being sent where I was and where I no longer am. I have moved. The energy of the words brushes by me, but does not reach me. Maybe it will hit me, but I will not be injured because I have moved. I am in movement. I have gotten off the line of danger. What James says does not concern me. It is HIS way of seeing things. He is speaking, not to me, but to a representation of me. This does not lead me to play down his words or act like he hasn't said anything. On the contrary. It is not necessary to let myself be hurt by words to react to them. My reaction comes from a position that is safer, more stable, and not unbalanced. The practice of *Aiki* exercises has physically ingrained in me this feeling of getting off the line of danger to the point of truly feeling that James's harsh words are aimed not at me, but at a representation of me. I no longer need to physically move to avoid the attack. I feel the movement as though I have made it. This movement brings the *irimi* principle to life. I move without backing up. I move by going toward the other person, to connect with him, from center to center. Like a sword striking at me, the words could have injured me. They end up in emptiness, there, where I am not, there, where I no longer am. They no longer interest me, except in a very minor way. Responding to words is like responding to a sword. The sword is not alive and neither are the words. What interests me is the person who is behind them: James. By moving and by connecting myself to his center, I get at the heart of things. The connection from center to center, from *hara* to *hara*, is a connection of presence, from person to person. The connection from emotional center to emotional center is an empathic connection: I go to meet the other person's emotion without letting myself be overcome or unbalanced by it. The connection from cognitive center to cognitive center is the center of what will become a debate of ideas and discussion, as well as shared understandings and misunderstandings. In the present case, it is the person-to-person connection that interests me because it is essential. The somatic center protects us from emotional and mental imbalances. Positioned lower in the body, it assures me a greater stability, but above all it connects me with my being and with the other person—two connected human beings. It is the space of our needs as persons, in all our humanity: respect, justice, listening, relationship, integrity, etc. By connecting myself to the other person—from somatic center to somatic center—I can once again see the other person as a human being. Before that, as long as I was in the line of danger, I saw only the attacker and the attack, which draws me into "survival" mode and activates my reptilian reflexes. I was incapable of having the least bit of empathy for him. He was only an enemy to strike down or at least neutralize. By moving, I have remained myself and I can go to meet him without resorting to combat. The question that automatically emerges is then, "What makes a reasonable, balanced person like James say that?" "What need is he trying to satisfy?" "What unmet need leads him to say that?"

Off the line of danger, connected from center to center, I take care to establish and maintain a relationship that offers the best security possible in this context. I could respond by a counterattack, but I choose to act in harmony with *Aiki* principles. Defeating the other person is not my goal. I do not try to harm him or humiliate him. Returning to a mood of healthy cooperation seems infinitely more efficient to me. James is my colleague; we have been working together for several years, and that will not end today. An aggressive counterattack would only inflame the situation and would damage our working relationship. If I win this battle, it's a good bet that this will lead to a war that would exhaust us needlessly.

James is worried about his proposal and no longer sees me as a colleague but as a competitor. To react harshly would reinforce him in this position. If possible, I prefer to bring him back to a place of cooperation.

> "James, we have been working together for almost ten years. You know just as well as I do that the energy that we invest in this sort of proposal is not lost if the proposal is not accepted. It brings us extraordinary experience that we can use again in all our future projects. We both know that we are each doing our best so that our proposal will be successful and that only one of them will be accepted. Just like you, I know the discouragement that we can feel at the idea of seeing a proposal that takes up our time, almost day and night, put on the shelf at a board meeting. It is difficult for this not to leave a bad taste in your mouth—all this energy wasted for nothing. But justifiably, you and I know that it is not for nothing. That would be to forget the pleasure of having worked it out and created it from nothing. The experience makes us even more effective in our future proposals.
> As for the question of my workplace relationships, I feel a bit vexed that you are bringing that up and I blame it on your anxiety, which is completely understandable. I know that you find it totally reasonable to spread the word around the office about a proposal that is dear to us. Not to do it would be to kill it off. You also know how strict the members of the board are and that they won't choose one project over another just to please one of us. They handle the company's finances and it's their heads on the block.
> So far, nothing tells us that my proposal has a better chance than yours to succeed. You explained to me the difficulties that you're running into now with your proposal and I understand that it gives you doubts. It's frustrating, and I've already gone through the same thing. I am ready to talk about it with you if you want, but not this way. Is that okay with you?"

My response blends with James's words. The energy of his words is used to my advantage to start a circular movement that transforms their meaning and reconnects them to other elements of our common experience: the learning that we acquire during the development of our prototypes, our pleasure in creating and building, and our knowledge of this competitive style of development that inevitably leads to one of the proposals in contention being dropped. Other elements are: enthusiastic communication with the decision-makers who will have to choose a proposal, the difficulties that are encountered during the creative process, and the frustrations that they bring. The discussion transforms the attack from a focus on persons in opposition into a focus on similarity of interests, on a work style that aims for excellence and whose price is known to all: the rejection of one of the paths in order to develop the proposal that is being retained.

If James can hear my words, he can return to proposals that are more equitable and our collaboration can go on without one of us feeling like he's up against the ropes or has been dealt a knockout blow.

A new balance can be found.

The *Aiki* movement started with the application of the *irimi* principle. By getting off the line of danger, I mobilized my energy into the shape of a triangle. I came into contact with his center. Rather than extending the triangle into a hurtful counterattack, I chose to switch to circle energy by reframing the meaning of what had been said. Through my movement, the energy of the initial attack ended up on the tangent, which fed the rotational movement. The result puts us in a new state of equilibrium that promotes our collaboration. The relationship has gone to square energy, which assures the continuation of activities in the new state of equilibrium. This state will last until a future incident will require us to find a new equilibrium.

incident leading to a new unbalance will require to find a new equilibrium..

The *Aiki* attitude blends perfectly with the process that is taught in non-violent communication. To refresh your memory, non-violent communication, created by Marshall B. Rosenberg, advises us to communicate while respecting a four-part process:

- Observation: describe the facts—what we see or hear—in order to distinguish what we observe from what we think about the situation

- Expression of feelings, of felt emotion, which expresses a need that is either met or not met
- Expression of needs: in nonviolent communication, a need is what brings us more life; certain needs are vital and others bring us security or more fulfillment
- Request: offer to connect or offer an action; be proactive

AikiCom adds a step that is a prerequisite to this NVC communication process: get off the line of danger. Without this, we risk being hit or injured and turning to our reptilian reflexes. By avoiding being hit with the full force of the attack—or what seems like an attack to us—we remain safe so that we can apply the four-part process. We take it upon ourselves to satisfy our need for security to initiate the NVC process, which will satisfy our needs for kindness, attention, openness, expression, empathy, and still more.

Having avoided the energy that is coming toward me—and, let me repeat, it has to do with my *perception* of what is happening—I can connect with the other person's energy. I connect from my center to his center, which is the seat of his needs and the cause of his action. The notion of need in the NVC meaning of the term is very close to the notion of positive intent in NLP. It allows us to "accept" an action, even an aggressive one, and remain *Aiki*, that is, to not give in to the temptation to counterattack. It leads me to go to meet the other person and to seek him at his source: at the need that he is trying to meet. Our needs are universal and I will of course recognize myself in this need because I share it by the very fact of being a human being just like him. I deliberately set aside the option of aggression, which I know will not bring the expected solution. I do not respond to it and I choose to lead the other person to new ground, that of the expression of our expectations, of our needs and about the way to find together a solution that respects the parties involved. I thus remain myself, centered, present to myself, and I give the other person the opportunity to come back fully to himself in his center. The violence very often loses its meaning and the dialogue begins again on a radically different level. But this will not always be the case. If the other person is not clear with himself, if he has dishonest intentions, if he has what may be called a "hidden agenda," the discussion will come to nothing, for the good and simple reason that it does not address the question, the dispute, the real reason underlying the conflict. The failed attack will then no doubt be followed by a new attack to which we will respond by again trying to bring to light the heart of the problem, and so on, until we realize that there is no favorable outcome to hope for and that this relationship is not what it seems to be.

Internal Conflict

Do I do my work or do I continue to watch this television program? Do I call Steven or do I wait for him to call back? Do I clearly say what I'm thinking or do I bite my tongue out of fear of his reaction? A day does not go by that we are not faced with these kinds of internal conflicts. This sort of conflict takes very diverse forms. Sometimes it's a choice between two alternatives that make us oscillate from one to the other and lock us into an infinite loop. Sometimes we remain undecided when we are faced with several options. We are looking for information that will help us to act. We find ourselves a bit like a swimmer who is caught in a river's whirlpool. He wants to move forward but he cannot. The rotational force of the whirlpool makes him spin around and his efforts are in vain. The waves keep him prisoner and keep him from moving forward. This is the whirlpool of our thoughts. The more we are irritated by the situation, the more the whirlpool grows in strength. Every effort seems doomed to failure. And often it is at the moment when we give up the struggle that the solution appears on the horizon. The waters become calm and a way out suddenly seems to open up for us. Here we are again in calm waters.

Internal conflict is similar to external conflict. Each thought, each emotion is like an enemy, an opponent. It's a little as though "I" were many. Many parts of me are struggling to impose their point of view. The more energy I put into the fight, the more fierce it is. This is the fast track to exhaustion. The *Aiki* attitude leads me to transform the internal struggle into a dialogue. Far more than in the case of a conflict with another person, I can become aware that each of these parts in conflict is part of a greater whole: me. In reality, there is no enemy, there are only partners. Each opposing energy is a part of me and it is up to me to find or restore the harmony that will again make me feel whole and fully myself.

The process is similar to a battle between two opponents on an aikido *tatami*. First find your verticality, come back to yourself through centering. Breathing creates the practice space, the internal *tatami* where these parts of me that are in conflict will move around. A full, deep breath contributes to reducing tension, opening up the opposing parts by putting them in contact, favoring communication. I then turn my attention to each of these parts. What do they want? What is important for them? What's their intent? Is there a way for them to satisfy their individual intentions while respecting the other parts involved? Each option is the best solution that can be found by a part of ourselves in order to satisfy something that is important to us. When I want to be clear with Steven, it is spontaneity that I want. I want to say what I am thinking, freely. I want to be myself. When I bite my tongue, it is out of fear of tainting our longstanding friendship, but it is also from wanting to please, to be liked. By exploring my internal landscape, I can reconcile these parts of myself and discover the intense feeling of a true relationship, in sincerity rather than in what has been left unsaid. I can recall previous experiences where I became more and more afraid of speaking and in fact this fear of a negative reaction was quite often stronger than the reaction itself. Most of the time when I was expressing myself sincerely—that is, from my heart—the other person could easily welcome my remarks even if they were difficult to hear. Speaking from my heart—without confusing sincerity with simply saying anything and everything, and especially any*how*—truly contributes to nurturing this true relationship that is so important to me. In this internal *randori*, the two opposing parts—the one who wants to speak and the one who wants to remain silent—meet in a new space, that of a true relationship that allows words and eases fear by nurturing the intense pleasure of being true and being in a sincere relationship. This new choice respects each of them and brings a deep reassurance. The fight has changed into a creative process that leads to a choice in which I find myself reunited, reintegrated, and reharmonized. I can go to meet Steven starting from myself, in verticality.

Struggling against Events

> Train strike today. My professional situation is critical and very tense. I cannot allow myself a day off and the idea of getting bogged down in endless bottlenecks brings down my morale. I could leave very early, but that would cost me, given my exhausting insomnia caused by my work-related stress. I very quickly end up cursing the unions, the railroad workers, the union representatives who defend rigid positions without making any concessions, the bosses who only think of saving their jobs or reaping personal benefits, my own bosses who chose to put the company in the most inaccessible part of town, my wife who wanted us to live in the country, in short, the entire world.

I only see the black clouds of the difficult situation that I am going through and this only adds another layer to what I am experiencing. I'm thinking about burnout, I'm thinking about giving up everything and taking a year off, but quickly family, social, and financial obligations come to mind and bring out a fit of anxiety in me. All this because of this darned train strike! Fighting against events that we have no power or control over is like Don Quixote tilting against windmills. The fight is lost before we even begin.

We need to feel that we have a minimum of control over what happens to us. Of course, when growing up, we learned that not everything is possible, that the world does not obey us. Premise No. 1 takes on its full meaning here. To move with the flow of events is to stop running into walls, accepting what we cannot change. *Aiki* work consists of transforming this passive, painful energy into an energy of life and learning that leads us to Premise No. 2. As Guy Corneau[140] said when talking about relationship conflicts: "In a couple, we do not evolve in the same way or at the same rhythm. Inevitably, there is friction." He adds with a knowing wink, "But this friction is what makes us feel alive, isn't it?" We need to encounter obstacles in order to find direction in our journey. This is the information that gives meaning to our path, to not doze off at the steering wheel of our life.

---

[140] Guy Corneau in a conference held at Namur, Belgium, following the publication of his book *N'y a-t-il pas d'amour heureux*, 2004.

Driving on a highway is an efficient way to travel large distances, but it is a dull, boring way to drive. And even the countryside joins with this monotony. On the contrary, when we drive on a winding back road, we are fully present. We watch our speed, slow down when approaching a curve to negotiate it smoothly, then get back to the optimum speed before the next curve. I can see each turn as a limitation or I can welcome it as an opportunity to follow the flow of things. In a decidedly less rural way, when I am stopped in a line of traffic at rush hour, I can decide to grumble and curse the authorities who do nothing to improve the transportation system, the other drivers (who should take public transportation), or my son who made me lose the precious ten minutes that would have allowed me to avoid this bottleneck. Or I could become aware of the contact of my hands on the steering wheel, of my breathing, of my presence in the car, looking around me and maybe smiling at the driver in the lane next to mine. Whatever my choice, the line of traffic will not move more quickly. In this sort of situation, I am the only one responsible for deciding if I want to fight against the situation or integrate it into the current of my experience and turn it into an opportunity for learning, for presence, or quite simply turn it into a moment for reflection.

Chapter 5

The *Aiki* Attitude

A Philosophy of Life

*A**ikiCom* is essential as an effective practice to live in a world that is not always easy. We struggle to manage conflict, be assertive, or understand the meaning of a retort. No doubt, this is what attracts people who lack the tools to defend themselves better, and no longer want to be pushed around. But *AikiCom's* reach would be very limited if it were only a tool box for conflict management. *AikiCom* succeeds in being both anchored in the reality of daily life and being a true philosophy of life. I will attempt to explain the basics of it to you by relying on the thoughts, models, and views of different authors who have all, in their own way, contributed to the *Aiki* process. I will begin with a philosopher who is known for his study of reciprocity: Martin Buber.

Martin Buber's Reciprocity

In his work *I and Thou,* Martin Buber sheds a lot of light on the profound nature of what I call the *Aiki* attitude. This serves as a basis for a true philosophy of life. Buber's doctrine is that the human being is defined by its encounter with a *You*. This *You* can be a thing or a person.

This encounter has nothing to do with our empirical discovery of the world that leads us to develop our knowledge. This discovery is an exploration of the surface of things, an analysis of its characteristics, its properties, and its behaviors. The things are then objects, the object of our process of exploration. This is the world of transitive verbs. I look at this, I handle that. This empirical learning about things is external but also includes internal experiences. This exploration is the exploration of the world of *It*, of *He*, of *She*. I know things and people empirically. For example, Martine has blond hair and she talks quickly. As long as I am distinguishing characteristics, I am in an *I-It* relationship, a subject-object relationship. This has nothing to do with the *I-You* relationship, which, according to Buber, is the foundation of the human being.

When *I* encounter a *You*, there is no longer a subject or an object. The *I-You* relationship is an encounter in reciprocity. It is an encounter with the totality of the person. No concept intervenes, no image, no memory. The part yields to the whole. The encounter does not take place in action. It seems passive, yet it cannot happen without the *I*. The encounter happens in the moment, in the present. In presence. Between *I* and *You*, there is no goal, no purpose, no means. We go from objective unity—that of subject and object—to a living presence.

This encounter can happen with a person, an object, and even an idea. If I look at a tree, I can judge its height, examine its leaves, the shape of its branches. I can also characterize it, name it, quantify it. Doing this, I am in the *I-It* relationship mode[141].

However, it is possible that under certain conditions I can be touched emotionally by this tree, that I will enter into a relationship with it. It then ceases to be an *It*. I am then struck by the power of what

---

[141] Martin Buber, *I and Thou*, page 58.

is unique about it. Its characteristics are still there but they are no longer distinct. The tree is in a relationship with me just as I am in a relationship with it. Every relationship is reciprocity. However, Buber warns us not to look for some form of awareness or soul in the tree. In this encounter, the tree cannot be seen through its qualities or parts, whether we are talking about its soul, its shape, its color, etc. What presents itself to me (as the *I*) is the tree itself, in its entirety.

When the encounter is with a person, it is the same but this experience of immediacy is more fuzzy because it is experienced in terms of feeling.

When I enter into a relationship with a person, the fundamental *I-You* connection is established, which results in the *other* no longer being a thing among things but a being among beings. He is not made of things or of characteristics; there is no more size, hair color, or eye color. "He is You and fills the firmament.[142]" *I* recognizes *You* in reciprocity and a dialogue is established.

The encounter with an idea—with a form—is, according to Buber, the eternal source of art.

> *"This is the eternal origin of art that a human being confronts a form that wants to become a work through him. Not a figment of his soul but something that appears to the soul and demands the soul's creative power. What is required is a deed that a man does with his whole being: if he commits it and speaks with his being the basic word [I-You] to the form that appears, then the creative power is released and the work comes into being."*[143]

This *I-You* relationship is far from being a mental abstraction, Buber tells us. It needs a body; it is incarnate. If not, it would only be an ethereal form of the *I-It* relationship, a product of our empirical experimentation, an experience in the world of ideas that constructs for us a representation whose goal is to escape from a certain commonplace mediocrity, the fruit of the absence of a living relationship. This conceptual world brings a certain comfort but let's not fool ourselves: it belongs to the world of *It*.

---

[142] *Ibid.*, page 59.
[143] *Ibid.*, page 60.

Aiki practice physically illustrates Buber's words. Aikido can be practiced in an *I-It* relational mode. Techniques are discovered and analyzed in order to execute them. They are named, catalogued, explained, and become a part of the set of movements to execute in order to be awarded a higher rank, *kyu* (from white belt through brown belt) or *dan* (black belt ranks).

Aikido is practiced on a *tatami* that brings together dozens of practitioners whom one knows more or less well and who display in a more or less visible way their level of experience (colored belt or *hakama*, the pant-skirt worn by aikidokas). When the teacher has presented a technique, the practitioners get up, choose a partner, and practice until the next technique. *I-It* practice is analytical. We try to reproduce the characteristics of the movement: the hand is placed here, you move there. The interaction with your partner also falls within this empirical approach: he was not chosen by chance. His size, his level of practice, the fact that you know him, that he is a man or a woman, an acquaintance or a stranger, his characteristics will make him a more or less suitable partner with whom the aikidoka can develop his empirical knowledge of *Aiki* movement.

But *Aiki* practice lies above all within the *I-You*. It then becomes a privileged space for *I-You* encounters. When the teacher has finished the demonstration of the movement and the students get up to find and go toward another partner, the magic of the encounter can happen. If this magic happens more through spontaneity than through a deliberate process, the practitioner's state of mind can create the conditions to favor its emergence. As Buber says, the *I* must go to meet the *You*. The *I-You* relationship is not an experience that one is subjected to, it requires putting oneself in the conditions of the encounter without necessarily giving rise to it. The process of centering and verticality leads us into the domain of the potential encounter. It is there that the magic can happen: time is suspended, causality vanishes, there is no longer an attack, a defense, an *uke*, or a *tori*. No more characteristic, no more belt, no more level, no more size. The person encounters another person, in his global nature. There is no more action; everything is action.

The *I-You* encounter is *kimusubi*[144] of aikido.

Vital energies and living beings are connected. The energies are blended. This is the reversal that Ueshiba, the founder of aikido, talks about. The transition from the *I-It* world to the *I-You* world is the inversion of the primacy of the physical body (what Ueshiba called the "body of flesh") with that of the spiritual body, the transition from the temporal and causal to the timeless, to synchronicity. When Ueshiba says that the movement springs forth, Buber responds that "here I and You confront each other freely in a reciprocity that is not involved in or tainted by any causality; here man finds guaranteed the freedom of his being and of being.[145]"

Buber asserts that *I* needs *You* in order to be fulfilled. In this excerpt from his work, he writes what Morihei Ueshiba could have written:

> *"The fiery matter of all my capacity to will surging intractably, everything possible for me revolving primevally, intertwined and seemingly inseparable, the alluring glances of potentialities flaring up from every corner, the universe as a temptation, and I, born in an instant, both hands into the fire, deep into it, where the one that intends me is hidden, my deed, seized: now! And immediately the menace of the abyss is subdued; no longer a coreless multiplicity at play in the iridescent equality of its claims; but only two are left alongside each other, the other and the one, delusion and task[146]."*

In the preface to Martin Buber's book, Gaston Bachelard highlights the vectorial character of Buber's approach: "It is thus in the domain of vectors and not in the domain of points and centers that we have to put ourselves...The I and the You are not separable poles.[147]" Quoting Fichte, who said that a man is only a man when he is among other men, Bachelard highlights one of Buber's messages: The *You* is the most

---

[144] *Kimusubi* comes from ki, the energy of life and musu(bi), the connection, the node. *Kimusubi* can be understood in aikido as being the union of two partners, a state in which Ueshiba said that there was nothing to do but to be there. We find this paradoxical union between action and passiveness.
[145] Martin Buber, *I and Thou*, page 100.
[146] *Ibid.*, page 101.
[147] Translated from Bachelard's forward to the French version of Buber's *I and Thou*, page 29.

basic attribute of the *I*. Without *You*, there is no *I*. The *Aiki* approach leads us to this through practice with a partner on a *tatami*. There is no individual practice. The magic only happens in interaction, in the encounter with the *other*, this *You* who is indispensable to me for me to be an *I*. Without experiencing this relationship, what is the flavor of things? In the world of *It*, what remains is mechanistic.

"Infinite things like the sky, the forest and light only find their name in a loving heart."[148]

What makes the *I-You* relationship unique with respect to the *I-It* relationship is reciprocity.

> *"This reciprocity is never clearly found on the I-It axis. It only truly appears on the axis where the I-You oscillates and vibrates. So yes, the person who is encountered worries about me like I worry about him; he hopes in me like I hope in him. I create him as a person at the very time when he creates me as a person.*[149]*"*

Isn't this the clearest definition of what love is? Without a doubt, if you distinguish between love and feelings. On this subject, Buber offers us an interesting distinction between love and feelings in terms of container and contents. Thus the *I-You* relationship is that of love without feelings. It encompasses the human being and is achieved through the *I-You* encounter in its reciprocity. From this relationship can emerge feelings that reside within the human being:

"Feelings dwell in man, but man dwells in his love. This is no metaphor but actuality: love does not cling to an I, as if the You were merely its 'content' or object; it is between I and You.[150]"

Thus, if feelings accompany the love relationship that is the *I-You*, they are not its substance. Morihei Ueshiba speaks in the same way when he talks about universal love—symbolized by the *Ai* of *Aiki*—which connects beings and the universe and is the purpose of his art of aikido.

To us, these considerations can seem particularly disconnected from our everyday reality. However, they are not so disconnected as it would seem. Juliette Tournand offers us a practical version of this in

---

[148] Ibid.
[149] Ibid.
[150] Martin Buber, *Je et Tu,* French version of *I and Thou*, page 47.

her book *La Stratégie de la bienveillance* (Strategy of Kindness). The concrete model that she develops is based on Robert Axelrod's reflections in his book *The Evolution of Cooperation*. This is in line with Martin Buber's thinking and confirms the pertinence of the *Aiki* attitude in the spirit of what Morihei Ueshiba wanted to pass on to us.

The Quadrants of Kindness

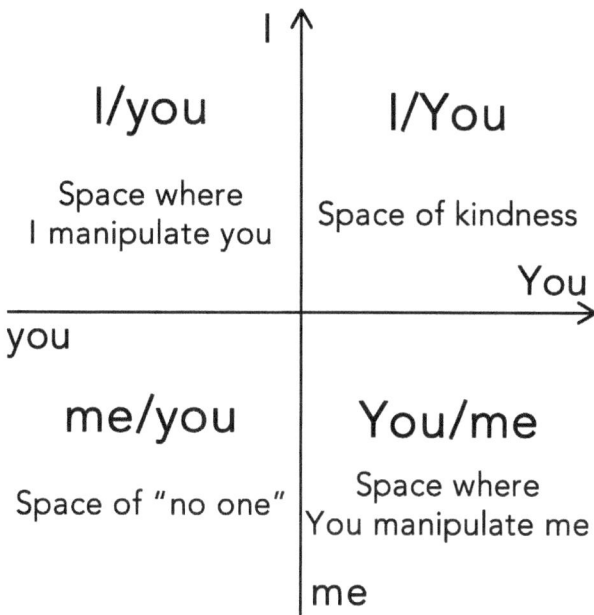

Figure 18 : The Quadrants of Kindness

Juliette Tournand defines the space in which we interact in the form of a grid that illustrates, in a very interesting way, Premises 3, 4, and 5 of the *Aiki* attitude. Two axes divide the space into four quadrants: the *I-me* axis and the *You-you*[151] axis. The *I* dimension is the one of my full presence as a person. This is "who I am" in my verticality, in my values (sky), my thoughts (cognitive center), my emotions (emotional center), my being, my humanity, my needs (somatic center) and the constraints I cannot escape from (earth). The *I* is a person who

---

[151] Translator's note: In French, the distinctions between the elements of the pairs I-me and You-you is clearer: Je-moi and Tu-toi. We have chosen to put "me" and "you" in lower case to highlight that **me** and **you** are seen and treated as things.

is fully recognized as such. If I move down this axis, towards the *me*, I thingify myself or I am thingified. I become the object of desire, an instrument, a means, a target—as marketing specialists would say. It is the same on the *You-you* axis for the person with whom I am interacting, the other person. In the *You*, I recognize the *other* as a person, in the *you*, I see the *other* as an "object."

Juliette Tournand defines the *I-You* space as the space of kindness. This is the space where I am fully myself and I recognize the *other* as a person, with his subjectivity, his thoughts, his emotions, his feelings, his body, his verticality. If I can distinguish these elements that make up the *other*, I recognize him fully as a person. In this space of the *I*, the *other* does the same. He is in connection with me and recognizes me as a person in my own right. The dynamic of the exchange can then lie within the spirit of the *I-You* relationship that Buber describes: a full and reciprocal acknowledgment of the *other* as a person. In this space, *I* can be and I accept that *You* are doing the same. Joined by our Humanity and distinct through our identity, we will try to resolve our differences in a creative manner through a dialogue whose characteristics we will examine below.

The nature of the situation will change if *I* transforms *You* into a *you* or if *You* transforms *I* into a *me*. One of us transforms the *other* into a thing. The *I/You* relationship will then change into *I/you* or *me/You*.

In the *I/you*, I push the relationship into the quadrant of the manipulation of the *other* to achieve my ends. The *other* is made to be an object, an *it*.

In the *me/You* situation, the opposite happens. The person I am talking to refuses me the chance to act according to my values, my choices, my goals. For him, I become an *it*, a means to satisfy what he aspires to.

The last quadrant of this grid is that of me/you, which is also the space of "no one" as there is no I or You. Each one gives up his responsibility. An uninhabited relational fog.

The Aiki attitude puts itself resolutely in the I/You space and creates its strategy in a kind approach that is, in many ways, close to the kindness strategy that Juliette Tournand describes so elegantly in her book La Stratégie de la bienveillance. Through centering, verticality, and connection to the Other, we call on our somatic intelligence to maintain ourselves in the space of kindness. Our body guarantees this space; this frees our mind, which is more inclined to calculations, anticipations, or reminders of the past than to the perception of the subtle slippage toward other parts of the quadrant.

Aiki practice teaches us to feel and trust subtle physical sensations that make us feel that we are leaving the I/You mode and veering toward the I/you or the me/You. If we expect our mind (cognitive center) to realize it, there is a great risk that it will happen too late. The somatic center is best suited to detect variations in the quality of the interrelationship with the other person. Our cognitive center can then support us in our creative process in order to return to the space of kindness.

Rapoport and Axelrod

The very notion of kindness can lead someone to think that *AikiCom* is part of a utopian and good-natured approach, which is certainly desirable, but disconnected from the hardness of real life. It's nothing of the sort. Experiments have studied and shown that cooperation is generally more effective than any individualistic behavior. This is food for thought for practical people who judge everything in terms of effectiveness. Referring to Robert Axelrod's work, Juliette Tournand brings up in her own work the tit-for-tat strategy that Anatol Rapoport applied during a tournament of experts[152] organized by Robert Axelrod within the scope of a game theory study of the optimal choices in the "prisoner's dilemma." Rapoport won this computer tournament by applying a simple and brilliant strategy that showed the power and effectiveness of the strategy of cooperation.

---

[152] This tournament was held in two innings and was played by university teams from departments of psychology, sociology, mathematics, and economics. Each team adopted a strategy that chose whether the next action would be cooperative or non-cooperative. The results were published by Axelrod in 1980 and confirmed the victory of Professor Anatol Rapoport with his "tit-for-tat" strategy.

The prisoner's dilemma features two prisoners suspected of having committed a crime. They are arrested and placed in separate cells with no possibility of communicating with each other. The police officer has no proof to incriminate them and is counting on the fact that one or the other of the suspects will give himself up or inform on the other to get him convicted. If neither of the accused speaks, the police officer will be forced to set them free after six months in prison. If the two suspects give each other up, the sentence that will be imposed on them will be five years in prison. On the other hand, if one of the suspects turns the other in and the latter remains silent, the one who spoke will be set free while the one who was informed on will receive a sentence of ten years in prison.

Suspect A → Suspect B ↓	turns in the other	remains silent
turns in the other	A and B: 5 years	A: 10 years
remains silent	B: 10 years	A and B: 6 months

Logically, the two accomplices should remain silent but since neither of them trusts the other, they mutually turn each other in rather than taking the risk of being turned in and remaining silent.

One of the essential parameters is the perception of each of the men of the "weight of the future" or, to put it another way, of the value of future rewards in comparison with the immediate benefit. If I am perfectly aware that my relationship with the other person is based on longevity, I can accept putting off a present gain to obtain a benefit that I judge to be greater in the future. If I do not have this perception, I will be a bit tempted to take my immediate benefit and run away. In the case of our two suspects, if each of them knows that he will end up seeing the other again and having a relationship with him in the future, there will be a strong temptation to remain silent and thus opt for the winning choice. If not, the preference will go more in the direction of trying to get out of the situation in the present moment rather than being the fall guy. This is how the two accomplices will be tempted to choose the unfavorable option of the double accusation.

The Conditions of Pragmatic Kindness

Juliette Tournand defines the conditions that allow the development of a kind, winning strategy. This kindness happens through cooperation that benefits everyone who takes part in it and nurtures a climate of optimistic confidence rather than forcing each person involved into exhausting and pointless defensive behaviors. The first condition is clarity.

Clarity

I am clear in my intentions, my attitude, and my words. It is through verticality that I show this congruity. The *Aiki* attitude is not something that I am subject to, it is a commitment, a decision—a decision to commit myself to the search for a rebalancing of energies, of a search for harmony and synergy, to create something new with the people in my circle. I constantly turn myself toward solutions that are suitable for everyone. This commitment is clear; I commit myself to cooperation and will do my utmost not to stop it.

The attitude of kindness is the embodiment of my intention to find harmony, to unite the energies. I do not yield to the least resistance; I receive it as an invitation to seek a new outcome. I do not try to impose my view or destroy the other person. If my techniques lead me to unbalance my partner, it is in order to invite him to get back into movement, to make the energy circulate. In aikido practice, this imbalance is an integral part of techniques. In daily life, this imbalance can be brought about by a question, a rewording whose goal is to make the other person wonder about what he is experiencing. Without movement, kindness cannot exist. But let's not fall into idealism or naïveté. We live in a difficult world and committing to the path of kindness does not mean accepting becoming a martyr or sacrificing yourself for a balance that the other person does not perceive or does not want to perceive, perhaps blinded by the desire for victory.

Reciprocity

Kindness in clarity requires reciprocity. If it's always up to me to yield to maintain a good relationship, if I am always helpful and I am consistently denied whenever I express my needs, I cannot say that I am in a relationship of kindness, but rather in a relationship where I step aside in favor of the other person. This is not about keeping a precise "balance sheet" of each gesture made by both people involved. The equilibrium is evaluated at the somatic center by a feeling that expresses the right balance. This reveals itself in the dialogue that is established between the two partners.

In connection, I remain continuously attentive. I am cooperative with my colleague, my friend, my partner, or my son, and I expect that the other person will do the same.

Reciprocity in kindness is applied by following these two rules:

If you stop cooperating, so do I

In the dynamics of cooperation, the first rule consists of reacting when we detect the first behavior that is interpreted as being non-cooperative and then talking about it. If I see that the other person has given up on this attitude of kindness, I in turn stop cooperating. This first rule may seem easy to apply. However, it is not. In a climate of good cooperation, when one of the people involved notices a dissonance, he will hesitate before bringing it up. Maybe he will tell himself that it is only an impression, that he is exaggerating. Maybe he will be afraid to disturb the good atmosphere and make the relationship a mistrustful one. You have to grin and bear it when you want to intervene in this way and sometimes we don't have the energy. By then, we are already too busy. However, reacting at the first deviation from the reciprocal relationship allows us to come back to kind reciprocity more easily. The emotional intensity is still at a low level. But we hesitate and we put off our intervention. We wait for the second occurrence of non-cooperation, then the third and the fourth and finally we explode when we've had enough.

Example 1

> Martina was just named manager of an administrative department. She is leading a team of six people. In this department, the work schedule is flexible. Each member of the staff takes care of marking down his arrival and departure hours and must make sure to work 38 hours per week. Martina has a lot of work and appreciates that the atmosphere is friendly. She lets her staff know that she is working with confidence and with the utmost flexibility to reconcile her professional life and her private life while at the same time being careful to respond in a timely fashion to the obligations

of her duties, which are pretty erratic in terms of the intensity of the department's workload. Martina quickly notices that the personnel in her department take advantage of the flexible time system by cheating on their arrival and departure times. Some surprise spot checks show Martina that some people arrive late or leave early, but the weekly balance sheet shows a full work week. She talks about this with her colleague who is running the department next to hers and finds out that he already knows about this. He is a bit lazy and has too much work to waste energy on this question. "You'll get used to it," he tells her. "Welcome to the club!" But Martina feels bad in this situation. She feels trapped between the desire for clarity and respect for the prescribed rules and the fear of ruining the atmosphere that is so dear to her in order to work well as a team. When I meet her in one-on-one coaching, I ask her to recenter herself. Martina clearly feels that she must tell her staff about this, even if her colleague who is in the same situation isn't reacting to it. Connected to herself, in her verticality, Martina also feels afraid of being criticized or judged as being strict, of causing her staff to withdraw into themselves: "If that's what she wants, she will no longer be able to count on us in an emergency." Together, we reframe this fear of displeasing others, this fear of sabotaging her own efforts. The tensions get back in harmony and Martina feels aligned in her decision to have a meeting with her staff to put the question on the table. When we see each other again, Martina is delighted and has calmed down. The meeting went far better than expected. Her staff explained how they had unilaterally corrected gaps in the system. When they are telecommuting, they can only post seven and one half hours of work, even for certain difficult projects. In the same way, on days when they are working to finish a project, the system does not allow them to register more than nine hours, even if they work more than that. Being attentive to the needs of her staff, Martina offers to clarify these situations when they come up by talking about them. In the days since this meeting, Martina hasn't seen any tension in her staff. On the contrary, she has clearly felt an atmosphere of listening, confidence, and mutual respect. Slight late arrivals have changed into a phone call to warn of the slight delay and extra work hours resulted in a flexible change in an employee's work schedule on the following days.

Example 2

Dennis's friends count on him. All year long, he stays in touch by e-mail, by sending invitations to have a drink or grab a bite to eat. Sometimes he lets some time go by before calling or sending an e-mail to one friend or another. The scenario is the same every time and his friends never take the initiative. Dennis is aware of the flow of life that carries us all, but he experiences it too. Why is he the only one to care about keeping the connection? He gradually realizes that he is carrying these relationships on his shoulders. He talks to his friends about it and they give various excuses, but nothing changes. Danielle, Dennis's wife, tells him that his tendency to take the initiative created a habit among his friends, who are not as devoted to this friendship. After having expressed his uneasiness at being in this asymmetric relationship mode, Dennis lets these relationships go and they fade away. He loses touch with a lot of them. Only Luke and Quentin end up understanding the message and stay in regular contact with him.

If you come back in the spirit of cooperation, I come back (title level 5 for formatting)

If, after having heard my feedback, the other person returns to reciprocal kindness, the second rule invites me to return to it too. This rule is also less obvious than it seems. If your colleague plays a dirty trick on you, not only do you cut off the cooperative relationship, but you will also tend to mistrust him and keep your distance from him.

"After what he did to me, he can no longer count on me!"

Lasting Relationship

Pessimists will note that the strategy of cooperation is only effective when the participants have a clear perception that their relationship will last for a long time. It is the only way for them to accept giving up an immediate gain in order to reap more in the future. If the relationship is not seen as long-lasting, it is in our best interest to choose to act selfishly, disconnected from the other person, thus winning a series of small, short-term victories. This reasoning is viable if you do not take into account the degree of interconnection that unites us or the unpredictability of life. These days, we are more and more connected and interconnected. Friends on Facebook, acquaintances on other social networks, friends, neighbors, colleagues, family members who may be either close or distant, weave a web that is difficult to cut ourselves off from. Since 1929, the theory of six degrees of separation has asserted that "everyone and everything is six or fewer steps away, by way of introduction, from any other person in the world, so that a chain of 'a friend of a friend' statements can be made to connect any two people in a maximum of six steps.[153]" We can well imagine that with the development of communication technology this number has diminished considerably.

The notion of a lasting relationship can be understood as being a question of duration but also in terms of recurrence, i.e., the clear perception that we will meet again one day.

Sociologists lean toward kindness's "contagious" effect. So, if you are in your car and another driver kindly yields the right of way to you, in the following minutes you will be tempted to make one or more kind gestures yourself. You will yield to a pedestrian who is trying to cross the street, you will let another driver enter traffic when a lane is closed, etc. These actions cause new actions by the people who have benefited from them, and so on. Ultimately, the action of the first driver will cause numerous responses. You thus become a vector of well-being around you and it is highly probable that you will benefit from the rebound effect later on. In a wider sense, the act of adopting kind behavior leads to better relationships that are more peaceful and recharge our batteries and encourage us to continue to move forward.

Ai and *Ki*—Love and Power

We would all like to get along with everyone, in perfect harmony. This is of course never the case and we have to come to terms with the reality of our differences. The two most common strategies consist of forcing the other person to submit to our demands or giving in so that we can have some peace. If we want to change things, we are tempted by the same choices: forcing the flow of things in spite of what others

---

[153] Wikipedia, Six degrees of separation, consulted April 27, 2015.

think or not doing anything and leaving things as they are. War or harmony, love or power, seem to have to oppose each other irreversibly. However, by the simple act of joining the Japanese words "Ai" and "Ki" we highlight the indispensable complementarity of these two vectors of change.

The term *Ki* represents the energy of life. It is *ki* that allows a wild plant to grow between two slabs of concrete in a city sidewalk. In a more general way, *ki* is the impulse that pushes every living thing to fulfill itself, to grow, to develop. It is the force that allows us to accomplish our life plan, to accomplish things, whether in the smallest everyday gestures or in our fundamental aspirations. Our life energy is at the base of our personal power. As long as it is connected to *Ai* it stimulates our creative ability.

The term *Ai* can be expressed as that which reunites what was separated. It is what reconnects what is fragmented and makes us see its unity. This is not about gathering together what doesn't go together. You connect *holons*, parts that are simultaneously entities in themselves, and parts of a whole.

Ai and *Ki* are thus two vectors of the same dynamic of life. However, they can move apart if they forget their common origin.

The life power of *Ki* without *Ai* can become self-centered, centripetal. By trying to develop the person and his individual plan regardless of the other person's needs, *ki* becomes a brutal and blind power. It turns the person into an insensitive robot or a tyrant.

An obsessional search for harmony and reliance on *Ai*—disconnected from *Ki*—rapidly leads to weakness and apathy. Homogenization, the avoidance of annoying topics, and the fear of collision or standing out can smooth out differences. The person sacrifices himself in favor of everything and forbids himself from using his own energy. This results in apathy, limp consensus, and hollow discussions where nobody commits himself. You prefer to not decide rather than ruin the atmosphere. The *I* and the *You* disappear in favor of a *We* that seems devoid of willpower.

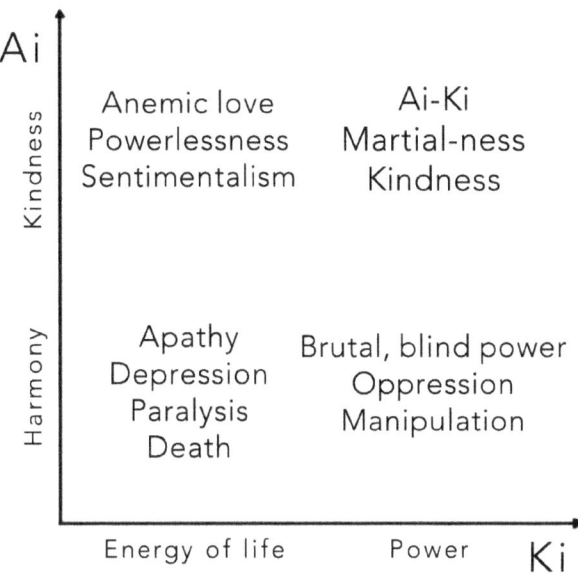

Figure 19 : The Ai-Ki Space of Kind Martial-ness

A couple is a magnificent expression of the beauty of the *Ai-Ki* union, as well as being an expression of its dark side.

The period that we call the "honeymoon" pushes lovers in the direction of *Ai* without *Ki*. The act of being together fills the individuals so much that they merge and no longer exist by themselves.

> *"What should we do?*
> *Whatever you want. What do you want to do?*
> *Do you want us to stay here or go out?*
> *And you, what do you want?*
> *Me? Whatever you want! What do you want?"*

The dialogue can go on like this for hours. The closely-bonded lovers no longer act from themselves, they act from the couple.

In the organizational dynamics of associations like, for example, non-profit organizations led mainly by volunteers, we also find this kind of behavior. Each person wants to respect the democratic side, listening to everyone, at any price. This behavior, when pushed to the extreme, paralyzes the group when the participants end up not making any more suggestions that come from themselves for fear of being accused of individualism, or of wanting to secretly take over the group.

Martin Luther King describes this connection between love and power in his book *Where Do We Go from Here?* He explains that power is necessary in order to accomplish our goals and that love and power are very often in opposition. In this way, love is often seen as an abdication of power while power is seen as an absence of love. And Martin Luther King asks us to change this way of thinking by becoming aware of the fact that love without power is anemic and mawkish while power without love is oblivious and abusive.

The *Aiki* attitude leads us to keep the connection between *Ai* and *Ki* and position ourselves clearly in the upper right corner of the graph in Figure 14.

The Stages of Dialogue

Example 1

> Michael is stressed. He is going to meet Sophie's parents for the first time. Luke, his brother, is supposed to lend him his car. This has been planned since the beginning of the week, but in the meantime the two brothers have argued about a book that Luke liked a lot. Luke claims that Michael folded the corner of a page. Michael believes that Luke is exaggerating and that the book is still in perfect condition. When Michael is leaving, Luke balks at giving his car keys to Michael. Knowing the importance of this dinner at Sophie's parents' house, Luke wants to force his brother to buy him a brand-new copy of the damaged book. He knows that, both literally and figuratively, he holds the keys to a smooth evening. Michael yields, but will not hesitate to get his revenge the next chance he has.

Example 2

> John responds aggressively because Lucy has spoken harshly to him. Lucy spoke harshly to him because John had reacted in a

distant manner. John had responded in this way because Lucy hadn't answered his text, etc.

Getting out of conflict and finding a solution that suits everyone is no easy task. Each of the parties concerned must be able to get in touch with the *Ai* and *Ki* dimensions, but this isn't easy. If one of the parties has more power or authority—or if he merely gives this impression, he will be tempted to impose his own solution.

It will then be difficult to reposition the dialogue in the space of martial kindness. In complex situations, causes and effects are often entangled in multiple loops that can sometimes go back very far in the common history of the parties concerned.

The situation can be difficult to unravel because each person has such a different—and highly subjective—view of the situation and of the sequence of events that led them there. In this sort of situation, nobody can pretend to have the solution that will allow them to get out of the deadlock and has even less power, by his separate action, to act to find a solution. The more complex the situation is, the more it will require acting in an *Ai-Ki* attitude, combining power and love, presence and connection.

Communication can then unfold. It sometimes begins by a polite exchange of ideas. This is Stage 1, that of approach. Each one talks about what can be said or heard. The real subjects are not addressed. Each one remains on guard and avoids revealing his view of things. The discussion is carried on with respect for the social conventions in place. At this stage, each individual maintains a view of the situation that conforms to the group's prevailing patterns of thought.

In Stage 2, the arguments take on more weight. The people in the discussion say what they are thinking. This is the *debate* stage. The people begin to defend their points of view. Each one states his view of things, presents his arguments, and tries to convince the other. The exchange becomes harder as the positions are asserted. Each of them identifies with his ideas and tries to pick apart the other's argument. The exchange takes on the appearance of a battle. Sometimes, at this level, the only possible outcomes seem to be to win or to die, to convince or to take the view of the other. While, in the preceding stage,

I had an overall view of the situation, that of my point of view or of the general point of view, here I am truly forced to see that there are other ways of perceiving things (even if, for me, they are less acceptable, distorted, or even altogether false).

Stage 3 is that of a dialogue that takes place with empathic listening. After having defended their ideas and their positions, the people in the argument choose to listen. They are interested in each other. While previously they saw, now they watch; if they were hearing, now they are listening. The points of view are no longer in opposition. They complement each other and enrich the overall image. The world is no longer seen as being external; they are all part of it and enrich their perspective by exchanging their points of view rather than putting them in opposition.

Stage 4 is that of *Aiki* dialogue, where something has opened up. The boundaries between the people in the argument become blurred. The words are no longer related to personal views, they bear witness to what is happening, to what is going through the group. The connections between the people take on a certain intensity. Time seems to stop and the sharing is complete. The people no longer speak in their own name; they are part of and participate in the emergence of a sort of deep intelligence that does not belong to a particular person but requires the presence of all.

The *Aiki* approach leads us to enter into connection with the other person and transform the stage of confrontational debate to lead to a dialogue in the sense described by David Bohm[154]. In the dialogue, each one is centered and present and is interested in the other's experience, in his way of seeing things. My view of things complements that of the other person. I discover, with curiosity, how the subjectivity of each person nourishes the group and enriches the global perception. I listen to the other person with empathy while recognizing him in his verticality. The other person is different but I can comprehend him (in the etymological sense[155]) and thus construct

---

[154] See *On Dialogue*, Routledge, 2014.
[155] Comprehend: mid-14c., "to understand," from Latin *comprehendere* "to take together, to unite; include; seize" (of catching fire or the arrest of criminals); also "to comprehend, perceive"" (to seize or take in the mind), from *com-* "completely" (see com-) + *prehendere* "to catch hold of, seize"
(http://www.etymonline.com/index.php?term=comprehend).

for myself a global view that goes beyond any personal perception that I had of the situation. If each of us does the same, we can reach a new stage of exchange where together we make up a whole. We move in a flow that is greater than ourselves. Morihei Ueshiba called this experience "being one with the universe." Our energies open up for us the doors of collective intelligence. The conditions are reunited to let future solutions emerge together. These solutions no longer belong to one or the other, they emerge from the global connection, in the flow. They are not definitively set or carved in stone. They circulate in the global movement that carries us. At this stage, we are no longer the originators of our ideas, we are contributors to this emergence. In aikido practice, this is the stage of mastery that, in *randori*, sees movements spring forth from our encounters with our partners. The techniques no longer have a name or a form.

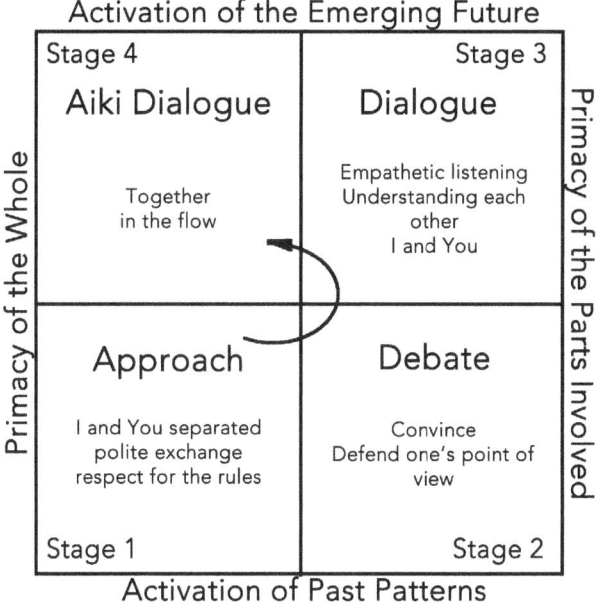

Figure 20 : Ai Ki Dialogue Quadrant

The above diagram is inspired by the one described by Otto Schärmer in his book Theory U. Theory U describes a process that is similar to the one experienced in Aiki practice but while Theory U talks about the importance of the physical dimension, it brings few concrete suggestions beyond practice that is filled with mindfulness, breathing, or visualization. The Aiki approach brings a physical practice to embody this U-shaped curve, which came from research conducted by Joseph Jaworski et al.

Living in the Flow

Living in the flow is a level of experience that is difficult to define. When we are in the flow, we are at the same time fully ourselves and fully connected to a greater Whole. This Whole can be a couple, a family, a team, a business, society, Humanity, the Universe. The *Aiki* experience allows us to distinguish two complementary aspects of this notion of flow.

When we perform a *randori* in aikido, several partners attack us and we perform the movements that emerge, without planning and without anticipating. We are fully immersed in the moment. The challenge is intense and while we feel like we are in full possession of our acquired technical skills, we feel that we can respond to it effectively. The attacks follow one another and the movements are linked together. The spirals follow one another and we whirl around on the *tatami*, going from one attack to the next. We have a feeling of joy, a feeling of being completely immersed in the activity. Nothing else matters. We know the rules of the game. The attackers are there to test us with kindness but without conceding. We know what we must achieve: we place ourselves correctly, keep our verticality, go in front of the attack, welcome it without opposing it, blending with the energy of the strike or going with the grab and then initiating a movement that comes from taking into account everything that is going on in the moment: force, intensity, direction, stability, available space... The feedback is instantaneous. Resistance gives way to variation, a new rotation. We instantly know the response to our action and we can change it again a fraction of a second later. From the outside, spectators only see an immense movement that encompasses, absorbs, and transforms all the attacks.

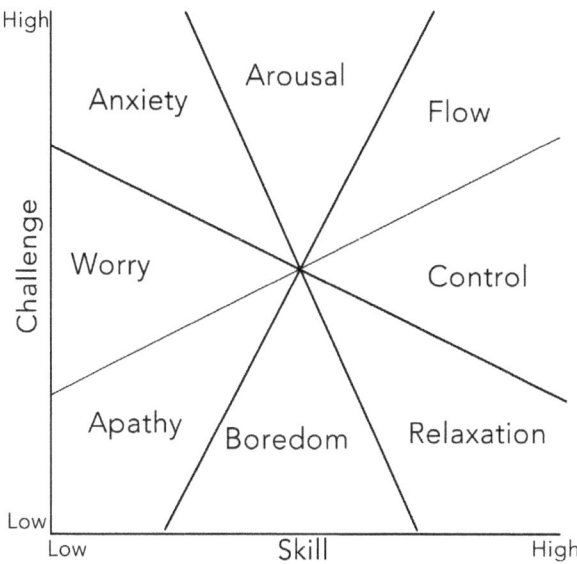

Figure 21 : The Zone of Flow

Mihaly Czikszentmihalyi described this sort of experience, which he called the "optimal experience" or "flow experience." According to him, flow experiences happen when we perform difficult but attainable tasks that involve us fully. In these moments that offer a delicate balance between our abilities and the difficulty of the task, we lose the perception that we have of ourselves. We are entirely immersed in the action. Time no longer exists and we feel pleasure in the moment. After the activity, we have the feeling of having lived fully, of being fulfilled within the action.

The skill-challenge balance is particularly interesting to study. If the task is too difficult for our abilities, we feel worried, which can be transformed into anxiety. If the task is too simple, the feeling of control and mastery can switch to relaxation, then boredom. Moreover, if the task is not very stimulating and the required skills to accomplish it are too basic, we sink into a sort of apathy.

Flow experience is an experience of intense concentration that can become harmful. Who hasn't experienced being completely immersed in an activity? The video game player, the Internet junkie, the movie buff, the avid reader of novels, are more than focused on their activity: they are absorbed by it. Nothing else exists, not even time. And when they come out, they either have the impression of having had a good time or, on the contrary, they realize that they have lost a part of their life. In this sort of situation, we talk about hyperfocus. This is the dark side of the force, the one that pulls us out of life instead of making us savor it through an activity that we love.

Martial practice causes flow experiences that combine concentration and perception. The fact that combat is involved seems to blend our inherited survival skills with our more modern skills of thinking and planning. Inherited skills are more rapid, intuitive, involuntary, and permanently connected with the environment in order to find sources of danger or pleasure in it and draw our attention to give direction to our actions. Modern thinking skills are slower and more costly in terms of effort, and they allow us to choose, to decide, to master our impulses, and to move away from our habitual actions to learn new behaviors, to organize our actions in order to reach a goal. We are permanently living between action that is guided by our attention, the result of our will, and reaction to stimuli that are perceived by our body and that reach our awareness to urge us to take them into account for our future actions. In the *Aiki* attitude, when I am in verticality, in the axis of being, I am present, I am not tense during the action. I am straight and I perceive with my entire body. As soon as a significant stimulus is perceived, a process of choice is at work that turns my *Aikisphere* toward what was noticed and the axis of action will focus our attention and energy for a maximum effect.

Being in the flow then becomes an experience where I am immersed in the flow of events that come to me and I guide my actions to do what I must in the moment. My actions seem to follow naturally. They take place without effort and give me a feeling of comfort, of ease, and of easiness.

This experience fits within a wider temporal framework that deserves our attention. It is about life goals, the goals that I set for myself and that other people may call their "mission."

Maslow described how our needs are part of a pyramidal structure[156]. The needs at the base of the pyramid must be satisfied

---

[156] A. H. Maslow, "A theory of human motivation" in *Psychological Review 50* (4) 370-96.

before taking care of those that are located at higher levels. At the top of the pyramid we find self-actualization. Since this term is not very clear, I prefer to talk about self-realization. Living fully would then express your uniqueness, not in a self-centered way, but in an altruistic and connected way. So that our life may have meaning, our purpose must go beyond us and be outside of ourselves. If we return to basic geometry, for there to be a vector there must be a point of origin and a direction that can be determined by setting another point. The meaning[157] of our life is given by this vector, which pushes us in a direction, on a path. A successful life is measured by the distance that is covered along this path. The destination has no importance except to indicate direction. What counts and is essential is the action that is taken in the here and now. Focusing your mind on your goal will guarantee you a life of frustration. The *Aikisphere* compass gives us our heading and guides our steps. On the way, we encounter obstacles: a branch, a stone, a tree. Our body detects them and changes its behavior in the moment, according to the circumstances. The *Aiki* attitude puts us in the flow of our life, connected to our environment and to others. Our verticality is the guarantee of our consistency and of our authenticity. It makes us act in harmony with our values (the sky) while taking into account reality and its constraints (the earth). In the present moment, I am centered and present (somatic center) and my life energy (*ki*) circulates fluidly among my three centers (somatic, emotional, and cognitive) to nourish my entire body. I have a feeling of being a living body that has borrowed a bit of energy from the universe in order to contribute to more harmony within myself and around myself.

Perception within the flow can be interspersed with questions: What is right for me, here and now? Am I on the right path? If I am running into so many difficulties, shouldn't I change my path or postpone some actions? These questions are the product of the cognitive brain; the responses emerge from the somatic center and are validated by the emotional center, which colors them with emotions.

Our life strategies and our career plans then become easier to appreciate. If I wonder about an action to take (Should I accept this

---

[157] Translator's note: In French, the word *un sens* can refer to both meaning and direction.

project, quit, tell him yes, refuse this offer, begin new training, move to another city, get married, divorce...?) the answer will be offered to me in the form of this question: Does this make me progress in the direction that gives meaning to my life? If the answer is no, the choice is easy. The choices will often be less clear. I may make detours that are not in the same direction as my path based on the reality of the moment. Less significant detours from my direction will be taken in order to account for the reality of the moment. This will be the case, for example, if it is important for me to write a book. Right after I sit down at my desk, my wife asks me to take a stroll in the forest. This stroll does not lead to the completion of my project, but the reality of the moment seems to favor giving myself time to relax with her.

In a memorable speech in front of Stanford University students, Steve Jobs talked about the effect of events on the future.

> *"Again, you can't connect the dots looking forward; you can only connect them looking backward. So you have to trust that the dots will somehow connect in your future. You have to trust in something—your gut, destiny, life, karma, whatever. This approach has never let me down, and it has made all the difference in my life."*
>
> *[June 12, 2005 commencement address; news.stanford.edu]*

Jobs explains here that thinking cognitively does not allow us to draw the right conclusions. And when he asks the students to believe in something, he invites them to map out a direction and to turn their *Aikisphere* in that direction.

The founder of Apple explained further:

> *"Your time is limited, so don't waste it living someone else's life. Don't be trapped by dogma—which is living with the results of other people's thinking. Don't let the noise of others' opinions drown out your own inner voice. And most important, have the courage to follow your heart and intuition. They somehow already know what you truly want to become. Everything else is secondary."*

(June 12, 2005 commencement address[158])

So, after having set aside the cognitive center as our guide, Steve Jobs advises us to listen to the somatic center (which he calls intuition) and the emotional center (the heart).

---

[158] news.stanford.edu

Conclusion

Quantum physics has opened up radically new perspectives in our way of perceiving the world. One phenomenon that has shaken our common sense the most is that of nonlocality. This theory seems to show that the world is fundamentally inseparable. In other words, everything is interconnected. The separating elements of time and space are no longer decisive in determining the dependence of one element upon another. Other modes of connection are possible. This is what David Bohm describes in his theory of implicate order. According to Bohm, there is a deeper, implicate order that cannot be described. Every description is only a language that merely expresses a view, "a projection in our explicate order of underlying reality, the implicate order.[159]" There really are no more separations or boundaries. Our universe is holistic and interconnected. While all this may seem abstract, it is possible for us to have a concrete perception of this wholeness through direct experience. This will be the case in what are called flow experiences, for example when we are admiring a magnificent landscape, listening to beautiful music or when we are simply immersed in an optimal experience[160]. Morihei Ueshiba, the founder of aikido, says the same thing. What he calls reversal is

---

[159]Translation of a quote found on Wikipedia, David Bohm, consulted September 3, 2015.
[160] Mihaly Csikszentmihalyi describes these experiences in his book *Living Well, Psychology of Everyday Life.*

nothing more than the switching of awareness from the explicate order that is expressed by practical physics to the implicate order that is expressed by a universe that is beyond the limits of temporality and of linear causality. In the same way, as we can experience wonderful moments while listening to a work of Mozart without expecting to permanently remain in the same marvelous state, *Aiki* practice leads us to color our lives with these special touches, with these magical moments where we are in touch with the feeling of connection, of a link between ourselves and others and with our entire environment. These moments radically change the manner in which we view the world in a lasting way.

With Edgar Morin's concept of ethics, this connection becomes an act of interconnection[161]. The miracle of life, marvel of the universe, creates structures that are constantly more complex, thus opposing the domination of the law of entropy that dismantles, scatters, and pushes to dispersion and uniformity. We own a part of the energy of life, which distinguishes us, as living beings, from the rest of inanimate matter. During a very brief period—these few decades that are given to us to live—we borrow a bit of vital energy and we have the illusory feeling of having the freedom to choose what we are going to devote it to. The intricacy of life and infinite interdependencies remind us that our control is not as perfect as we would like, but it is nevertheless significant enough to offer us the luxury of asking. What meaning do we give to our life? Should we live in a consumerist daze or mobilize ourselves to get back into action? This bit of energy of life makes me think of the story of the hummingbird. One scorching day, a piece of glass acted like a magnifying glass and set some twigs on fire. The fire very quickly spread to the trees and then the entire forest. The panicked animals ran to the nearest river while seeing the dreadful spectacle of their home being destroyed by flames. Only a hummingbird, this tiny bird, continued to stay busy. He flew continuously from the river, where he took one or two drops of water in his beak, to go pour them on the flames. A fox who was watching him mockingly asked him: "What are you doing, little hummingbird? Don't you see that you're

---

[161] The "act of interconnection" is a translation of the French word *reliance*, which was defined by Edgar Morin to give a more active characteristic to the word *relié* (connected). "Relié est passif, reliant est participant, reliance est activant" (MORIN, Edgar. *La Méthode. Tome 6 Éthique.* Paris, Seuil, 2004, page239).

knocking yourself out for nothing?" The hummingbird answered: "I'm doing my part."

It is up to us to contribute to carrying on the energy of life, which is sorely lacking in the universe. The force of the phenomenon that we call love is the strongest manifestation of our deep need to carry on life just like we transmit the flame from one candle to the next. This is the call to universal harmony that Morihei Ueshiba wanted to pass on to us. The universe is inherently hostile to life. Not that it wants to do away with it, but because it applies the second law of thermodynamics, which is constantly returning to maximum disorder. Take some printing blocks and arrange a poem with the letters. Then throw the blocks on the ground. See how the blocks spread out on the ground. It's likely that you will no longer be able to see the poem or any other intelligible writing. This is the law of entropy. And life is the "anomaly" that goes against this fate. If we return to the human dimension and to the concerns of our daily life, we notice that it is the same. Our relationships are living processes. We are the constituent elements. To keep them alive, we have to invest a part of our vital energy if we do not want to witness their death through decomposition. It is an extreme privilege to be the creators of a fleeting work of art, which allows us to understand ice sculptors who spend hours creating works that will not survive thawing. Everything is impermanence, the Buddhists tell us. Everything changes except change, barroom philosophers tell us. The message is the same and the outcome is identical. We are the hummingbirds of life and we do our part. Some do this more awkwardly than others, who burn themselves out without even taking a single drop to its destination.

Evolution has given us awareness and by doing so has given us a new impossible mission: structuring and putting the chaotic world of our thoughts in order. A hard task! This developmental outcome puts in our hands a saw that allows us to cut the branch of the tree of evolution on which we are sitting. The power of our mind is also a formidable weapon of mass destruction: destruction of the feeling of belonging and of the cohesion of the forces of life. The extraordinary ability to categorize and to distinguish in order to identify and give meaning, conceals from us the view of the deep order of nature and of life. We create our own identity and shelter it behind the shield of our ego, which nourishes our illusory experience of being unique, apart from, or separate. The perpetuation of life shrinks so that it only aims at the suboptimum, at the survival of an individual rather than that of the species or even of life as a whole. The energy of life shrinks and goes so far as to choose to destroy life—that which is developing around oneself—to perpetuate as long as possible this ego/organism, against all logic. This is the fate of closed systems that loop infinitely without feeding themselves with what comes from elsewhere or from others. Reasoning gets carried away and "goes off the rails." The ego, this virtual entity that gives us the feeling of being ourselves, is a prerequisite in the process of individuation. One must have *been* in order to connect. Life invites us to develop ourselves in all the complexity of our unique being, thus creating a new structure of order. It is then up to us to tie ourselves to other living beings and to thus participate in the miracle that some call the zoosphere, this gigantic system made up of all living beings. Without individuation, the work cannot be accomplished. The *Aiki* approach leads us on the path that goes from individuation to interconnectedness. Centering and verticality bring us back to ourselves, in our being and our individuality. We can then go to meet the *other* and invest our *Ki*, our vital energy, in the dynamic of exchange and communication. Conflicts that are only the expression of our differences enrich the global system. This is the fundamental mechanism that makes a group of individuals greater than the same individuals taken separately. *Aiki* practice makes us more aware. It guides our attention not only toward the energy that we bring but also toward the *other's* energy. We develop our ability to gather all this energy and blend with it for maximum effectiveness. We then live in the flow, attentive to subtle variations of life, nurtured by our individual differences, together creating more than we could have imagined being able to do on our own. This energy in movement makes up the *Aiki* struggle. This is not a destructive struggle, but a mobilization that turns itself in the direction of the flow of life. Marshall Rosenberg defined needs in non-violent communication as what gives life, what nurtures it[162]. *Aiki* struggle is the struggle of life against the forces of entropy. And we are all the heroes of this epic tale.

---

[162] Marshall Rosenberg, *Nonviolent Communication: A Language of Life.*

Illustrations

Figure 1 : Illusion 21
Figure 2 : The Position of the Center of Gravity 68
Figure 3 : The Skeleton Protecting the 3 Center 69
Figure 4 : Cognitive Center: Creating Meaning 95
Figure 5 : Maslow's Hierarchy of Needs 97
Figure 6 : Tai sabaki, step diagram 101
Figure 7 : Turning the Action toward the Objective 106
Figure 8 : The Aikisphere 109
Figure 9 : Moving the Energy to the Tangent 141
Figure 10 : Aikisphere as a compass for the Aiki attitude .. 151
Figure 11 : Taking a triangle stance 160
Figure 12 : The Triangle 161
Figure 13 : The Circle 166
Figure 14 : Homeostasis and Change 169
Figure 15 : Maze 170
Figure 16 : Taking a square stance 170
Figure 17 : The Square 172
Figure 18 : The Quadrants of Kindness 197
Figure 19 : The Ai-Ki Space of Kind Martial-ness 207
Figure 20 : Ai Ki Dialogue Quadrant 211
Figure 21 : The Zone of Flow 213

Terminology

Aikidoka: the Japanese way to refer to someone who practices aikido. Similar to karateka for karate or judoka for judo. In the USA, the term aikidoist is often used.

Dan: rank corresponding to black belt levels. First dan, or *shodan* (*sho* represents first, new, or a beginning) is the first black belt level.

Dojo: (from *do,* the path and *jo,* training). The *dojo* is the place that is devoted to practice, where we seek the path.

Hakama: wide-leg pleated pants worn by aikidokas. The *hakama* is a traditional garment in Japan. Practicing aikido with a *hakama* intensifies the feeling of movement in the hips and therefore in the *hara.* On a symbolic level, the *hakama* features seven pleats that represent the seven qualities of the *samurai*: kindness, honor, courtesy, wisdom, sincerity, loyalty, and piety.

Hanari or *hanare*: a term used in *kyudo* to describe the moment when the archer releases the arrow.

Keikogi or *gi* (from *keiki*, training and *gi*, uniform): the uniform for practicing a martial art.

Randori: defensive exercise against one or several attackers.

Reishiki (from *rei*, greeting and *shiki*, ceremony): the set of rules of etiquette and behavior in a *dojo*.

Kyu: rank identifying the practice levels before the black belt. In aikido, each *kyu* (numbered in reverse order from 6th *kyu* to 1st *kyu*) is characterized by a belt color (white, yellow, orange, green, blue, brown).

Sensei (literally, in Japanese: the one who walks ahead, the one who was there before me): *sensei* is the teaching title in the Japanese martial arts. *Do* is the path, the way, and the *sensei* is the one who is ahead of me on the way.

Shoshin (*sho*, the beginning and *shin*, mind): *shoshin* is the beginner's mind, a concept used in the martial arts and in zen. The beginner's mind is characterized by modesty and curiosity and it does not anticipate because it does not yet "know." This state of mind must be present at every level of practice. Its final result is the state of *mushin* or the non-mental state that is like a mirror that instantly reflects what is happening in front of it, without anticipation or the interference of one's will, without reference to the past or projection into the future.

Tai sabaki (literally, in Japanese: *tai*, body and *sabaki*, to avoid, to turn): in aikido, *tai sabaki* refers to a particular movement that allows the *tori* to move while turning to end up next to the *uke*.

Tatami: floor covering in *dojos* for practicing martial arts. The *tatami* is the floor covering in traditional Japanese rooms.

Tori (literally, in Japanese: to take or to choose): in aikido, the *tori* is the one who performs the technique; he or she is attacked by the *uke*.

Uke (literally, in Japanese: to receive or to undergo): in aikido, the *uke* is the one who attacks and then receives the technique.

Bibliography

Anaxagoras of Clazomenae in *Aristotle Metaphysics*. Book I.

Axelrod, Robert. *The Evolution of Cooperation*. Revised edition. New York: Basic Books, 2006.

Bach, George R., and Ronald Deutsch. *Stop! You're Driving Me Crazy*. New York: Putnam, c. 1979. (French edition: Arrête, tu m'exaspères. Éditions du Jour, 1985.)

Bandler, Richard, and John Grinder. *The Structure of Magic, Vol. 1, A Book About Language and Therapy*. Palo Alto: Science and Behavior Books, 1975.

Bateson, Gregory. *Steps to an Ecology of Mind* (1972). See "Form, Substance and Difference" (p. 459).

Bohm, David. *On Dialogue*. London: Routledge, 2014.

Buber, Martin. *I and Thou*. Translated by Walter Kaufmann. New York: Touchstone (Simon and Schuster), 1996. (French edition: *Je et Tu* prefaced by Gaston Bachelard, Aubier Philosophie, 2012.)

Capra, Fritjof. *The Tao of Physics: An Exploration of the Parallels Between Modern Physics and Eastern Mysticism*. Boulder, Colorado: Shambhala, 1983.

— *The Turning Point: Science, Society, and the Rising Culture*. Toronto; New York: Bantam Books, 1983.

Castaneda, Carlos. *Journey to Ixtlan: the lessons of Don Juan*. New York: Simon and Schuster, 1972. (French edition: *Le voyage à Ixtlan*. Éditions Gallimard, 1988.)

— *Tales of Power*. New York: Simon and Schuster, 1984.

Coelho, Paulo. *Le Manuel du guerrier de la lumière*. Éditions 84, 2012.

Csikszentmihalyi, Mihaly. *Vivre, la Psychologie du bonheur*. Paris: Éditions Robert Laffont, 2004.

— *Living Well, Psychology of Everyday Life*.

— *Flow, The Psychology of Optimal Experience*. New York: Harper Perennial Modern Classics, 2008.

Corneau, Guy. *N'y a-t-il pas d'amour heureux: comment les liens père-fils et mère-fille conditionnent nos amours*. J'ai lu, 2004.

Damasio, Antonio. *Descartes' Error: Emotion, Reason, and the Human Brain*. London: Penguin, 2005.

d'Ansembourg, Thomas. *Cessez d'être gentil soyez vrai!: être avec les autres en restant soi-même*. Montréal (Québec): Les Éditions de l'Homme, 2001.

— *Being Genuine: Stop Being Nice, Start Being Real.* Encinitas, California: PuddleDancer Press, 2007.

Denys-Struyf, Godelieve, *Les chaînes musculaires et articulaires,* Bruxelles (Belgium): ICTGDS 2000.

Dilts, Robert, Grinder, John, Bandler, Richard, and Judith DeLosier, *Neuro-Linguistic Programming: The Study of the Structure of Subjective Experience, Vol I*, Meta Publications 1980

Eliot, T.S. *Four Quartets.* London: Folio Society, 1968.

Ferry, Luc. *Apprendre à vivre: Volume 2, La Sagesse des Mythes*. Paris: J'ai lu, 2010.

Gendlin, Eugene. *Focusing*. New York: Everest House, 1978.

Gershon, Michael D. *The Second Brain: The Scientific Basis of Gut Instinct and a Groundbreaking New Understanding of Nervous Disorders of the Stomach and Intestine*. New York: Harper Collins Publishers, 1998.

Gibran, Khalil. *The Prophet*. New York: Alfred A. Knopf, 1923.

Gilligan, Stephen. *The Courage to Love: Principles and Practices of Self-Relations Psychotherapy*. New York: W.W. Norton, 1997.

Goleman, Daniel. *Emotional Intelligence.* New York: Bantam Books, 1995.

King, Martin Luther, Jr. *Where Do We Go From Here: Chaos or Community?* New York: Harper and Row, 1967.

Labonté, Marie Lise. *Au coeur de notre corps: Se libérer de nos cuirasses*. Pocket Evolution, 2014.

Laborit, Henri. *L'agressivité détournée. Introduction à une biologie du comportement social*. Éditions de Poche, 1970.

Lakoff, George, and Mark Johnson. *Metaphors We Live By.* Chicago: University of Chicago Press, 1980.

Lamboy, Bernadette. *Devenir qui je suis, une autre approche de la personne*. Desclée de Brouwer, 2003.

Lavoisier, Antoine. *Traité élémentaire de chimie*, 1789.

Lenoir, Frédéric. *"Malraux et le religieux" Le Monde des Religions*, septembre-octobre 2005.

Lorenz, Konrad. *On Aggression*, New York: Harcourt, Brace & World, Inc., 1966

Mandelbrot, Benoit B. *The Fractal Geometry of Nature*. New York: W.H. Freeman and Company, 1982.

Maslow, A.H. "A theory of human motivation" in *Psychological Review* 50 (4) 370–96, 1943.

Merriam-Webster's Collegiate Dictionary, Eleventh Edition, Springfield: Merriam-Webster, Inc., 2005.

Midal, Fabrice. *La voie du Chevalier*. Petite Bibliothèque Payot, 2009.

— *L'esprit de la chevalerie*. Paris : Presses de la Renaissance, 2005.

Millman, Dan. *Way of the Peaceful Warrior : A Book that Changes Lives*. Tiburon, California: H.J. Kramer, 2006.

Morin, Edgar. *La méthode Vol. 6 : Éthique*. Éditions du Seuil, 2004.

Nietzsche, Friedrich. *Untimely Meditations*. Edited by Daniel Breazeale. Cambridge, United Kingdom: Cambridge University Press, 1997.

— *Considérations inactuelles*. Paris Gallimard, 1990.

Plato. *The Allegory of the Cave, Book VII of The Republic*.

Pranin, Stanley. *Aiki News* No. 18, August 1976.

Robbins, Anthony. *Unlimited Power: The New Science of Personal Achievement*. New York: Free Press, 1986.

Robinson, Byron. *The Abdominal and Pelvic Brain*. Hammond, Indiana: F.S. Betz, 1907.

Rosenberg, Marshall. *Nonviolent Communication: A Language of Life*. Encinitas, California: PuddleDancer Press, 2003.

Scharmer, C. Otto. *Theory U: Learning from the Future as It Emerges*. Cambridge, Massachusetts: Society for Organizational Learning, 2007.

Senge, Peter. *The Fifth Discipline.* New York: Currency Doubleday, 2006.

Tolle, Eckhart. *The Power of Now: A Guide to Spiritual Enlightenment.* Vancouver, British Columbia, Canada: Namaste, 2004.

Traversi Bruno, dir., *Les carnets de Takemusu Aiki, Carnet d'étude fondamentale sur la pensée de Morihei Ueshiba n°1 : Le Corps et le Sabre*, Éditions du cénacle, 2010.

Trungpa, Chögyam. *The Sacred Path of the Warrior.* Boulder, Colorado: Shambhala Publications, Inc., 2010. (French edition: *Shambhala: La voie sacrée du guerrier.* Points Sagesses, 2014.)

Ueshiba, Kisshomaru. *The Spirit of Aikido.* Translated by Taitetsu Unno. Tokyo; New York: Kodansha International, 1987.

Ueshiba Morihei, Takahashi Hideo, *Takemusu Aiki, Volume I, II and III.* Translation, annotations and introductive texts by par Kuhihara Seiichi, Régnier Pierre, Traversi Bruno, Editions du Cénacle, 2006, 2008, 2011.

Vanhenten, Christian. *Au-delà de la Magie, la Méta-PNL*, Bruxelles : Editions de la Bienveillance, 2006

Varela, Francisco, Evan Thompson, Eleanor Rosch. *L'inscription corporelle de l'esprit.* (Original title in English *The Embodied Mind*, Cognitive Science and Human Experience)

Vézina, Jean-François. *Danser avec le chaos, accueillez l'inattendu dans votre vie.* Montréal, Québec, Canada: Éditions de l'Homme, 2012.

— *Les Hasards nécessaires.* Montréal, Québec, Canada: Éditions de l'Homme, 2001.

Watzlawick, Paul, Janet Helmick Beavin, and Don D. Jackson. 1967. *Some Tentative Axioms of Communication. In Pragmatics of Human Communication - A Study of Interactional Patterns, Pathologies and Paradoxes.* W. W. Norton, New York.

Wilber, Ken. *A Brief History of Everything.* Boston: Shambhala, 2000.

— *Sex, Ecology, Spirituality: The Spirit of Evolution.* Boston: Shambhala, 2000.

www.ingramcontent.com/pod-product-compliance
Lightning Source LLC
Chambersburg PA
CBHW070314230426
43663CB00011B/2121